SUFFOLK
IN ANGLO-SAXON TIMES

SUFFOLK
IN ANGLO-SAXON TIMES

STEVEN PLUNKETT

TEMPUS

Frontispiece The Roman fort and medieval Church of St Peter & St Paul, Burgh Castle. Thought to be the site of Fursa's monastery *c.*633-651. Reassigned to Norfolk in 1974. *Photograph: Author*

First published 2005

Tempus Publishing Limited
The Mill, Brimscombe Port,
Stroud, Gloucestershire, GL5 2QG
www.tempus-publishing.com

British Library Cataloguing in Publication Data.
A catalogue record for this book is available from the British Library.

ISBN 0 7524 3139 0
Typesetting and origination by Tempus Publishing Limited
Printed in Great Britain

Contents

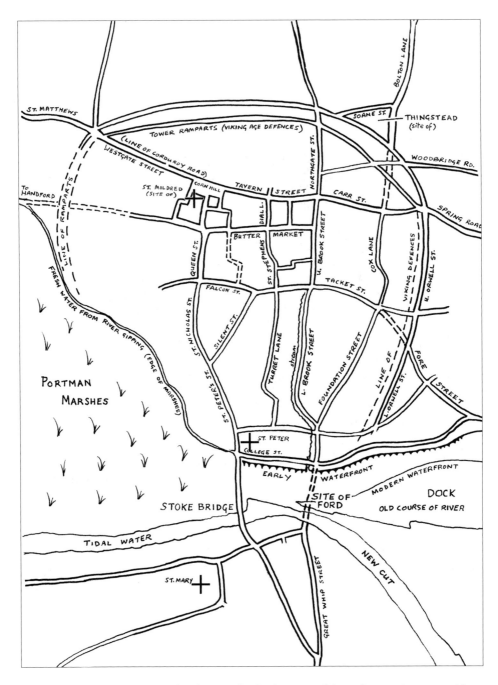

Map 1 Ipswich *(Gipeswic)*. Street plan showing the development of the early town (compare with colour plate 13)

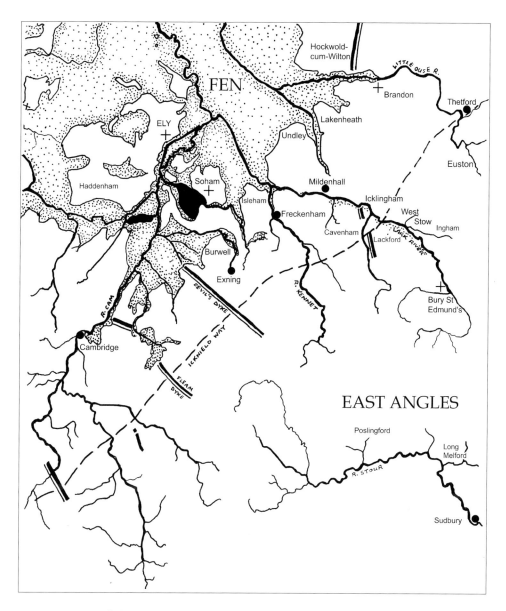

Map 2 Western Suffolk in relation to Ely and the Fen (ancient Fen contours after Cyril Fox, 1923)

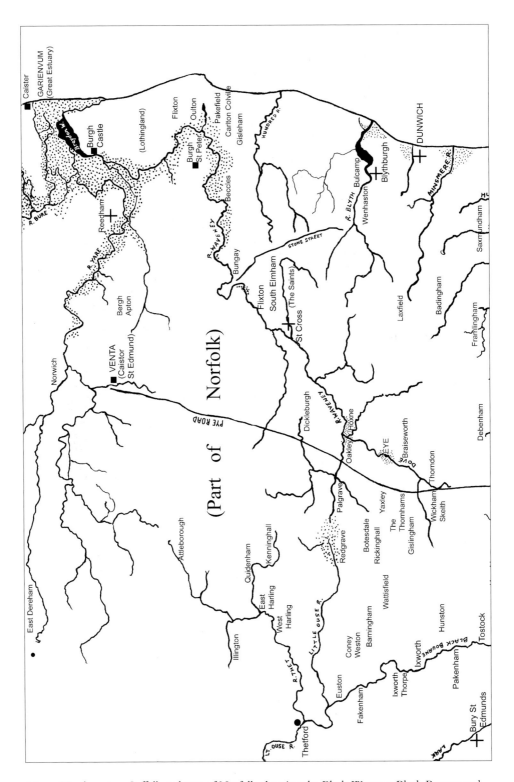

Map 3 North-eastern Suffolk and part of Norfolk, showing the Blyth, Waveney, Black Bourne and Little Ouse rivers

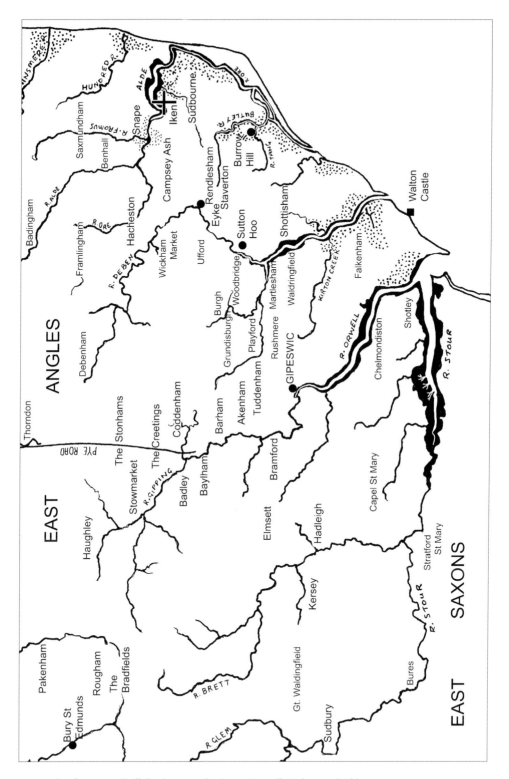

Map 4 South-eastern Suffolk, showing the Stour, Orwell, Deben and Alde rivers

Preface

This book offers a narrative of Suffolk affairs from the Anglo-Saxon migrations of the fifth century AD down to the onset of the Viking wars and the overthrow of King Eadmund in 865-70. Suffolk, Norfolk and parts of Cambridgeshire (including Ely) were not then separate entities but collectively the territory of the kingdom of East Angles. It was not until the tenth century, long after the first Viking onslaught and the English reconquest, that the shires gained their separate existence. Many towns and communities have developed continuously since before that time: Suffolk took its shape from part of an older reality.

Sites, discoveries and expositions have opened windows of inspiration for today's inhabitants of Suffolk and for many thousands of visitors. If one wishes to learn about Anglo-Saxon history in general, Suffolk is a very good place to begin. In different ways the archaeology of West Stow, of Sutton Hoo and of the urban origins of Gipeswic (Ipswich) have all been fundamental to modern understandings of that period. By offering a connected view this book may help non-specialist readers to envisage the wider context and to find their bearings within it. If so, perhaps specialists will forgive the necessary, but almost facetious, compression of debates which begs many questions and lays few claims to original scholarship.

Having accepted the challenge to write this account without an apparatus of notes and references I have kept my narrative in the Anglo-Saxon past rather than the scholarly and archaeological present. The principal sources are included in the reading list. The chronological framework is provided by the reigns of the East Anglian kings in whose dates I have adopted a moderate course. Their royal and ecclesiastical affairs are seen in their English, British and European contexts. That perspective leads us far from East Anglia at times, because distant events shaped and illuminated the land and people that afterwards became Suffolk.

The term 'Angle Saxon' appears in the eighth century to differentiate the English from the continental Saxons, and refers to their mixed Germanic origins.

From the introduction of the Old English language in the fifth century, down to the unification of English rule in the tenth and the Norman Conquest in the eleventh, spans a series of historic transformations. Archaeologists speak of its early, middle and late periods, each with distinct economy and artefacts. The present work is mainly concerned with the early and middle 'Anglo-Saxon' periods, spanning some 450 years leading up to the wars of King Ælfred the Great against the Vikings. Eadmund's martyrdom, which in Ælfred's own time came to symbolise the passing of a great era, completes the theme of our narrative. The materials for the late period, including the Viking wars and English reconquest, the Benedictine reforms and refoundations and the ages of Canute and Edward the Confessor, are extremely copious and culminate in the Domesday Survey. That must be a different chapter; this nutshell is already full.

Suffolk's sites and archaeological resources are rich and have much to tell, especially where, in the early period, historical details are lacking. A historical view (for East Anglia always sporadic) emerges with the spread of Christianity and literacy during the seventh century. All these evidences, physical or historical, are fragmentary and open to much study, debate and interpretation. I first visited Sutton Hoo on a walk from Shottisham with my father in 1964, and saw the hollow of the ship in the mound. I hope a reader who feels as I did then, drawn to see that episode in a longer narrative continuum, will enjoy this gathering from the things which are well-attested and from others which of their natures must be more speculative.

A NOTE ON HISTORICAL SOURCES

Sources for earlier East Anglian history are extremely varied. They include the earliest general commentaries, the *de Excidio Britanniae* of Gildas (*c*.540), stories told by Procopius in his *Gothic Wars* (*c*.555) (and the related *Fulda tradition*), Bede's statement about the English settlements (*Historia Ecclesiastica I.15*), and certain details in the *Historia Brittonum* (*c*.825) formerly attributed to the Welsh monk Nennius. For the fifth and sixth centuries written sources concerning East Anglia are so slight that we depend mainly upon the archaeology of settlements and cemeteries, the intrinsic and comparative study of artefacts, and their much-debated meaning.

Vernacular sources include the *Anglian Collection*, brief pedigrees of the ruling houses in succession from Woden. It is inferred that an oral tradition of heroic narrative poetry existed, precursors of works such as *Beowulf*, the *Finnsburg* fragment or *Widsith*. Sam Newton's study of the genealogies in relation to *Beowulf* shows the poem's direct bearing on the early East Anglian kingdom. The *hearpe* or six-stringed lyre, which in East Anglia was cultivated in the sixth and seventh centuries, accompanied such recitations: but if poems of the kingdom's early formation were composed they have not survived.

The vernacular *Anglo-Saxon Chronicle* was compiled in Wessex for a patron of Ælfred's time. Its early pages have Kentish, South and West Saxon but not East Anglian invasion narratives. Taciturn about East Anglia, it is, however, the primary source for the death of Anna and foundation of Iken (654), the execution of Ethelberht II (794), the death of Bishop Alfhun and the opening of Wihtburh's tomb (798), the East Anglian revolt against Beornwulf (825) and the death of Eadmund (869-70). It does not contain the muddled but plausible series of annals for the reigns of Wuffa, Tyttla, Raedwald and Sigeberht, nor the important ones for King Beonna and Ethelberht I (749, 760) copied by twelfth-century chroniclers from sources now lost.

Some East Anglian material in the *Chronicle* is derived from Bede's *Ecclesiastical History* (731), including Eorpwald's baptism (632) and Felix's preaching (636), though Bede's episcopal years for Felix, Thomas and Berhtgils contradict the *Chronicle* dates. Bede, polemic, highly selective and partisan in his silences, is our principal source for the seventh century. With access to various sources, including royal and church archives, he is the key authority for Raedwald, Eorpwald, Sigeberht, the family of Anna, Ealdwulf and the East Anglian Church and bishops.

The literature of Saints' *Lives* or *Passions*, familiar to Bede, provides confirmatory or additional material, as in Eddius' *Life of Wilfrid*, the *Vita Fursei* and the later *Virtutes Fursei*, or the Whitby *Life of Gregory*. Where Bede says nothing, we have the contemporary *Life of Guthlac* by Felix (mentioning Ælfwald's sister Ecgburh), but only eleventh century materials (the Slesvig *Breviary* and Folcard's *Life*) for Botolph apart from brief notices in the *Chronicle* and the anonymous *Life of Ceolfrith*. Goscelin of St Bertin's *Life of Mildburg* contains the details of Iken's exchange with Much Wenlock. The late *Liber Eliensis* references to Seaxburh, Eormenhild and Werburgh are reinforced and enlarged in the Mildryth cycle of *Lives*, parts of which David Rollason credits to eighth-century sources.

The Continental missions are documented through authentic *Lives*, and through *Letters*, especially of Boniface, Lull of Mainz and Alcuin. Levison gives compendious references. Stenton (whom I have often followed) accepts a kernel of truth in the Richard legend (*Vita Ricardi*), and the Boniface *Letters* attest Eadburgh's existence and accomplishments. Ælfwald's letter to Boniface (*c*.747 - Haddan & Stubbs III, p.387-88) and Alcuin's to Tidfrith (*c*.800 - Dümmler 301, and *cf*. 302) are primary East Anglian documents, as are the Professions of Bishops Tidfrith (798), Hunferth (*c*.816) and Ethilwald (*c*.865) (Birch 286, 375 and 528 respectively). Attendances at the great Councils are recorded. Fictional aspects to variants of the Ethelberht and Kenelm legends convey the conflicting loyalties of St Albans towards the martyrs and towards their Mercian founders, but the Hereford-derived *Passion of St Ethelbert* has some authentic features. Meanwhile regnal coinage and moneyers establish authentic sequences continuous into Eadmund's time.

East Anglia and Suffolk were reshaped in the aftermath of the Viking wars. The devastation of records had been great: no pre-Viking charter survives. Bishop Theodred's *Will* highlights the cult of St Æthelberht (not Eadmund) at Hoxne, and we learn of the lay brethren at *Beodricesworth*, that is, Bury St Edmunds. Æthelwold's endowments of Ely in 970, mentioning Sudbourne as the administrative centre of the Five-and-a-half Hundreds or *Wicklaw* during the 940s, the Stoke Charter and many other grants are recorded in *Liber Eliensis* (twelfth century). Both Abbo's *Passion of St Eadmund* (Ramsey) and Folcard's *Life of Botolph* (Thorney) arise from the Reform period interest in relics, and both are very short of firm historical material. Many later sources for Eadmund's legend are assembled in Lord Francis Hervey's *Corolla*, where Professor Whitelock is our indispensible guide.

Geffrei Gaimar, who owned an early copy of the Chronicle, incorporated variant information in his early post-Conquest *L'Estorie des Engles*. The *Annals of St Neots*, a twelfth-century source, give some notice of Eadmund and Guthrum. The monk Florence of Worcester in his *Chronicon a Chronicis* (*c*.1118) gathers important notices including episcopal lists. Symeon of Durham (*c*.1130) brings Hunberht into Eadmund's martyrdom. William of Malmesbury (d.1143) in his *de gestis Regum* remarks that he has only outlined East Anglian affairs because *plena gesta regum nusquam potui invenire* – he was not able find a full account anywhere. The *Histories* of Henry, Archdeacon of Huntingdon (fl. 1154) contain details of the Battle of the Idle (616) and of Anna's death at Bulcamp (654), possibly on early authority. Various early sources are combined in the *Flowers of History* of Roger of Wendover, which include the annals for Wuffa, Tyttla and Raedwald, and for Beonna. Roger (d.1237) was precentor at St Albans, became Abbot of Belvoir, but was afterwards deposed for his extravagance.

Finally, the book inevitably draws upon scholarly works of synthesis by which the framework and context are underpinned. Gibbon's *Decline and Fall* was indispensible. The study of *Roman Suffolk* by Moore, Plouviez and West, and the *Historical Atlas of Suffolk* by Dymond and Martin were also fundamental, as of necessity were the *Suffolk Landscape* and *Suffolk in the Middle Ages* of Norman Scarfe. Stenton's *Anglo-Saxon England* and Campbell's *The Anglo-Saxons* provided continual food for thought, and Levison's noble study of *England and the Continent* a visionary example. Stanley West's *Corpus* of artefacts is a rich source. I found a wealth of authoritative observation in the *Making of England* by Webster and Backhouse, yet sometimes turned to Rapin for a theme or a reference. Rupert Bruce-Mitford's monograph on the *Sutton Hoo Ship-Burial* remains an awesome tribute to its subject and a mine which will not soon be exhausted. The sources are listed: the path through them is my own.

Acknowledgements

I wish to thank all the friends and colleagues who, by encouragement or advice, have made the completion of this book possible. I owe the decision to attempt it to Peter Kemmis Betty, who invited me to do so (at the suggestion of Helen Geake), and to Norman Scarfe, Stanley West and Keith Wade, whose example, kindness and encouragement have been the foundation of all.

I have sought advice in many quarters from those engaged in specialist areas of work. What I made of their information, and the shortcomings, are my own. I owe my knowledge of Burrow Hill and my first experiences of Anglo-Saxon excavation to Valerie Fenwick. More recently I have received advice from Stuart Boulter, Robert Carr, Joe Caruth, Tom Loader, Edward Martin, Faye Minter, Richard Mortimer, Colin Pendleton, Jude Plouviez, Andrew Tester and Chris Topham-Smith, as to the particulars of their sites. Where artefacts were concerned, Noël Adams, Martin Allen, Angela Evans, George and Isabel Henderson, Graeme Lawson, Chris Mycock, John Newman, Arent Pol, Ian Riddler and Susan Youngs kindly shared their valued opinions.

My friends at Ipswich Borough Museums and Galleries, especially Robert Entwistle, Sally Dummer, Martin Sanford and Dominique Rogers, have remained most kindly helpful in providing information and access to the collections and archives since I ceased to curate them. I also remember with gratitude the collaborations with Ian Drake, Maggi Hayward and Liz Dodds on various Anglo-Saxon projects for the museum, and those with Mike Burgess and the late Lew Holmes who made the reproduction Sutton Hoo cauldron and Burrow Hill cauldron-chain (respectively) for the museum display.

In dealings with the finders of artefacts I have always experienced the most courteous welcome, and must record the long-sustained friendship and support of David and Mary Cummings and their family, of Peter Murrell and the kindness of Lord de Saumarez, in giving access to their marvellous finds from Coddenham and elsewhere over the past 14 years. I am very grateful to be able to illustrate the finds of Alan Calver, Andy Humphrey, John French and Darren

Clarke; and for the opportunity to study the finds from the Eye neighbourhood made by Paul Kemp through the Portable Antiquities Scheme, thanks to the friendly expertise of my colleague Faye Minter.

Among many other kindnesses, John Blatchly arranged for me to consult Sir Henry Savile's and Spelman's editions, and other primary sources in Latin, in the historic Town Library of Ipswich courtesy of the headmaster of Ipswich School. He also helped me track down the Witnesham rider. John Fairclough honed my Latin readings, shared theories, and commented on drafts. I recall many exploratory conversations with Sam and Teresa Newton in 2000-2002 with great pleasure. Robert Carr very generously placed his photography at my disposal, which in addition to those separately credited include the best of the Suffolk County Council images. Similarly the best of the Ipswich Museum photographs were taken by Douglas Atfield during the 1990s.

I warmly acknowledge the courtesy of the Trustees of the British Museum, the Ashmolean Museum (Oxford), the Trustees of the Annie Tranmer Trust, Lord de Saumarez and the team of David, Mary and Francis Cummings with Peter Murrell, the Suffolk County Council Archaeological Service and Portable Antiquities Scheme, the St Edmundsbury Borough Council (West Stow Anglo-Saxon Village Trust and Moyses Hall Museum), the Norwich Castle Museum with Norfolk Archaeological Service, the Ipswich Borough Council Museums and Galleries, and the Syndics of the Fitzwilliam Museum, Cambridge for having granted permission to reproduce copyright images of objects in their collections. All were extremely generous. All coin images are greatly enlarged.

I wish moreover to record my personal gratitude to Martin Carver, Barrie Cook, William Drummond, Margaret Elwood, Janet Fairclough, Anna Gannon, Helen Geake, Mike Hardy, Tim Holt-Wilson, Cliff and Rosemary Hoppitt, Ivan Howlett, Graeme Lawson, Ivor Lawson, the Mael family of Iken, Robert Markham, Chris Mycock, Tim Pestell, Kate Sussams, Vaughn Gledhill, the Warren family of Melton, Leslie Webster, Gareth Williams and Donna Wreathall. I owe much more than thanks to the many people of Suffolk who have shared the journey through thick and thin. This is part of their story.

Ipswich, August 2004

In gratitude to my parents, who together
chose Suffolk for scenes of my childhood.

I

The end of Roman Suffolk

There is something of Christmas Past in the old oak woods at Staverton, between Butley and Eyke north-east of Woodbridge. The roots of the giant holly trees in Staverton Thicks grow close beside those of the oaks, and their trunks soar upwards to the canopy from the leaf-mould below. One can see why the holly, berried and evergreen, was thought to sustain the life of the oak, and was brought in beside the blazing hearth at midwinter. In the old carol it also became the example of Christ's Blood and the Crown of Thorns. Staverton, though variously managed for many centuries, has never been fully cleared. Its ancestral woodlands once spread over the estate beside Rendlesham, where the kings of East Anglia had their palace in the seventh century after Christ. Sixty-five years ago Basil Brown discovered the fabulous burial of one of them in a great ship under a mound at Sutton Hoo, overlooking the river Deben. Presumably the oaklands were their places of recreation and hunting. The lofty spaces of their wooden halls, domestic or dynastic, naturally breathed the spirit of the forest. Oak [*Ac*] was the wood of the Ship and the Hall. One can sense their ancient energies at Staverton.

There are many places in Suffolk where one feels such an invocation of the Anglo-Saxon past. Suffolk is traditionally composed of two counties, East and West, of which Ipswich and Bury are the county towns. Suffolk and Norfolk come into focus as distinct regions during the tenth century, after the former kingdom of the East Angles had been submerged in the Viking wars and brought back under English rule by the descendants of King Ælfred the Great. The names of Suffolk and Norfolk, the south and north folk, preserve a memory of the old kingdom, *Estengle*, which also extended into Cambridgeshire. Suffolk's share of that inheritance was extremely rich, for this part of the kingdom had benefited especially from the patronage of the Wuffinga family, the former royal house of the East Angles. Christianity first came to them from Kent into Suffolk, where their power was focused around the south-eastern havens. The sites of the first East Anglian bishopric (and probably also the second) and its earliest recorded monasteries lay within what later became Suffolk. The county towns both owe their origins to royal patronage of the early seventh century, Ipswich as the original trade capital of the kingdom, and Bury St Edmunds as one of its earliest monasteries and probably its first royal martyr shrine.

Anglo-Saxon civilisation in Suffolk began almost two centuries before that, during the great age of European migrations which attended the collapse of the Western Roman Empire. Peoples from the north continental and Scandinavian coastlands occupied and settled eastern and southern Britain, where they converged in various ways with the native population and established their own industrial arts and customs within new communities. Then arose the shared experience of the English in the formation of their language and kingdoms, their domestic, religious and urban institutions. For the former part of the story the archaeology of cemeteries and settlements is the principal guide through fragments of myth, history and legend, since there was at first no written literary tradition among the migrants, and that of the native population had been eclipsed. The royal and ecclesiastical history of East Anglia can be sketched from the seventh century onwards, from written records and later from the regnal coinage, and is a framework for the interpretation of its archaeology. The written history accentuates East Anglia's political and ecclesiastical relations within Britain, while archaeology also reveals its cultural relations with Scandinavia, northern Europe and beyond. On this national and international stage their affairs were played out, and Suffolk's Anglo-Saxon topography preserves its part of that grand narrative.

THE FACE OF LATE ROMAN SUFFOLK

For more than 350 years Roman imperial government and civilisation shaped the province and native Celtic population of *Britannia*, the most northerly part of its Empire. The last Roman strata in our archaeology were laid down soon after AD 410 when the imperial (civil and military) government was officially withdrawn. British and migrant populations both contributed to the early Anglo-Saxon society of East Anglia, although the extent and method of their convergence is richly debated. Among the derelict sites of former villas, abandoned towns and dwellings, the landscape they occupied also included the Roman stone-built shore forts and parts of the road system which were maintained. As Anglo-Saxon identity coalesced in Britain from diverse origins (not least from continental homelands which had never been conquered by Rome), the immanence and vast authorising example of that imperial past shaped the insular consciousness. Its influence was irresistibly renewed through the expansion of the spiritual empire of Roman Christendom and was at length embraced and appropriated by the Anglo-Saxon rulers.

Our story therefore begins not in the forest-girt halls of pagan Germanic chieftains but in the organised world of eastern Britain under Roman administration.

When Roman armies invaded Britain under Claudius in AD 43 northern Suffolk formed part of the territory of the Celtic nation of the Iceni (pronounced *Ickeni*), but the southern area lay within the sphere of their neighbours the Trinovantes. Both peoples had a developed agriculture and a structure of aristocracy in their society. Under Roman governance two urban centres developed, one at *Venta Icenorum* (Caistor St Edmunds, south of modern Norwich) as the Market of the Iceni, and a more important one at *Camulodunum* (Colchester) established as a Colony of veteran legionaries under the first governors after the Roman invasion. *Camulodunum* possessed stone architecture and both centres were laid out with public buildings and rectangular street grids.

The east coast was then a frontier of Empire, for the lands north of the Rhine were not conquered. The great series of stone fortressess defending the south-eastern British shore was probably reorganised under Constantine the Great. He was acclaimed Emperor in York in 306 on the death of his father Constantius Chlorus at the Imperial palace there. A fort (*Garianonum*) enclosing about 6 acres, with stone walls over 2m thick and 6m high and with turret bastions, stood (and still stands) at Burgh Castle. To north and west it overlooked the vale of the lower Yare where it flows north-east to its mouth. Another at Walton (Felixstowe) controlled access to the Deben and Orwell havens; its site now lies a little way offshore. By the late fourth century, and perhaps from Constantine's time, their command lay under that extremely important official, the Count of the Saxon Shore through Britain. The coasts were vulnerable to attacks by pirates from Germany and from northern Britain: the cavalry units stationed in some of these forts were presumably to intercept raiding parties once they had landed. Camouflaged ships were used to monitor and intercept raiders before they reached the coast. Other key fortresses stood at *Branodunum* (Brancaster, Norfolk), at Caister-on-Sea north of the Yare estuary and at *Othona* on the southern promontory of the Blackwater estuary (Bradwell-on-Sea, Essex).

The countryside which they protected was in a developed state of management. A network of roads was established throughout Suffolk, some of which are still used today. Most of the land was already being farmed when the Romans arrived; farmsteads and small settlements flourished along river valleys and also across the higher clay lands, the woodland being cleared extensively. Market towns developed at important road intersections near river fords within the larger Roman communication system. Up to 13 have been located in Suffolk distributed evenly across the countryside. They were laid out informally. Goods and produce were brought to market and redistributed into their hinterlands by road and river. Manufacturers had workshops, millers ground and weighed the grain and familial sentiments consecrated the cemeteries. Their collective economies, trade and taxation were formally administered.

The largest farmsteads were the villa estates, centred upon a residence built in Roman style with masonry foundations, bathhouses or rooms with hypocaust heating, patterned flue-bricks, tiled roofs, painted plaster walls and sometimes tessellated pavements. More than 20 have been identified in Suffolk at sites long-established under Roman rule. Most numerous in central and western parts of the county, they clustered near the small towns, attracted by their commerce or controlling it. An impressive one stood at Castle Hill (Ipswich) on rising land overlooking the Gipping valley route to *Combretovium*, an important centre a few miles upstream. Substantial buildings or enclosures were constructed beside the Gipping mouth at Handford as it flows into the tidal waters of the Orwell; a watercourse through Portman Marshes may have been engineered to serve a mill at that time. Castle Hill villa had two tesselated pavements: a jet plaque found there which depicts the Phrygian god Atys shows an interest in Eastern mystery cults. Perhaps this villa had some official connection with the haven. The villa at Rougham (near a large settlement at Sicklesmere at the head of the Lark valley) is associated with impressive burial tumuli suggesting a partly Gallic culture. The mounds at Eastlow (Rougham) can be compared to those at Bartlow (Cambs), just beyond Haverhill, towards the Roman walled town at Cambridge and the town at Great Chesterford. A similar burial stood at Mersea Island near Colchester.

Two Roman roads through Suffolk are listed in the *Antonine Itinerary*, a venerable document describing routes through the Empire prepared during the second century. The Fifth and Ninth Iters follow the same route between London and Colchester. The Fifth was a road to Carlisle: after Colchester it reached *Villa Faustini* (a major estate named for the Faustinus family) and passed *Icinos* and *Camborito* before reaching *Duroliponte* (Cambridge). The Ninth Iter went to *Venta Icenorum*. It crossed the Stour at *Ad Ansam*, fording at Stratford and reaching a village at Capel. Bronze lion-mounts from a couch and fine glass mosaic tesserae show the refinements of a nearby villa. Then the road headed towards Castle Hill, but after fording Belstead Brook at Copdock it veered north along the west side of the Gipping valley to the town at Baylham Mill (Coddenham) called *Combretovium*. This had developed as a militarised centre in the first century, but grew into a town with numerous dwellings and industrial fringes including mortarium kilns. A superb silver- and niello-inlaid bronze figure of Nero (found at Barking) and a relief-cast mirror-case found in the area of the town reveal sophisticated occupants during the early, military phase.

Combretovium was a major road intersection from which routes extended west, north and north-east. The Ninth Route continued through an important centre called *Sitomagus* to *Venta*. The Pye Road (modern A140) formed the direct route from *Combretovium* to *Venta*. This passed northward from Beacon Hill to cross the valley at Stonham, site of plentiful occupation including a bathhouse some distance east of the road. The Creetings, Mickfield, Crowfield and Mendlesham were densely occupied. At Stoke Ash, crossing the Dove tributaries, John Fairclough and Mike Hardy suggest that the road met a large and complex estate associated with the late Roman hoards from Eye and Hoxne just to the east. These indicate a great household nearby handling official finances and possessing sumptuous gold jewellery and silver tableware, including some spoons

Barking: bronze statuette of Nero (first-century). *The British Museum*

inscribed for a wealthy Roman named Aurelius Ursicinus. The road crossed the Waveney by a town at Scole where various excavations by Norfolk and Suffolk archaeological teams have revealed houses and industrial sites, including a small reservoir apparently serving a brewery.

Roads east and north-east from *Combretovium* skirted the estuary complex. One led to a town at Hacheston, crossed the Deben to a villa at Farnham, and forded the Alde (at Stratford St Andrew) and the Fromus to reach a town at Knodishall on the Hundred river. The north-eastern road led to Wenhaston town, where it forded the Blyth and returned north-west along the Stone Street to the Waveney crossing at Bungay. Going south-west from *Combretovium* one passed the Long Melford town (a Stour ford) to another at Wixoe. Melford linked northward past Sicklesmere and the Rougham villa to join the Peddar's Way below Pakenham town in the Black Bourne valley (tributary of the Little Ouse), and thence north past villas and other settlements at Ixworth and Stanton Chair. In the clay land below the Little Ouse and Waveney headwaters a dense concentration of kiln sites around Pakenham, Wattisfield and Rickinghall show the importance of the pottery industry there. Separate, smaller industries also extended west towards Lakenheath and into the Lark valley. A late Roman hoard of jewellery and spoons of similar quality to the Hoxne finds was discovered at Thetford, from which a cult of Faunus there has been inferred.

In the west the Icknield Way and Peddar's Way, and the river waterways, provided important routes along the Fen Edge up to the Hunstanton area. The Roman town of Icklingham stood amid dense occupation including villas along the Lark valley and beside the Fen margins to the north-west. Votive hoards of pewter are among the evidence for the special religious significance of this area in Roman times. Pre-Christian religious expression is represented by figurines, amulets and gems found in many parts of Suffolk. A group of ritual 'crowns' (including two bronze circlets which bore applied images of gods), probably worn during religious ceremonies, were found at Cavenham Heath: another group from Hockwold (Norfolk) shows a similar cult functioning just north of the Little Ouse. Bronze figurines from Icklingham, presumably from a sophisticated votive shrine or temple, include a panther statuette and a group of bronze heads. An extremely wealthy presence is indicated at Mildenhall where a hoard of almost 40 items of silver tableware included the massive platter sculpted with scenes of the Bacchic dance and the face of Oceanus. This allegory of the Dionysian creation is a masterful work of late Roman art.

Icklingham also provides important evidence for early Christianity. The foundations of a probable flint-built church and a (separate) smaller apse-shaped building on its eastward axis, associated with a Christian cemetery, were excavated in 1974. Three large lead tubs or cisterns from Icklingham carry the chi-ro monogram for the name of Christ. A pit near the apse contained a stone baluster from an important building, perhaps the baptistery. British Christianity had gained its first martyr when Alban was beheaded at Verulamium (the

Icklingham: Roman lead cistern with Chi-ro monogram. *Ipswich Borough Museums*

Roman city where St Albans afterwards arose) during a persecution. Constantine suspended the oppressive edicts of Diocletian and at Milan proclaimed that all Christian rights and property should be restored. At the Council of Arles the bishops of Britain (including Eborius of York, Restitutus of London and another) joined those who condemned the heresy of Arius. The subsequent Council of Nice formulated the Creed of the Co-equal and Consubstantial Persons of the Holy Trinity. Constantine besieged Byzantium in 324, and built there the Christian city of New Rome (Constantinople). With sole dominion he exhorted all his subjects to embrace Christianity. Constantine and his army are said to have beheld a noontide vision of the Cross inscribed 'In this sign Conquer'. His uncovering of the Holy Sepulchre at Jerusalem (where the True Cross, the Nails and the Holy Lance were displayed) became a founding mystery of Roman Imperial Christendom.

Julian, last survivor of the House of Constantine, had been immersed in the study of pagan philosophies when he was called to the joint Prefecture of Spain, Gaul and Britain in 355. His accession as Cæsar coincided with violent barbarian inroads into north-eastern Gaul. In campaigns of 357-9 he three times crossed the Rhine, subdued the kings of the Alemanni and contained the Franks who dwelt beyond the river. The nearer Franks he subjected by arms and treaties in Batavia and Brabant, the original seat of their ancient kingdom. Having reopened and occupied the Rhine, he had a fleet of 600 ships built in the Ardennes to supply grain from Britain to his military stations there. This presumably affected Suffolk's harbours and agriculture. Based in Paris, his influence was felt in Britain through his near friendship with the civil administrator Alypius. After Julian's death (as Valentinian again faced the Alemanni in Gaul) Caledonian and Saxon attacks in 367 threw Britain into turmoil. Army pay was said to have been hoarded and discharges freely sold; as soldiers deserted to find subsistence the highways became infested with robbers. General Theodosius, a Spaniard, landed an Imperial army in Kent, probably at Richborough, and overwhelmed several looting parties even before reaching London. Obtaining a civil governor from Trèves, in two campaigns he drove the Caledonians beyond the northern Wall, and then defeated the Saxons in a naval battle off the Orkneys. The stone walls fortifying the core of *Venta* may have been defended in the later fourth century. The coastal fortifications were doubtless active: but normal life was withdrawing from the coastal areas, as Jude Plouviez's researches into coin loss in different areas of the county indicate.

THE COLLAPSE OF ROMAN POWER

The western advance of the Huns from the Caspian shores during the late fourth century drove those in their path before it. During the 370s they burst through Scythia, impelling the Gothic nations across the Danube and into the eastern Empire. The Goths (many of whom were Christian) were settled as refugee nations but were then abused by their new masters. In a mighty battle they destroyed Valens and his large army at Hadrianopolis in 378. The migrating Goths, Alani and Vandals also spread widely through the lands north of the Danube and the Imperial frontier. (In this age the Swabian peoples, *Swæfe*, observed a boundary drawn along the river Eider, *Fifeldore*, by their northern neighbour Offa, ruler of the Angles of southern Denmark.) Forty thousand Alemanni, expecting the western Emperor Gratian's departure to assist Valens, launched a fresh invasion into Gaul. Gratian, in alliance with the Franks, defeated them in Alsace and subdued them beyond the Rhine. He then proceeded east too late to save Valens, and having elevated Theodosius (son of the General) to the Eastern Empire he returned to Paris.

Britain gathered a huge following under Magnus Maximus, a man of Spanish birth long established in the island. In an exodus of perhaps 200,000 civilians and soldiers they invaded Gaul in 383 and were immediately acclaimed. Gratian was deserted at Paris and assassinated at Lyons. The loss of military strength from Britain proved largely permanent: many emigrants settled in Armorica (Brittany). Emperor Theodosius had newly achieved the enlistment of the vast Gothic armies under the Imperial banner. He associated Maximus to the Western Empire beyond the Alps, but destroyed him in 388 when ambition led him into Italy. Similarly in 392-94 he crushed the civil war of Eugenius conducted by Arbogast, Frankish-born general-in-chief of the Gaulish armies. Theodosius established catholic doctrines of Christianity throughout his Church, as distinct from the Arian doctrines favoured by the Greeks and received by the Goths. Great churchmen of his time included Martin of Tours, Ambrose of Milan and Jerome. His final edict effectively made pagan worship a treasonable, capital offence. Having unified the Empire under his own power he died in 395 making the absolute division of East and West. They fell to his sons Arcadius and Honorius respectively, both of minor years. He entrusted their supervision to his general-in-chief Stilicho, of Vandal extraction.

Alaric the Goth invaded Italy in 403-04. British and Rhenish garrisons were urgently redeployed to relieve Honorius at Milan, and valiantly opposed the Goths. Honorius left Rome for the safety of Ravenna, where the Imperial court became permanently settled. Meanwhile the nations migrating north-westwards across Germany – other Goths, Vandals, Alani, and now Burgundians and Swabians imbroiled in their destiny – had swollen into an immense confederation below the Baltic. Led by Radagaisus, possibly out of Mecklenburg, they burst in great numbers across the upper Danube and into northern Italy, where their campaign collapsed at Florence. But the western arm of their invasion broke across the Rhine into Gaul, driving out her citizens, bishops and common people in displaced multitudes. Britain, becoming isolated, learnt of the sack of Strasbourg, Arras, Rheims, Amiens and Tournai in consternation.

The British twice invested leaders, Marcus and Gratian, in the Imperial Purple, and twice murdered them, before acclaiming Constantine (III) from military ranks to direct their fortunes. Entering Gaul with the remaining British forces, he stabilised hostilities by battles and treaties, and won the acknowledgement of that people and of the province of Spain. Stilicho, Italy's loyal defender, fell victim to Ravenna intrigue and was executed there. Alaric, king of the Visigoths and their leader under Honorius, renewed his hostility towards Italy's worthless ministers. Having led his nation in arms to the gates of Rome, he thrice laid siege to her, demanding and receiving vast recompense of treasure. At last the Gothic army gained entrance to the Eternal City and stripped her citizens, her temples and public buildings of their precious goods and ancient trophies. Alaric then marched north and showed his obedience to Honorius by resting a short way outside Ravenna. At that moment, in 410, Honorius sent a 'Rescript' or letter to the cities of Britain and Armorica to allow their need to conduct their own government and defence. Constantine was besieged at Arles in 411 and disposed of while being led, captive, into Italy. But the myth of Rome's unassailable endurance was shattered.

The flow of Imperial finance into Britain ended and its official civil and military administration was not restored. Hoards of Roman coin in Suffolk, from the official reserves represented by *solidi* found at Eye and Hoxne to the pot of small bronze coins from Little Bealings, show that Constantine's was the last rule in which Roman coins were issued there. The late hoards from Tuddenham St Martin (not far from Castle Hill) and (in the north-west) from Brandon, Freckenham, Icklingham and Mildenhall all end with Arcadius and Honorius. They show Roman wealth and occupation in early fifth-century Suffolk distinctly focused in these areas. However, the near-15,000 silver *siliquæ* of the Hoxne treasure, which included two of Constantine, contained many circulated and clipped coins. The impressive jewellery and tableware buried with them had therefore remained the coherent possessions of a powerful Romanised family in north Suffolk for perhaps a decade or two after the official withdrawal. It is less certain when the magnificent treasures of Mildenhall and Thetford were buried, owing to the lack of coins as evidence.

Hoxne: silver *siliqua* of Constantine III, *c.*408-411, from the Hoxne hoard. *The British Museum*

Buckles and belt-fittings from late Roman official costume, civil or military, are found in various parts of lowland Britain. They represent a class of officialdom similar to that active on the Gaulish Rhineland frontier. In Suffolk their distribution, known principally from metal-detector finds, is more widespread than that of the late coin hoards. In the north-east there are examples from Gisleham and Wenhaston. On the upper reaches of the Alde they are at Badingham, at Sweffling and Little Glemham: on the lower Deben, at Ufford, Waldringfield and Shottisham, and at Walton itself. Near the Gipping Stowupland, Barking and Great Blakenham (on the middle stretch near *Combretovium*) have produced specimens. On the north bank of the Orwell there is a buckle from Nacton and belt-fittings have been found at Hintlesham and Somersham beside its tributary, the Bourne. An example from Little Oakley (Essex) reinforces the coastal-estuarine distribution, while others lie inland between the Brett and Stour rivers (Brent Eleigh and Lawshall), and one far to the west at Wixoe. In the Lark valley they are located at Icklingham and West Stow and on the southern tributary at Little Saxham. Around Worlington (Mildenhall) and Freckenham they form part of a cluster spreading north to Lakenheath, as part of the intensive occupation of the Fen Edge area. Finds from Ixworth and Hinderclay also place these late Roman officials on the Black Bourne and at the head of the Little Ouse respectively.

How far these may represent the continuation of hired military defence after the official withdrawal is not determined. The former distributive industries ceased: the potteries, including the fast wheel and the updraught kiln, were rapidly abandoned. Archaeology, lacking later coin-dated horizons, finds the native occupation and agriculture of East Anglia invisible, and the town markets soon falling empty. Without adequate provision and defence, formal urban life dwindled to the occupation of decaying buildings. British rulership wearing some Roman name and manners became focused in northern, central, southern and western parts of the island.

Raids by the Irish and the Picts of the north (*Caledonians*) continued. In one of these a Briton named Maun had been captured by raiders and taken to Ireland. Escaping, he resolved to convert that nation to Christianity; a compatriot, Bishop Palladius, went before with limited success. After training in Rome, Maun took the name Patricius and returned to Ireland to spend the remainder of his long life preaching and baptising. St Patrick's example and Gospel struck deep, permanent roots: austerity, discipline and isolated contemplation taught them the pilgrimage of the soul, and prepared them for their missionary pilgrimages into the post-Roman world. The British Church was visited in 429 by two Gaulish bishops, Germanus of Auxerre and Lupus of Troyes, who found its orthodoxy untainted. Germanus saw St Alban's tomb at Verulamium and deposited precious relics. He healed the daughter of a tribune, whose rank reveals an organised military structure. He also defeated a large army of pagan Saxons who, at the British shout of 'Allelulia', fled thinking the sky would fall on their heads. Germanus made a second visit after 435.

The British monk Gildas (writing a century later) tells that as raids were renewed there was widespread famine and plague, and a return to living by hunting. Then, in council with their senior ruler, the Britons decided to employ foreign soldiers from beyond the Roman frontiers to defend them, making a treaty (*foedera*) to provide supplies (*ammonæ*) by monthly allowances (*epimenæ*) for their services. (This was an established Roman practise quite distinct from the regular enlistment of auxiliary units from allied nations.) The soldiers they invited were Saxons, who first arrived in three ships or 'keels', in their language *cyuli*, which the Romans called 'long ships'. They were planted on the east side of Britain and, having prospered, were joined by a larger contingent. After a long time they demanded greater allowances, found fault in their hosts, and swore to break their treaty and plunder the whole island. A north Gaulish chronicler, writing in 453, told that Britain had passed 'into the control of the Saxons' a decade earlier, in 441-2. However, that was a very temporary or partial view.

People from the lands around the lower Elbe and Weser rivers in north-west Germany were already appearing in East Anglia early in the fifth century. A very early 'supporting-arm' brooch resembling examples from Gudendorf was found at Shottisham, on the same spot as a Roman belt-fitting. At Waldringfield on the Deben, above Kirton Creek, a bossed urn containing ashes and a miniature pair of metal shears represents a pagan Saxon funeral of this time. Along the Gipping, an early Saxon-made urn was placed in a grave at Coddenham near old *Combretovium*. Supporting-arm brooches of a kind known at Perlberg-bei-Stade (on the south bank of the Elbe estuary) have been found at Coddenham, Stonham Aspal and Mildenhall, and a Mahndorf type at Pakenham (near Ixworth). On the upper Deben there are examples from Kettleburgh and Debenham, and others show a central-southern focus at Bures and Little Waldingfield. Three 'upturned foot' brooches reinforce the Lark valley distribution at West Stow, two being of an early type also known in Huntingdonshire. The very earliest cruciform brooches are from Coddenham, Wenhaston and Mildenhall, and there are two of Witmarsum type from Ixworth and Hinderclay.

These distinctive earliest continental brooches are therefore found in the same areas as the late Roman hoards and belt equipment. A striking instance at Scole (on the Norfolk border) showed a woman buried wearing both a Germanic supporting-arm brooch (a fourth- or fifth-century type) and a hinged Colchester-type brooch of early Roman date, and also a glass bead necklace. The continental artefacts represent the first visible Germanic presence at some sites which later became established immigrant settlements; but archaeology has not shown that their owners interacted with organised sub-Roman populations. If indeed the newcomers did enter treaties of military service, the burden of their provision must have fallen to the British. The succeeding British organisation in Suffolk is unknown. There is growing evidence that in central Suffolk a landscape was maintained by pastoral farming or management. Certainly many of the roads were kept clear and in good order.

NATIONS IN TURMOIL

The Angles, centred in the southern part of the Danish peninsula, were already expanding towards the Elbe and mixing with Saxons to their south and west around the Weser. The Frisians occupied lands near the river Yssel and along the Frisian Isles: the Frankish peoples inhabited the lower Rhine, and the Boructari near them the Ruhr. The Vandals, Swabians and others who had entered Gaul during the rising of Radagaisus proceeded across the Pyrenees into Andalusia, where they fought both the Roman and the Visigothic armies between 416 and 426. Having united with the Alani and occupied Andalusia and Cartagena, some 80,000 people (including an army of 15,000) were led by their Vandal King Genseric (r.428-77) to the invasion of Pro-Consular North Africa in 429, the siege of Hippo Regius in 430 (in the last days of St Augustine) and to the conquest of Carthage and Sicily in 439 and 440 respectively. Theodoric, Alaric's son, made the seat of the Visigothic kingdom at Toulouse. At the same time the Franks under Clodion, based between Louvain and Brussels, crossed the Ardennes to occupy Tournai and Cambray and conquered the Somme, making their camp at Artois. Here they were confronted by the Roman *Magister Militum*, Aetius, but Clodion held his kingdom from the Rhine to the Somme, and his son Meroveus was adopted by Aetius and became a Roman ally.

However, the elder brother of Meroveus allied himself with Attila, King of the Huns (based in Hungary), who turned his vast following towards an invasion of Gaul. These included Gepidæ, Vandals, Ostrogoths, Heruli, Burgundians, Franks, the Rugeri and the Thuringians (who occupied the region of Gotha (Erfurt), Weimar and Eisenach). Having marched to the confluence of the Rhine and Neckar, they poured with hostile fury into the Belgic provinces across the Scheldt. Troyes and Paris were saved, but Tongres was ruined, Metz was burnt and its people massacred, and Attila proceeded to Auxerre and to the siege of Orleans. Aetius agreed an alliance with Theodoric of Toulouse, and rallied to his banner Visigoths, Gaulish barbarians, Franks under Meroveus, the Saxon colonists of Bayeux and the Burgundians of Savoy. Attila retired back across the Seine to avoid entrapment in central Gaul and, after a battle between the Franks and Gepidæ, the two immense forces met in 451 at the Mauriac Plain near Chalons, 27 miles from Rheims. Aetius was successful, but Attila, still commanding huge armies, proceeded across the Alps to north Italy and to the occupation of Aquileia and Milan. He then returned to Hungary, where he died in 453.

Meanwhile, a new British appeal to the Romans for defence against raiders having failed, Vortigern, their senior king, sought help from 'the Nobles of Angle-kin.' Gildas states that many Angles and Saxons came, were settled as federates in the east of Britain, and were joined by reinforcements. An early chronology for the story of Hengest, given by Nennius and affirmed by John Morris, places his historic arrival at Thanet in *c.*428. His revolt, when, demanding more land and supplies, he turned on Vortigern and his followers and drove them out of Kent in great fear to London, may belong to the decade following. The conventional arrival date of 449 arose in connection with a letter, 'The Groans of the British', sent to Aetius when he was in Gaul preparing to confront Attila. It declared that the British were being slaughtered or driven into the sea by the barbarians. Tidal inundations were pinching the unhappy natives between the advancing Saxons and the advancing seas. The letter was perhaps written by independent Britons wishing to resist Vortigern and his 'virulent plantation' of Saxons.

Aetius did not respond, and could not have done so: even Attila laid some claim to Britain at this time. In 454 Aetius was murdered at Rome by his own Emperor Valentinian III, who met a similar fate a year afterwards. Genseric the Vandal King immediately entered Rome and for two weeks methodically stripped out everything of value, carrying it all back to Carthage in his fleet together with thousands of Romans: all her skilled, learned and professional people. Roman civilisation in Britain now looked more to Gaul than to Rome for the example of leadership. It was becoming obvious that Rome would never again come to Britain's defence.

2

The posterity of Woden

THE ANGLIAN MIGRATION

In 1830 a large larchwood ship was unearthed at Ashby Dell, Suffolk, in a vale (possibly a silted waterway) near the Yare estuary a few miles from Burgh Castle. Fifty-one feet long and 8 in the beam, with benches and oar-rests for 14 oarsmen, her stem and stern posts rose 9ft above the keel. Her form and early, lashed construction resembled the larger fourth-century oak ship buried at Nydam (Denmark), but without iron rivets. This travelling vessel, probably not a funeral ship, proclaims the northern maritime communications of the East Anglian seaboard. During the fifth century, water-levels were rising. To the west, the Great Fen (partly drained in Roman times) was frequently inundated (Map 2). From the Midlands the Nene and Welland rivers pass north across it to the Wash. Its southern tributary, the Great Ouse, rises near Banbury (Oxon.). Meeting the Cam south of Ely and turning north to the Lark, today it follows the western slopes of East Anglia to emerge near King's Lynn, but formerly it joined the Nene to reach the sea at Wisbech.

The river Lark, rising in central Suffolk, flows north-west through Bury to Mildenhall and thence to the Fen. Further north the Little Ouse is joined from Suffolk by the Black Bourne, and then at Thetford by the Thet from Kenninghall and the Harlings in Norfolk. Flowing west past Brandon, it falls into the Fen and joins the Great Ouse. Various navigable tideways once flowed through the Fen expanses of wetlands and reed-beds. In the eighth century the monk Felix knew of it 'with pools, intermittently with dark sluggish vapours and waters poured forth, occasionally with thick woods on intersecting islands, from south to north as far as the sea'. Abbo, there in the 980s, wrote of its wide marshes with countless stretches of fen water often 2 or 3 miles across. The west margin of Suffolk and Norfolk overlooked many miles of such terrain. Similar fenland spread into southern Lincolnshire, surrounding the lower Witham most of the way upstream to Lincoln. Increased water levels also made the eastern rivers swollen, their unembanked channels opening through salt marshes to the sea. Much of the Suffolk coastline (with its archaeology) of that period has been lost into the sea, in some places to a distance of miles.

Adventus Saxonum

The story of Hengest in Kent is the epitome of a turning point, when the policy of defence by barbarian soldiers under treaty dispossessed the British. Hengest is commonly identified with the continental exile-hero named in early English heroic narrative poetry, the *Freswæl* section of *Beowulf* and *The Fight at Finnsburg*. Finn Folcwalding, ruler of the Frisian people, had married into the ruling Danish *Scylding* family but had slain his brother-in-law Hnæf. To avenge the kin-feud Hengest (an exile adventurer in Hnæf's service) led the Danes against Finn, who was killed defending his Frisian hall. The lands of the Saxons around the lower Elbe and Weser were at this time the scene of mixing cultures resulting from the pressure of groups expanding southwards from the Danish peninsula and westwards from East Holstein. Their varied customs and ornaments are represented, for instance, in the cemeteries of Perlberg-bei-Stade or the Galgenberg near Cuxhaven. Their shelving coastlands were also affected by rising sea water. These folk were pressing westwards upon the Frisian lands and people and establishing colonies among them. Swabians were moving westward onto the Elbe above Hamburg. The legend of Hengest, the roving hero-warrior, relates to these coastal movements into Frisia, and shows how men displaced from their former allegiances may have gathered into leagues under distinguished leaders to find adventure or destiny in Britain.

The Venerable Bede (writing before 731), who assigns the immigrant settlement of East Anglia, Northumbria and the English Midlands mainly to the Angles, notes that in addition to Saxons and Jutes the nation at large included Frisians, *Boruhtware* (Bructeri), Danes, Huns and Rugini (the last of whom may have dispersed from Attila's forces). *Bructeri* probably denotes Franks of the Ruhr. Procopius, during the 550s, specified a strong Frisian presence in Britain. There is no legendary East Anglian narrative of a military conquest as there was for Kent or Wessex and the archaeological evidence is also lacking to show it. Medieval chroniclers (Wendover's tradition) compress into one annal (527) the statement that pagans from Germany occupied East Anglia, some of whom invaded Mercia and made many wars against the British. The East Saxon kingdom is simultaneously created.

Archaeology, on the other hand, presents its highly complex picture of new cultural settlement in eastern Britain, in which Germanic and Scandinavian industries, ornaments, building techniques and funeral customs predominate. Their affinities are notably with Saxon, Angle and Frisian identity, but also closely with western Norway during the later decades of the fifth century and the first half of the sixth. That Norwegian dimension (noted further below) is not suggested by Bede. It is conventional and probably true to explain this in terms of the migrations of peoples from continental and Scandinavian homelands directly into eastern Britain, who mixed into a new culture progressively in the course of generations.

By *c.*500 many were settled in stratified and culturally mixed communities in East Anglia, and others were becoming so. The former Roman market centres and villas had decayed rapidly through disuse rather than by hostile action. Without the hand of Roman management some regeneration of woodland is likely to have occurred, especially in the heavier clay lands of central Suffolk, its traditional woodlands: its timber became the building material of a new society. However, pollen or soil evidences from central northern Suffolk indicate that open pastoral farming was never abandoned there, and point to the survival of organised rural populations.

The campaigns attributed to Hengest and his heir Æsc precede the 24-year reign of Æsc said by the *Anglo-Saxon Chronicle* to commence in 488. The South Saxons led by Ælle fought the British near Selsey Bill and, having driven many of them into the Weald forest, besieged the Roman fort at Pevensey in 491 and massacred every last man. Other migrants had come through the Thames to the settlements of Middlesex and Surrey, and some found their way further west below the Chilterns or towards Oxford. As the century neared its close the assaults on Portsmouth and elsewhere along the southern coast of Britain introduced a new power, perhaps combining British and Anglo-Saxon leadership, which the later West Saxon dynasty attributed to the founding energies of Cerdic and Cynric.

Occupation and settlement of the Suffolk valleys
Estuarine settlement of eastern Suffolk shows early and continuing occupation of the Blyth near Wenhaston, and a more numerous presence along the Alde and Deben in the Sandlings, the light and often heathy land lying towards the coast. A field of Bronze Age grave mounds about a mile north of the Alde, commanding the brackish fen at Snape, was adopted as a burial ground by settlers nearby: others moved past the fen to Blaxhall. Some penetrated the Chillesford marshes and were established at Butley. Along the Deben, houses of continental kind, post-constructed around sunken floor spaces, arose near the site of the former town of Hacheston: the burial grounds of Ufford and Hasketon indicate occupation nearby. Cemeteries came into use at Bealings, Tuddenham St Martin, Rushmere and Playford, approached by Martlesham Creek, a large tributary of the Deben emerging just below Woodbridge. There is as yet little evidence of early settlement beside the lower Stour, though it is hard to believe that those fertile leagues were not exploited.

From Walton, occupied perhaps near the fort itself, the Orwell formed the seagate of the Gipping valley and its north-westerly route. An early grave found at Ipswich in 1911 leads inland to other burial grounds at Akenham, Barham, Claydon and Great Blakenham. This occupation extended notably around Coddenham (well established during the fifth century), into the Creetings and north up the Pye Road to the Stonhams. Above Thorney and Stowmarket the tributaries descended from the central clayland, partly afforested, between the watersheds of the Gipping, Lark, Black Bourne and Brett. The Pye Road linked the settlements near Stonham and Coddenham north to the Dove valley. Cemeteries developed at Thornham, at Yaxley and Braiseworth and around Eye, an isle (*Heia*) connected navigably to the Waveney. Early finds at Hoxne, Oakley and west to Palgrave show cemeteries around the Waveney headwaters. The southern bank of the Waveney was certainly populous during the early sixth century, a fact now being realised through recent excavation and discovery. Several rivers which meet at the Yare Estuary then converged in the wide sea inlet to the west of Burgh Castle. North of the Waveney a separate focus of activity was established around Venta, with cemeteries for instance at Caistor and Markshall of mixed Saxon, Anglian, Anglo-Frisian and Swabian appearance.

A large series of settlement complexes and cemeteries extended down the Lark valley, notably at Bury, Culford, West Stow, Lackford, Icklingham, Tuddenham, Eriswell, Mildenhall and Holywell Row. If the Lark followed the Nene route to the Wash at Wisbech, its westwards communications lay in the direction of Ely. It is not clear whether the settlements of the Black Bourne and Little Ouse (such as Ixworth or Grimstone End) looked to them, or northwards to the Nar and Wissey in Norfolk and so to the east side of the Wash. Taken with the important sites at Lakenheath, and to the south at Exning, Freckenham and elsewhere, Suffolk's western cultural area was orientated towards the Fen. Their material affinities in ceramic and metalwork ornaments lie with their neighbours from Fordham, Isleham, Soham and Burwell across to Cambridge, with others further up the river Cam and towards St Ives on the Ouse, and with the communities of western Norfolk. In archaeological terms they are part of a larger Fen-hinterland occupation which also extended west on the Nene and Welland and north into Lincolnshire. Similar occupation was becoming established north and south of the Humber estuary. The Fenside occupation gave control of the upper Icknield Way, the main route around the southern side of the Fen. Myres and others long maintained that it formed a path of invasion or reinforcement from East Anglia into the Thames valley during the later fifth century, a view now less favoured.

It is tempting to conclude that whatever British population remained in East Anglia in the late fifth century (perhaps a very large one increasingly integrated with the migrants) did not play a major part in the resistance centred in the south and west. Gildas says that Britons who surrendered were enslaved and that others fled to the hills. They found a leader in Ambrosius Aurelianus, a patrician, whose parents had worn the purple but had been slain in the Saxon wars. This figure of Roman heroism rallied the British for many years with varying success. Many actions doubtless took place across central and southern Britain. A list of early battles (attributed to King Arthur) in Nennius' ninth-century compilation includes three fought in Lincolnshire near the river Douglas. The situation culminated some 44 years before Gildas wrote, in the year of his birth.

At the famous battle or siege of Mount Badon the British thoroughly defeated a confederation of Anglo-Saxon armies under the ultimate command of King Ælle of the South Saxons, who is described as the first Overlord of the southern English peoples.

This historic battle took place either shortly before or after the year 500, probably in central southern Britain. In consequence of it, the advance of Anglo-Saxon control was held back for some decades. But it was too late for western British rulers to reconquer East Anglia. The defence of the lands east of the Fen had begun to shape Eastern Angle identity. A distinguished Anglian person at Lakenheath wore a gold bracteate (disc pendant), made in the late fifth century probably in Slesvig or southern Scandinavia. Its embossed design shows a Roman Imperial bust and an image of Romulus and Remus suckling the she-wolf, both derived from Roman coin prototypes. There is a surrounding text in runic letters which may refer to the she-wolf. What it meant to its owner is uncertain, but it evoked the image of Rome and the kinship of the wolf together in a form brought from the Anglian continent. It is not, however, only the wealth of an immigrant class but the continuity of East Anglian settlement through the age of Mount Badon which assures us that the growth of the new culture was not arrested in this region.

Undley, Lakenheath: gold bracteate pendant. *The British Museum. Photograph: R. Carr*

West Stow, Lark valley – an Anglo-Saxon 'village'

The West Stow settlement, active *c*.450-650, was excavated and reconstructed under Stanley West's direction. A presence early in the fifth century is indicated by three 'upturned-foot' brooches like examples from Glaston (Hunts.), among the earliest continental types found in England. There are other early Germanic forms with lozenge-shaped terminals, and distinctive early pottery. The inhabitants occupied a heathy knoll beside the river Lark, fronting a section between fords on the Icknield Way and a Roman road. A few households each had a central hall for living quarters, surrounded by a group of smaller buildings used for ancillary occupation and activities. Cattle were kept in the meadows beside the river, and the surrounding fields, probably developed for arable use in Roman times, provided such crops as wheat, barley, rye and peas. The drier, sandier lands above were suitable for sheep grazing and woodland nearby was managed by coppicing and provided pannage for pigs. Fishing and fowling, and other forms of hunting, added to the food resources. The cemetery of mixed interments and cremation burials lay near the Roman road. In one grave a Roman stone coffin had been reused.

The halls, on average some 9m long, were built with heavy rectangular posts set into the ground, vertically-planked walls and a door usually in the centre of the south side. The posts were tenoned above into a wall-plate from which the rafters rose to the roof tree, which was covered with thatch of reed or straw. The hearth, probably central, provided fire for warmth and for cooking in small cauldrons suspended above it. (Examples, probably made on the continent, are found in Suffolk: the Vestland type with concave sides (e.g. Ixworth Thorpe) is found widely from Norway to Germany, while a more globular form (e.g. Brightwell Heath) seems particularly connected with Gotland.) The smoke rose and filtered through the thatch. Textiles, bedding and wooden furniture, storage chests, wooden vessels and osier baskets have not survived, but miniature cooper-made tubs with bronze fittings were among the more delicate vessels. One hall slightly larger than the others had an internal partition, perhaps to define sleeping quarters. The crafts of weaving, antler-working and pottery were practised at West Stow. The houses and outbuildings were rebuilt at least once during the life of the village, before the community moved to a new site.

The outhouses, a few associated with each hall, were built over a flat-bottomed pit over 4m long. They had evolved from simpler dwellings characteristic of the continental homelands. At West Stow and elsewhere in Suffolk the sunken floors were not trampled, but were covered with a raised, planked floor just above ground level. At either end of the pit, one (or sometimes three) upright posts were driven in: a floor frame was suspended from them, and on it the planked walls were erected. The pits provided storage and allowed circulation of dry air under the floor. Henry Thoreau dug one under his cabin at Walden Pond, describing the space as for storage of root crops and maintenance of even temperature: he noted that the excavated shape was preserved by never being exposed to sunlight.

These buildings could have been used as sleeping quarters or as stabling for farm animals, but were certainly also connected with the ancient and necessary industry of weaving. Several at West Stow contained loom equipment, and three looms were apparently in use in one hut when it burnt down. Clay loomweights, bone needles and pickers were associated; bone and antler-working were important village industries. Combs, used principally for grooming, and perhaps ritually, were made from sawn sheets of antler which were drilled, riveted and decorated. Early examples from West Stow and Pakenham include several with triangular or pedimented backs like the Eye example, continuing a late Roman type, and others typically Frisian in shape.

The Anglo-Scandinavian technology of the warp-weighted loom replaced the Roman two-beam loom, which did not use weights. At Grimstone End (Pakenham) in the Black Bourne valley in a settlement which flourished during the sixth century, fire destroyed two looms in their huts built across the ring-ditch of a large Bronze Age burial mound. When excavated in 1953 the weights still lay as they had collapsed. A beam supported by two upright posts formed the loom frame, which could be dismantled for storage. It was leant against a wall at an angle while in use. The hanging warp threads were weighted in bunches by unfired, ring-shaped clay weights of about 1lb each, suspended just above the floor. The loom was particularly suitable for making woollen four-shed twills with chevron or lozenge patterns like the mineralised fragments found in East Anglian cemeteries of this period. The Grimstone End looms were

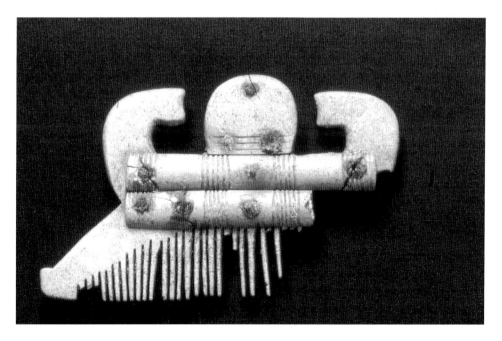

Pakenham: comb of Frisian type. *Ipswich Borough Museums*

Pakenham: collapsed loomweights *in situ* (1953). *Ipswich Borough Museums*

Loom reconstruction based on the Pakenham weights. *Ipswich Borough Museums*

extremely large, weaving textiles up to 8ft wide. This technology spread around England with the settlers. Weaving was seemingly done by women working in small groups: there was division of labour in measuring and weaving the warp, in working the heddles and passing the skein of weft. Weighted spindles were used to spin the yarn, and at Grimstone End a bell of folded iron, probably for the bell-wether of the flock, suggests the local source of the fleece. Swords for beating-in the weft (some actually made from old weapons) are found in women's graves, for instance at West Stow, at Holywell Row (Mildenhall) and at the distinctive cemetery at Spong Hill, North Elmham (Norfolk).

Burial Customs: cremation and furnished inhumation
Heathen burial customs travelled with the early East Angles from their homelands. Various distinct rituals were observed, often within the same cemetery. After cremation of the body on a pyre the ashes were buried, commonly in a pottery urn and sometimes with token possessions. Others buried their dead in formal costume with brooches and ornaments or with weapons, and with additional goods or vessels. Cremation, at first the stronger custom, gradually yielded precedence to furnished burial. The furnished graves seem to represent a wealthy stratum within the communities, and many cemeteries included graves without grave-goods, suggesting a poorer class. In fact, these unfurnished burials may often denote a difference of custom rather than of wealth. Cemeteries were built up over generations of use, sometimes through distinct phases. Some thousands of graves have been excavated in East Anglia, a prolific if also fragmentary source of information about the people who formed the communities. Hardly any cemeteries have been completely excavated to show their full historical and cultural profile.

Cremation, largely abandoned by the Romans in Britain during the second century, was an extremely ancient Germanic custom in northern Europe. Its reappearance in Britain is concentrated especially in East Anglia, in the Midlands between the river Trent and the Icknield Way (including the Soar valley and as far south-west as Cirencester), and through Lincolnshire around the Humber into Yorkshire. After early appearances in the south-eastern corner of Britain, where a much stronger Frankish influence operated, it quite rapidly became unfashionable there. Pyre-burning no doubt had a very cohesive effect on the communities of mixed origins which practised it. To others of different custom it may have seemed atavistic. The fire, sufficiently intense to reduce bone to calcined fragments, usually left few other residues, though an impressive group of fire-distorted brooches has recently been found at Yaxley. These show that the dead were burnt in costume with token possessions. Sacrificed animals might also be laid on the pyre. Small items were occasionally added before the urn and ashes were buried. Not surprisingly, the great majority of Anglo-Saxon ornaments survive from furnished inhumations rather than from cremations.

The pottery urns, shaped without the wheel and fired under a bonfire, contrast totally with Roman products. They do not merely imitate the continental homeland technology, forms and styles, but extend them into this new territorial sphere. J.N.L. Myres recognised (and James Campbell illustrates), in urn-fragments from Markshall cemetery near *Venta*, work of the same potter who made an urn used in a cremation burial at Wehden, Lower Saxony, during the mid-fifth century. Of course the pot may have been imported rather than the potter – it was a particularly splendid one, burnished, with embossed and sculpted features, and modelled human faces not unlike those which peer from early Saxon button-brooches. But the role of potters in relation to the groups or families they served apparently survived the sea crossing. Their vessels, which employ techniques of burnishing, and of bossed, modelled and incised, combed and stamped ornament, have a strongly organic appeal. Their makers remained aware of changing continental fashions.

Stanley West argues that the Lackford cemetery, beside a Romano-British ritual site, formed a regional focus for groups who favoured cremation. They may have gathered from various surrounding communities or farmsteads to use this burial ground. Beginning in the mid-fifth century perhaps a thousand burials, almost exclusively cremations, occurred here while the custom survived. Some 530 have been found contained in urns, fewer than 50 of which contained artefacts or goods. The older examples include Anglian types, like those of eastern Slesvig and Funen, Saxon wares like those from the Lower Elbe-Weser region, and Anglo-Frisian examples typical of the mixed settlements in Frisia. That cultural mixture is also found in smaller cemeteries where many fewer were buried over the same period, and where (as at West Stow) burial with grave-goods was also practised. A Swabian bowl was found at *Venta*, and the name Swaffham in Norfolk, Suffolk and Cambridgeshire is taken to show the presence of Swabians there. Early Frisian artefacts like the comb from Pakenham, and place names Freston and Friston show direct communication with that culture. One Lackford grave included a large pair of burnt red deer antlers, perhaps for a pagan mumming ritual or totemic dance.

The vessel from Eye figured by Akerman enclosed with the ashes a miniature iron knife, shears and tweezers, and a pediment-backed comb resembling late Romano-British production, like several found at Grimstone End and elsewhere. W.H. Brooke drew other Eye urns in 1818, including a shouldered urn with scored swathes like hanging festoons. The series in the Ipswich Museum illustrate a range of forms. The very early open shallow urn from Coddenham has combed decoration. A globular grey example from Culford has embossed knobs around the shoulder, and a narrow neck and rim. Miniature implements were added to these ashes. A *Buckelurn* excavated at Fakenham on the lower Black Bourne is a hybrid with foot and stem supporting a bellied and stamped vessel with large diagonal bosses, a narrow neck and rim. Two burnished black urns from Snape cemetery, ovate in profile, have only slight bosses created by

Eye: cremation urn sketched by W.H. Brooke, 1818. *Courtesy of William Drummond*

finger pressure within: both apparently contained child burials. Others from the early excavations at Snape include tall vessels with combed panelling and zones containing stamped decoration.

The bodies which were laid out in the grave with costume and other accessories project to us an image of the dead person. The arrangements were made by the funeral parties and there is great discussion as to their cultural, social and economic meaning. The ornaments closely associated with women, in particular, suggest a kind of national costume, probably consisting of a tubular woven twill dress fastened at the shoulders with brooches, and tied at the waist with a belt or girdle. Preserved textiles on some brooches (e.g. Hadleigh Road cemetery, Ipswich) show they were used singly to fasten a twill shawl or overgarment above a linen undershirt. In archaeology this costume is represented especially by the metal brooches and bead necklaces, by the various girdle-pendants and accessories, and also by sleeve-clasps (for the cuffs). These small ornamental metal plates in linking pairs were in certain florid types supplied with an additional plate to mask the sleeve gusset above the cuff. The costume therefore included sleeved garments: preserved or replaced textiles show that the cuffs were sometimes trimmed with colourful band- or tablet-woven braids.

Objects often associated with women include the spindle-whorl and implements of the girdle, including real keys or long bronze key-shaped plates which may betoken guardianship, the small knife and girdle-ring, and the comb.

Above Culford: cremation urn with bosses. *Ipswich Borough Museums*

Left Coddenham: pair of sleeve-clasps. *de Saumarez/Cummings Collection*

Brooches, buckles and small knives occur in graves of both sexes and often a vessel of pottery, wood or glass, a bronze bowl or stave-tub might be placed with them, probably for food or drink offerings. As the 'spindle-half' had been represented, so the 'spear-half' often assumed a military aspect in death. The spears, blacksmith-forged, frequently had long double-edged blades and were mounted on shafts of ash-wood about 2m long. The circular shields were often made of lime-wood, probably covered with hide. Normally all that survives is the pointed iron boss which protected the central hole for the hand-grip. Swords (valued weapons signifying personal status) were more seldom buried, and acquired virtue with their history of use.

These burials project an ideal or mythic sense of nationhood expressed by this costume in life, and rendered or consecrated to the grave, to the Land, in death. By that projection nationality became historical as successive generations continued their customs. A woman buried at Westgarth Gardens (Bury St Edmunds) dressed with sleeve-fasteners, beads and two small-long brooches, held a fossil sea urchin (a 'fairy loaf') in her right hand as a talisman. Good omens might therefore follow the dead in their forming role as ancestral guardians of landed nationhood. But even within their pre-Christian society, which some believe to have been comparatively egalitarian or collective, that mythic process became absorbed in organisation. Martin Carver saw a conceptual link between the tribute of the costume to the grave, and the more fiscal exactions imposed upon the population as formal rulership developed.

Handford, Hadleigh Road: spear-heads and shield-bosses from the late sixth century cemetery.
Ipswich Borough Museums

Brooches, markers of cultural identity

Great scholarly attention surrounds the brooches, which show various continental and Scandinavian affinities and distinctive regional developments. The small-long brooches, for instance, form a large category with a distribution in the Lark valley at Bury, Icklingham, Cavenham, Lackford, Eriswell, Mildenhall, Lakenheath, Freckenham and Exning, and in the Dove watershed between Wickham Skeith and Eye, but also in the south-east, notably at Coddenham, Bealings, Playford, Rushmere and Tuddenham, and at Snape, Ramsholt and Ufford. Their use continues from the late fifth through the middle of the sixth century. The brooch headplates are of various shapes, square, trefoil, cross-shaped or horned, and have counterparts in the Angle and Saxon areas of the continent. The trefoil types are thought to imitate southern Scandinavian cruciform brooches of the late fifth century.

The Cruciform brooch characterises the Migration Age in northern Germany and Scandinavia, and in Anglian England. Examples are very widespread and numerous in Suffolk, and more so in Norfolk. The earliest types (which include a southern group north-east of Sudbury) are shaped like a long pin with a bow, a knob on the head and an animal's head at the tip. Those from Wenhaston, Coddenham, Ixworth and Mildenhall are among the important markers for migration during the middle or later fifth century: new examples from Eye, Yaxley and Braiseworth show the Dove valley similarly active in these early stages. A woman of Westgarth Gardens (Bury) wore both an early cruciform brooch and an equal-armed brooch of the fifth century (Nesse type).

Little Waldingfield: early cruciform brooch, front and side view. *Suffolk County Council*

As the cruciform brooch evolved, flanges appeared on the head below the knob, and the animal's head terminal grew in characterisation. Side-knobs were attached to the 'wings' of the headplate and later became a cast-in feature of many brooches. Much larger display forms were adopted, the varieties and uniformity of which both seem to hold clues to changing patterns of social organisation and patronage. In Suffolk they are especially profuse in the Lark valley and other western settlements, but they also have an important presence along the Orwell and Gipping, for instance at Creeting, Coddenham and Akenham, and at Tuddenham nearby. Fine large examples, including one with empanelled groups of S-motifs, were among burnt ornaments from cremations newly found at Yaxley in north Suffolk.

The cast saucer-brooches, sometimes gilt, are rarely found in Suffolk, and do not illustrate any focused cultural group. A gilt example from Butley carries a simple interlace motif. A Coddenham specimen with human faces as quadrants resembles one from Horton Kirby in Kent. But gilding and ornamental casting made its appearance early in a new and more exotic variety of the cruciform brooch. They were embellished on the bow, arms and footplate with florid relief-cut castings. Two handsome examples from Icklingham typify the earlier development, with a frontal mask at the foot, and panels of zoomorphic abstraction applied or cast into the outline. This ornament, with its masks and animal scenes crowded with staring eyes, short limbs and loops for bodies, is associated with a phase in the history of north Germanic and Scandinavian migration spanning the late fifth and the early sixth century. In their later developments florid cruciform brooches are often gilt. Finely-carved gilt bronze belt-fittings in related style from Icklingham, Eriswell and Coddenham, and newly from Hacheston and Sutton on the Deben, suggest the expression of individual authority and wealth in personal attire.

The Great Square-Headed Brooches are another distinct type but, like the large cruciforms, are heavy, conspicuous vehicles of ethno-cultural display. Individual specimens occur in richly-furnished graves, usually with beads, knives and vessels, in such cemeteries as Holywell Row, Mildenhall, Lackford and Lakenheath, in Norfolk at Bergh Apton and Morning Thorpe, and among inhumations at the mainly cremation cemetery of Spong Hill (North Elmham). They have a large square headplate, a high bow and an elaborate footplate with expanding arms or knobs, all decorated with stamps and chip-carved ornament prepared for the casting. Large gilt examples found at Baron's Road, Bury and at Lakenheath show animals formally disposed on the headplate, and masks with staring eyes hidden among the ornament. These have derivatives, like the fragmentary brooch from Cavenham.

A distinguished brooch is represented by fragments newly found at Witnesham near Ipswich. In solid silver, gilt, its modelled carving and rich ornament includes faces around the headplate frame. The brooches were more usually bronze castings gilt by mercury process. The earlier forms, which include one

Akenham: pair of cruciform brooches
found before 1853. *Ipswich Borough Museums*

Lakenheath: florid cruciform brooch. *The
Ashmolean Museum, Oxford. Photograph: R.
Carr*

Bury St Edmunds, Barons Road: square-headed
brooch. *Drawing, after S.E.West 1998*

from Holywell Row, Mildenhall (Grave 11) and another provenanced only to
Suffolk, have parallels in Jutland and Anglian Slesvig-Holstein, and in southern
Norway. They can be attributed to southern Scandinavian influence on England
at the beginning of the sixth century. Their long series of types show diverging
progressions or communicating focuses of style and manufacture. There is a
separate evolution in the Kentish sphere in communication with the Franks.

Examples from Lakenheath, Mildenhall, West Stow, Lackford and Tuddenham
in Suffolk form part of a distribution group including the Cambridgeshire
cemeteries at Girton, Barrington, Wilbraham or Great Chesterford, and with a
sparser spread between Lincoln, Leicester and Northampton. John Hines discerns
the Scandinavian influence operating in eastern England independently of Kent,
and continuing to do so as the various Anglo-Saxon types make their appearance
in East Anglia. The third and ultimate phase of their use, extending beyond
the middle of the sixth century, shows three distinct series strongly focused in
Suffolk and Norfolk. In sixth-century Scandinavia the comparable square-headed
brooches are distributed mainly in western Norway, then a particularly rich area.
Designs of continental square-headed brooches were probably influenced both
from Norway and Britain.

A significant number of the grave-groups containing them, from Bergh
Apton and Spong Hill in Norfolk through Suffolk and Cambridgeshire into
the east Midland settlements west of the Fen and in south Lincolnshire, also

include sleeve-clasps, with a clear bias towards the more ornate forms. Suffolk examples of this combination are at Lackford and Little Eriswell. Dr Hines makes the case that the sleeve-clasps ('definitive for the Anglian English culture-province') were introduced from the last quarter of the fifth century onwards under immediate Norwegian influence. Their influx and distribution may still be explained in terms of the movement and migration of people, maintaining direct links between eastern England and west Norway during the sixth century. The costume, like the ornament of the large brooches, gave a significantly Norwegian aspect to the early Angle identity in Britain.

THE RULERSHIP OF THE ANGLES

The emergence of East Anglian ruling power and the origins of Devil's Dyke, the long earthwork between Reach beside the Fen and Stetchworth in the woodlands of north-western Essex, share a similar obscurity. As described by Abbo, the Dyke is 'a foss sunk in the earth, fortified by a mound equivalent to a wall of considerable height', and was built to deter or repel attack from the west. It is an immense monument to a centralised power controlling populations based in the eastward lands, approximately Suffolk and Norfolk. It is the largest of a series of similar earthworks, including the Black Ditches below the Lark near Mildenhall and the Fleam Dyke between Fulbourn and Balsham (Cambs.), which defend the principal land route south of the Fen, and the upper end of the Icknield Way. Opinions have varied as to whether its origins lie more among the prehistoric defences of the region, or in the formation of Anglo-Saxon East Anglia, when it was certainly defended. If the latter, then it begs the question of when and how a sufficient power may have emerged to create it. It was of paramount importance to East Anglia during the second quarter of the seventh century, but had perhaps stood in the consciousness of the emerging state long before this. At times of alert, it gave Exning the importance of a frontier settlement.

The Continent and eastern England
The powers beyond the North Sea were laying the foundations of great dominions. One of the two principal Frankish branches, the Ripuarii, founded a kingdom at Cologne in 460 and, spreading up the Rhine, eventually confronted the Alemanni, and defeated and subjugated them in 496. The other branch, the Salii, were continuing their own expansion south and westwards. New settlements arose on the southern shores of the Channel. The personal sophistication of their King Childeric I (d.481) is revealed by the contents of his grave at Tournai. It contained several golden ornaments with inlaid cellwork of cut garnets. His personal gold seal-matrix bore a frontal portrait and inscription in classical style, presenting a Roman style of authority.

Childeric's famous successor King Clovis I (481-511) drew the Frankish kingdoms together. After a great victory at Soissons in 486, and the defeat of the Alemanni at Tolbiac (not far from Cologne) in 496, Clovis was converted and baptised by Bishop Remigius at Rheims. He conquered the Burgundians and held them in tribute: his campaigns from 507 against the Visigoths added Aquitaine to the Frankish Empire, with Poitiers, Angoulême, Bordeaux and Toulouse. The Christian Church in France therefore retained an unbroken continuity from its Roman origins. The Eastern Emperor Anastasius (491-518) conferred Consular or pro-Consular authority on Clovis, whose sister was married to Theodoric of Bern, the Ostrogothic ruler of Italy (493-526). In 511 the Frankish Empire was partitioned between the sons of Clovis, Theodoric (511-34) in Austrasia (the kingdom of Metz), Clodomir at Orleans (511-24), Childebert at Paris (511-58) and Chlothar I of Neustria. The kingdoms finally reunited under Chlothar until his death in 561. Childebert at one time is said to have held some power in Britain. Protected by Theodoric the Ostrogoth, the less powerful successors of Genseric the Vandal (d.477) were still acknowledged by the Eastern Empire. The Vandal position in Africa failed under Gelimer in 533.

The dynastic struggles of the Scandinavian peoples in the decades after 500 form the social background of the Old English heroic poem *Beowulf*. The Swedish ruler Ongentheow held his power at Old Uppsala in Uppland. Hygelac King of the Geats (of southern Scandinavia) slew him in a great battle at Ravenswood in 510. Hygelac himself was killed in *c.*521 while conducting a raid on the Franks of the Rhine for booty and prisoners. Theodobert (son of King Theodoric of Metz) repelled the raiders: Beowulf, whose mother was Hygelac's sister, avenged his uncle's death and escaped by a heroic feat of swimming. He did not know, as he rose exerted from the Rhine waters, that he should be numbered among the first heroes of English legend.

Beowulf's father Ecgtheow had caused a blood feud among the Wulfings and took refuge among the south Danes. The affair was settled by the intervention of Hrothgar, the Danish ruler in Sjælland. Beowulf therefore rendered service to Hrothgar at his great hall of *Heorot* – the primary narrative of the poem. Later, in 532, Ongentheow's son Ohthere died, and his brother Onela seized the Swedish power: he was married to Hrothgar's sister. He drove Ohthere's sons, Eanmund and Eadgils, out of the country, and they found refuge with the Geatish ruler Heardred (Hygelac's son). Onela therefore attacked the Geats in 533, slew Heardred and Eanmund and left Beowulf to rule them. A few years later Eadgils, assisted by the Geats, reopened the war. Onela was slain in a great battle on the frozen surface of Lake Vänern, and Eadgils made himself ruler of the Swedish house.

In 531 Theodoric invaded and subjugated Thuringia. Two separate traditions indicate that many people were emigrating from Britain back to the Elbe and Weser homeland in search of land to settle. Arriving at Hadeln (beside Cuxhaven, near the Galgenberg and Westerwanna cemeteries) they came to the attention of Theodoric, who enlisted them in his Thuringian campaign and then gave them some of the conquered lands north of the river Unstrut. The Thuringian colonists from the Elbe lands were called Angli and Varni. Procopius (in Constantinople) heard that many families from Britain sought new homelands in the kingdom of the Franks each year, and recorded that their king (Theodobert, ruling 534-47) sent Angles among his embassy to the Emperor Justinian (527-65) at Constantinople to reinforce some claim of dominion in Britain. If Anglian expansion into central and central southern Britain was for some time arrested after Mount Badon, the growing population must have been in the east. Their various dialects had increasingly merged into English variants of Anglo-Frisian speech. Many returning emigrants may have come from East Anglia itself or have come through it to the coast. Some may have died here leaving artefacts brought from more central parts of Britain. John Morris points to a concentrated area of English settlement between Boulogne and Lille whose place names appear to reflect a population derived from Norfolk, probably colonised there under Frankish royal patronage.

Procopius gives a story which shows that the Angles had ruling families with dynastic interests and large military resources. At a time when some of the Varni were settled near the Rhine mouth, a sister of a ruler of the Angli of Britain, with a second brother, led a large army in 400 ships up the Rhine. She went to assert her prior marital claim over a prince of the Varni, a people associated with the Angles. Despite being betrothed to her, at his father's death the prince had attempted to marry his own stepmother, Theodobert's sister, since the political friendship of the Franks offered greater benefits. Thus the Angles of Britain asserted their rights in the world of Frankish diplomatic influence, which now dominated the Rhineland, some Frisian territory and most of Gaul. Kent's relations with Frankish culture had been the closest in Britain from the later fifth century onwards, and so this story seems to belong to a more northerly, perhaps East Anglian society.

Tokens of an aristocratic class
Who then were these rulers of Angles? Christopher Scull proposed the model by which customs of inheritance favouring the eldest son might naturally result in local and regional powers, and ultimately in formal rule. If senior male heirs sought brides of their own class outside their immediate communities, this would create a network of kinship amounting to a class. Their patronage of craft specialisation and exchange might then be expressed in attire, possessions and gifts, promoting competition among them. He envisaged that junior heirs consolidated more local positions, in the earliest phases forming rural settlements around origin-households. (The custom of Borough English, by which the youngest son inherited, was known in various parts of Suffolk: the senior heir may not necessarily have been the eldest.) Early territories are inferred from the groups named in the *Tribal Hideage*, a later Mercian compilation for calculating

tribute. Like the Wissa of west Norfolk, mentioned in another source, they were focused upon river systems.

Patrilineal inheritance was profoundly important among the early ruling families. The rulers of the Old English kingdoms who claimed to be their descendants expressed their right by ancestral affiliation to pre-migration figures. These they declared to be the collective posterity of the god Woden. Woden was a Mercurial figure. The Angles in Britain (especially in the south Midlands) attached his name to certain places. If its early German form, *Wuotan*, may signify movement or striding (Old English, *wadan*, 'wade'), a medieval commentator, Adam of Bremen, found in it the concept of *wod*, madness. Motion and alteration may introduce positive, transforming arrangements, or chaos and disarray. Among characteristics later attributed to Woden were the powers to bind runes, riddles, word-charms, oaths, contracts and music. Hence, by powers, contracts and music the rulers became heirs of Woden. The leadership of peoples in movement, those of the kin who could guide new nations to their destinies and so bring about new order, were the posterity of Woden. The sacred oaths which bound them were fastened on the Spear which led them: it brought them to the field of slaughter overseen by Woden.

The East Saxon rulers, exclusively, derived their ancestral line not from Woden but from a manifestation called Seaxnot, whose worship (together with that of Woden and Thunor) the continental Old Saxons of Thuringia first renounced during the eighth century through the teachings of an Englishman. As they did so, the English Christian rulers were compiling ancestral tallies proclaiming their own descent from the same gods. Wendover and other medieval chroniclers associate the foundation of the kingdom of East Saxons (Essex) with the name of Exwine or Eorconwine and a founding date of 527. Gildas informs us that international seaborne trade was busy in the Thames and Severn in his own time, the 540s: London may still have been largely British in population. The grandson of Ambrosius Aurelianus was then among the British rulers. But Gildas wrote on the eve of a calamitous Yellow Plague, which spread around much of the known world and destroyed several millions of people. King Maelgwyn the Great of Gwynedd, perhaps most powerful of the rulers whom he addressed, fell victim to it. We do not know how it struck the villages or halls of East Anglia, but various English dynastic claims seem to have become consolidated in its aftermath, as scholars perceive the end of the Migration Age, the *Volkerwanderungzeit*, during the 560s.

Aristocratic values were expressed in individual burials of unusual wealth or custom. The distinctive ritual of horse-burial may bear witness to an equestrian class, where it is found in eastern England and in northern Europe. An outstanding equestrian grave, hitherto largely unnoticed, was uncovered during crag diggings in 1820 at Witnesham just north of Ipswich, on land belonging to Revd C. Eade of Metfield. The farmer Charles Poppy, who was present and kept some of the finds, described his discovery to D.E. Davy in May 1824, to

P. Meadows in July 1828, and to Major Moor of Bealings in September 1846. Both Davy and Meadows independently call him 'very intelligent'. All that is known is recorded in Davy's Suffolk Collections (Witnesham, Fols. 410-411).

On a side bank at the farm, within 6ft of the surface, was found the skeleton of a man about 5.5ft tall carefully laid east and west, with a lance alongside, a helmet with a silver ornament at the front of it and 'other perfect specimens' and 'military accoutrements'. Within a yard's distance were the bones of a horse of full riding size with saddle and bridle. Of the bridle only the bit curb and buckles remained, but the wood of the saddle and some of the leather remained in perfect shape: it was raised some 4 or 5 inches at the back, where the edge was covered with iron or copper. In front the saddle pommel was high, with a round silver 'plate' on each side; the finder described it as 'similar to cavalry saddles of the present time.' There were also two larger plates on the hind part, described as 'button like ornaments, the top of them covered in tin foil, circular, an inch and three quarters in diameter.' A stout iron ring and supposed stirrups were buried with the saddle. On a separate occasion at the same pit the labourer found and reburied 'many pieces of armour.' Mr Poppy saw 'a breast plate or two and some other portions.' The labourer explained 'he was not aware what these iron things were.' Perhaps they were shield bosses and similar equipment from a surrounding cemetery. They should not be confused with the full *cart load* of bones found on the opposite side of the valley in around 1800.

Annotated sketches by W.H. Brooke (recently found by William Drummond) show that a bridle-and-bit, and bones of horses, were among objects excavated at the Eye cemetery in 1818. Henry Prigg found buried horses in cemetery contexts at Mildenhall. A related bridle-bit with fixed mouthpieces and rein links was found in a horse grave in the Anglo-Saxon cemetery at Great Chesterford (Essex). Discs recovered from a mound-burial at Allington Hill, Bottisham (Cambs) are likely to be funerary horse-trappings. More recently, dramatic examples of this sixth-century custom have been excavated at Sutton Hoo and RAF Lakenheath cemeteries, both with owners bearing shield and spears, and another is identified at Snape.

Joe Caruth's excavations at Lakenheath revealed two such graves, one of them a remarkably early and complete example. The dead man lay in a coffin near the south wall of a large rectangular pit, with his horse beside him. The pit was surrounded by a barrow ring-ditch enclosing a square area, near to which were children's graves. The man was buried as a warrior with sword and spear, and with a shield resting on his coffin. As at Witnesham his horse wore its saddle and bridle in death, and also had a bucket of provender. The mouthpieces of the iron bit have applied silver attachments, while the bridle includes gilt bronze cruciform fittings set at the strap crossings, with chip-carving in the central field and applied silver terminals. Fittings from the headband and browband are long ovals with a mask at the top with staring eyes, and crescent-shaped at the foot. Their ornament (from the Style I repertoire) is of the second quarter of the sixth century and of high quality, a commission of worth. Among the finest works in related style are fittings for drinking-horns made perhaps in the 520s and buried much later in the mound-grave at Taplow (Bucks). As they reflect formal mead-drinking in an aristocratic Hall ceremonial, so the Lakenheath bridle fittings (and the horse itself, no doubt sacrificed for the occasion) denote achieved status among noble kindred or companions.

Heroic or aristocratic mound-burial saw a revival during the sixth century in Scandinavia as well as in Britain. The transition from the Age of Burning to the Mound Age is given a mythic association with Frey at Uppsala, and with King Dan the Proud in Denmark (buried in royal estate with war gear and a saddled horse), in late literature such as the *Heimskringla* Prologue. The real mounds at Old Uppsala are associated with the Swedish rulers. The renewal of the English custom may also have been a response to local examples of Bronze Age mounds, around which their early settlements and burial sites often clustered. At Snape, among mounds already perhaps 20 centuries old, Anglo-Saxons had cremated their dead since the fifth century AD. Soon after the middle of the sixth, a new and remarkable ceremony was enacted there for one very important burial. A clinker-built ship at least 14m long and about 3m in the beam, presumably hauled the considerable distance from the north bank of the Alde, was laid deep under a large new mound. The dead person was placed in the ship with precious

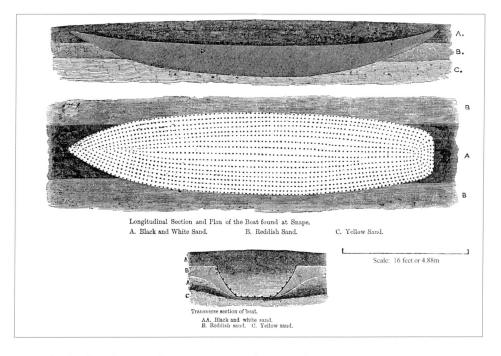

Snape: the ship-burial excavated in 1862. *Drawing, after N.F. Hele 1870*

goods, including a glass claw-beaker of sixth-century type, some spears and a gold ring with beaded filigree work, set with a Roman intaglio.

The grave had already been plundered when Septimus Davidson and Dr Hele investigated it in 1862. William Filmer-Sankey, the modern excavator of Snape, shows that this burial took place in a cemetery already used for urned cremations. Some had been disturbed when the ship-grave was prepared, and the funeral pots were carefully re-buried. Following the ship-burial, at least 21 inhumations took place in a group of satellite graves surrounding it. One, particularly rich, was of a man buried in warrior-fashion with weapons, an iron-bound bucket, ornaments and other attributes, within a small log boat. It was also associated with a buried horse with a bridle. The dugout boat ritual alludes to the ship-grave as the founding burial of this later phase at Snape. The excavator drew comparisons with small boat-graves found on the Isle of Bornholm in the Baltic Ostsee.

At Sutton, overlooking the Deben opposite Kingston and Woodbridge, a cemetery developing at the crest of a coombe also witnessed various customs. One group here had Kentish connections, for they cremated their dead and buried their ashes without vessels under moderate-sized barrows formed from circular surrounding ditches. The inhumation graves included men presented as warriors. One bore over his breast a shield with fittings of exceptional quality, of gilt bronze with applied sheet silver. They represent an eagle or predatory bird, and a long creature, probably a fish or a dragon. Like insignia or totemic images, they suggest allegiances in the dead man which are simultaneously temporal and spiritual. The shield also carried an ornamental gilt stud on the boss, and a group of metal discs fastened to the board.

Among the cremations one was buried in a small pit, the ashes contained in a fine bronze hanging-bowl. This had three openwork escutcheons or hook-plates and another decorative casting centrally within. Such bowls were apparently produced by British or Celtic craftsmen during the fifth and sixth centuries, and appear, complete or in fragments, with some frequency in Anglo-Saxon contexts where

Snape: gold ring with Antique intaglio, from the ship-burial. *The British Museum. Photograph: R. Carr*

they were much valued. This bowl's escutcheons, essentially sub-Roman in character, are very like a detached plate found at Eastry (Kent), a place of early administrative importance and a royal dwelling during the seventh century. The link shows direct communication between East Anglia and Kent during the sixth century, at two sites later closely connected with their ruling dynasties. A stamped pottery vessel, probably of the later sixth century, was included with this Sutton cremation.

Kingdoms: from East Anglia into Mercia

The late 550s mark a distinct horizon in the formation of English powers. At that time King Ida died after ruling for some years in the northern coastal kingdom called *Berneich* (Bernicia), centred upon his stronghold at Bamburgh. Northumbrian ancestral tallies show him as the nephew of King Ælle of the South Saxons. At Ida's death Northumbrian power transferred to another King Ælle, of a rival dynasty centred at York in the ancient province of *Deur* (Deira). At this same time Ceawlin, son of Cynric, obtained the kingship of the West Saxons or Gewissæ, after joining his father's wars against the Britons of Wiltshire during the 550s. His power was such that in 568 he drove Æthelberht (Eormenred's son) back into his kingdom of Kent, from which he had apparently been expanding.

The ancestral tallies of the later rulers of East Anglia and Mercia provide clues to the origins of their power. These genealogical lists of the so-called *Anglian Collection* reflect eighth-century interests. They show the paternity of ruling kings ascending into sequences of names, often in alliterative pairs, from older traditions of ancestry. They span the migration and early state-formation periods, numbering a few generations in each dynasty. They are likely to compress affiliations more complex and remote than direct paternal lineage. As that of Kent included Hengest and Æsc, and of Wessex the names Cerdic and Cynric, they are sources adapted to legend, to myth even.

The Mercian tally refers to Icel, the fourth name after Offa of Angeln. During the eighth century Felix, the East Anglian biographer of St Guthlac, described his subject as an Iceling and therefore of Mercian royal descent. He clearly expected the East Anglian king Ælfwald, his patron, to recognise and honour that ancient name. Icel appears fourth in sequence before Creoda, the immediate forebear of the later Mercian dynasty. John Morris envisaged the rulership of an Iceling dynasty centred in Norfolk from the later fifth century, which later led the conquest, consolidation and rule of the English Midlands. In doing so its power within East Anglia was lost to an independent dynasty based around Rendlesham. He finds Icel at Ickleton (Cambs.) and Hickling (Norfolk), but Norman Scarfe showed that the ideal form, Icklingham (in the middle reaches of the Lark valley) probably has a different explanation. Icel's successor Cnebba may have lent his name to a Roman shore fort in East Anglia called (in the seventh century) *Cnobheresburg* or *Urbs Cnobheri*, usually taken to be Burgh Castle. He might also be the leader named Cnebba who was slain fighting Ceawlin of Wessex in 568 at *Wibbandun*, according to the *Anglo-Saxon Chronicle*.

The development of an early Middle Anglian province may be reflected in the regions grouped together in the *Tribal Hideage*. East Anglia's engagement with the Anglian peoples from Kesteven through the lands of the Nene and Welland towards Leicester and towards the Avon headwaters was reinforced through the middle and later years of the sixth century. The production of florid cruciform brooches, in which East Anglian examples had provided a stimulus to the Midland fashion, spread to the Kettering region and elsewhere. The later types of square-headed brooch especially associated with East Anglia are also distributed, more sparsely, in that region between Lincoln, Leicester and Northampton. Their transmission into the Midlands implies the westward movement or dispersal of the industry, or of the women who wore them.

Two distinctive late East Anglian groups of square-headed brooches are represented in the cemetery at Handford, where the Gipping valley emerges into marshes at the head of the Orwell estuary above Ipswich. Stuart Boulter's excavations have revealed sixth-century occupation on the Ipswich side of the river including eight-post houses with (untrampled) sunken floors. On rising land, on the opposite bank beside the Hadleigh Road, a cemetery (possibly connected with this occupation) was in use during the later sixth and early seventh centuries. The graves of more than 160 people buried there were investigated by Miss Nina Layard in 1906-07. Thirty-five contained necklaces made of amber, coloured and patterned opaque glass, melon-shaped or polished clear glass beads. Altogether seven square-headed brooches and a hybrid, made perhaps around 550-70, mostly associated with the longer strings of beads, marked the wealthier burials. Plain annular brooches were worn in some other graves, sometimes with amber and crystal beads. Among the male burials at Handford was a high proportion containing spear and shield. The command of south-east Suffolk depended upon the control of this waterway, and a militarised community here may be a realistic explanation. By contrast, the partly excavated cemetery nearby at Boss Hall, Bramford had no square-headed brooches, but one fine florid cruciform type. However, the cultural divide is not complete, for a pair of silver bracelets of beaten and stamped silver found here are like the ones

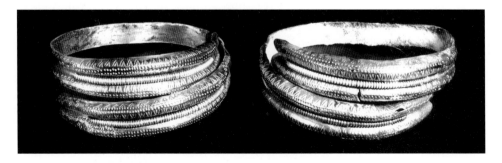

Bramford, Boss Hall: silver bracelets from a woman's grave. *Ipswich Borough Museums*

found with square-headed brooches at Barrington (Cambs.), Holywell Row, Lackford and Icklingham.

Two of the Handford square-headed brooches, which have enrolled animal heads in spiralling cuts on the shoulders, belong to a type (Hines XVII) also found at Finningham and Eriswell in Suffolk, south of Cambridge at Barrington, and in Norfolk at Kenninghall, Bergh Apton, Bircham and Burnham Norton. West of the Fen they appear at Ruskington near Sleaford (Lincs.) and at Market Overton (Rutland). Handford had five of another type with large gaping animal heads (Hines XVI), also of gilt bronze with applied sheet silver detail. Others like them are found at Westgarth Gardens cemetery (Bury), at Lakenheath and Holywell Row, and across southern Norfolk at Bridgeham, Kenninghall (2), Morning Thorpe (3), at Bergh Apton and Catton, at Spong Hill and Hunstanton. There are Midland examples, for instance at Billesdon and Willoughby (Leics.), at Market Overton (Rutland) and Great Chesterford (Cambs.). Another type (Hines XV) occurs in the Lark valley, around Cambridge, and at Nassington, Wakerley and Market Overton west of the Fen.

The localised presence of these particular groups, for instance at Handford, Kenninghall, Morning Thorpe and Bergh Apton, must tell us something about the movements of their owners. They are thought to have been made in East

Handford, Hadleigh Road: square-headed brooch.
Ipswich Borough Museums

Anglia. Three Handford examples show riveted repairs owing to poor casting – does this suggest they were locally produced? The uniformity of each group suggests they served as display insignia of status among kin, perhaps received in token of marriage or maturity. Thus household patrons may have controlled their manufacture and ownership, and their distribution could reflect marital commitments. Perhaps they imitated some fine prototype (like the Witnesham brooch?) worn by the matriarch of an extended household or family tribe. Some owners, marrying within their community, might be buried near the point of production; others possibly dispersed to lives, eventually to graves, elsewhere. A brooch of the larger kind at Westgarth Gardens (Bury), worn in death with a necklace of beads very like those available at Handford, suggests that their owner had moved from one settlement to the other. Two Kentish keystone-garnet disc-brooches from graves at Handford may similarly have come there as possessions of Kentish womenfolk.

Settlements in the Waveney valley

Populous centres were developing along the south side of the Waveney. That the nobility were not confined to the halls of the Deben and Alde, or of the Lark valley, is shown by the barrow site excavated at Bloodmoor Hill, Gisleham (north-

Handford, Hadleigh Road: silver-gilt keystone garnet brooch. *Ipswich Borough Museums*

east Suffolk) in December 1757. The high mound (now lost) may at some time have been used for the Hundred-Moot of Mutford. Enough survives to show a distinguished burial, including a necklace of roughly-shaped garnets, a large jet bead and oval crystal gemstone, and a gold coin of Avitus (c.455), converted with a loop into a pendant. There was, furthermore, an onyx intaglio pendant set in gold. This is now lost, but a wax impression taken in 1758 shows first-century Roman work, a naked helmeted Dioskuros holding a wand, standing beside his horse. As at Snape, antique gems were prized by this early Anglian noble. A sixth-century cemetery nearby yielded beads of amber and coloured glass. More recently cruciform and small-long brooches have been found there.

Between Pakefield and Carlton, adjacent to Bloodmoor Field, Richard Mortimer has recently excavated a settlement of the sixth and seventh centuries. The inspected area contained at least eight timber-framed houses and 39 'sunken-featured' buildings. They stood on a sand ridge on the south-eastern side of a valley tributary to Lake Lothing, at the lower end of the Lothingland peninsula. The timber houses form a close-knit group and include some cross-aligned to form a courtyard. The village overlies Roman occupation so as to disregard its alignments and uses: there was no apparent continuity. A small cemetery of 26 burials lay at the centre of the occupation, and the site also had pits, oven-bases

Gisleham, Bloodmoor Hill: impression of lost onyx intaglio. (diam. c.2cm)
Ipswich Borough Museums

and a large midden-heap worthy of Chanticleer. The cemetery grave-goods included a wooden casket with a barrel-lock, a circular gold pendant with suspension ring, and a high quality gold and garnet disc-brooch, probably of seventh-century date. They used handmade wares, but received a few imported vessels and many lava quernstones.

Finds of unfired loomweights showed that textile weaving was important here. Two of the graves, near together, contained pairs of shears, and one of them also a pair of heckles, all presumably from sheep-minding and wool processing. The large looms at Grimstone End described above were in use at the same time – the later sixth century. Textile production was a primary, organised activity in these communities. The pottery industry was gaining a wider kind of social and economic organisation. One particular workshop distributed large amounts of its ware into west Suffolk and Norfolk. Identifiable by their stamps, combed patterns and other design features, these vessels occur in cemeteries from Castle Acre in the north to those near the Fen south of Lackford, but especially in the Illington (Norfolk, Thet valley) and Lackford cemeteries and surrounding areas. They were not only used as cremation urns: the same potters made a great deal of the domestic pottery (food vessels) used at West Stow at that time.

Another settlement, no less complex than the one at Carlton, has been partly excavated at Flixton (by South Elmham) on the south bank of the Waveney. Even in its upper reaches the Waveney flows through broad water meadows, which are overlooked by a long range of hill spurs. During the sixth century, cemeteries were formed at Flixton around two Bronze Age barrows some 500m apart. One grave included a fine dark glass claw-beaker, and others include inhumations with brooches and beads, with broken pottery and a woman's chatelaine, and a male with shield and weapons. Many new settlements or cemeteries were created near ancient mounds or earthworks during the fifth and sixth centuries. Some think this was a contrivance to justify their land-taking by appropriation of its antiquity. But in pre-Christian consciousness ancestral and other animate powers might really be feared or propitiated. By dwelling near ancient hallowed sites, communities invoked the protection and benign influence of their guardians over hearth and harvest. This appears to have been a very widespread practice.

The settlement itself was about 500m from the cemeteries. It covered an area some 300m long by 50m wide along a gravel ridge, was dominated by a very large Bronze Age mound, and overlooked the barrows of the cemetery on the neighbouring ridge. Among the buildings so far excavated are six 'halls', probably family houses (of which the largest measured 13m by 5m, but most 9m by 4m), some containing internal posts possibly to support upper storeys. There were five smaller post-hole buildings approximately 5m long, an unusual hybrid structure, and eight small 'sunken-featured' buildings. The ring-ditch of a barrow stood in one corner of a large rectangular enclosure some 60m across, and several buildings were also contained within these boundaries. At their centre was a smaller, ditched enclosure about 9m square, containing a circular pit. Some think it could represent a pagan Anglo-Saxon sanctuary. There are also evidences of domestic industry (spindle-whorls and loomweights), slag from ironworking, and sherds of imported Rhineland pottery.

A ruling culture beside the Deben

Beside the river Deben urned cremation continued on the hill spurs at Rendlesham, and the cemetery at Ufford remained in use. We have already mentioned the unurned cremations under barrows in an existing burial ground at Sutton Hoo, downstream from Rendlesham, where other cremations with valuable bronze vessels and a military inhumation including superb shield-fittings have also been found, showing an increasingly complex social organisation with varied cultural affinities. Perhaps during the 570s, a new area was brought into use nearby on a riverside bluff further along the same ridge but separated from the other gravefield by a broad coombe. It was reserved for a series of exceptionally elaborate burials, including both cremation and inhumation. The wealth, selection, rituals and layout of their contents imply that these people had held the foremost social importance, thus far separated even from their aristocratic counterparts in the older cemetery nearby. They had enjoyed an unusually sophisticated material culture with contacts ranging from the Mediterranean, North Africa and the Near East to the centres of north German and Baltic rulership.

This gravefield, the renowned Sutton Hoo cemetery, is witness to the emergence of the most distinguished, powerful elect recognisable within East Anglia during the late sixth century. In this domain of south-eastern Suffolk, this *regio* with its broad coastal waterways, the independent rulers of the East Angles established the seat of their hereditary power. Their earliest activities on that field included the building of three substantial mounds to enclose the remains and offerings for three cremation burials. Their position on the crest of the ridge was conspicuous from the opposite bank, for instance from Woodbridge or from Kingston (Kyson), near the emergence of the estuarine tributary of Martlesham Creek. Ufford, Rendlesham, Kingston and Sutton form a complex of sites around the fordable headwaters of the Deben estuary, midway between the Roman shore fort at Walton (possibly inhabited during the sixth century) and an extended community near the former Roman township of Hacheston. In the dawn age of written English history, the East Anglian rulers associated with Sutton Hoo rose to supreme power among the English and stood in that right beside the senior kings in northern Europe.

Wuffa is the name given to the father of the East Anglian royal house, from whom they took their name *Wuffingas*. According to the East Anglian tally, the descent of his authority from Woden begins with Caser, signifying Cæsar, an imperial Roman title. We will return to that unique claim. Wuffa's later forebears are grouped in three alliterative pairs, Tyttman and Trygil, Hrothmund and Hryp, Wilhelm and Wehha, the last of whom Nennius calls the first to rule over the East Angles. Wuffa succeeds Wehha in the tally. Wuffa's name might suggest a mythic founder embodying a family or clan totem of the wolf. Others find in him the historic founder. Late chroniclers, including Roger of Wendover, state that he was ruling in 571, and we presume he is dead when the annal for 578 records that Tyttla (his successor in the tally) took up the helm of the kingdom. Bede, who seemed to know the tally, described them as father and son: yet they may already have been partly fictional.

Anyone wishing to explore the family origins of the Wuffings, and the premises upon which their power arose, should begin with Sam Newton's masterful study of their relationship to the historical and legendary materials of *Beowulf* and other geneaological sources. One part of his inquiry shows how the Wuffing name might express a remembered connection with the continental Wulfing people, among whom Beowulf's father Ecgtheow had caused a feud. The name Hrothmund, fourth before Wuffa in the East Anglian tally, might refer to one of the sons of the Danish ruler Hrothgar and his wife Wealhtheow, whose marriage sealed a pledge of peace between the Scylding and Wulfing houses (the two sons appear as youths in the poem (1.1189): Hrethric was later killed, but of Hrothmund, born perhaps soon after 500, no more is told). If so, this was an extremely distinguished claim, and one which might link Hrothmund personally with the occupation of East Anglia, perhaps as an exile leader, before Wuffing dominion was consolidated.

There are echoes in the landscape, like (for example) the place name of Helmingham beside an upper tributary of the Deben. The Helmings (mentioned both in *Beowulf* and *Widsith*) were the people from whom Wealhtheow came, but we cannot know whether, or in what way, those of Suffolk were connected with them. The survival of legends later incorporated in the poem, presumably in the context of minstrel recitation, shows that they held enduring importance to English patrons in the formation of their new ruling cultures. In that light, heroic names may have been projected into the Suffolk landscape retrospectively. Whatever the true history of Wuffa and his forebears in buiding the East Anglian kingdom, their names now represent a process rather than a historical narrative, and became absorbed within the founding myth of East Anglian royal identity. In that illustrious environment they could, with hindsight, be recognised as the progeny of Woden. That hindsight was intensified as the prospects of Christian kingship came into view.

3

The spell of Sutton Hoo

TYTTLA, 578-599

Tyttla appears next after Wuffa in the East Anglian dynastic tally in the *Anglian Collection*. Roger of Wendover's chronicle (compiled *c*.1235), which has Wuffa ruling in 571, makes Tyttla's reign begin in 578. Are these dates derived from authentic tradition, or are they merely a late attempt to fit the names from the tally into a historical framework? Bede (writing before 731) had a form of the tally, for he identified Tyttla as father of Rædwald and Eni. The Sutton Hoo cemetery appears increasingly active in the last decades of the sixth century, so aristocratic occupation nearby was sustained or intensifying. As Mercian, West Saxon and other powers developed and expanded, their frontiers became defined through conflict or competition. From them the energy of expansion rebounded into the social stratification of their kingdoms, reflecting military structure into aristocratic culture. The weapons in their richly-furnished graves suggest warrior status, and other artefacts show their sophisticated European contacts or evoke the customs of the Hall. Such were the nobles surrounding the Wuffing leader to whom tradition has fastened the name of Tyttla.

The look of the nobility
The royal Hall and surroundings formed the seat of education for a future king. Here the doughty troop (*duguth*) and the youthful blades (*geoguth*) made their oaths, participated in drinking ceremonies, remembered traditionary history and heard its recitations, and advanced in degrees of seniority. Loyal service within the household, among the *gesiths* or royal companions, the thegns, the officers, reeves and servants, was itself an instruction in social order. Board games taught forethought and strategy, and the dangers of immoderate gambling. The guests, ceremonies, weddings and seasonal feasts of the household and of the court contained roles which must be learnt and manners which must be exemplified. The athletic sports of swimming or oarsmanship, the noble recreation of falconry,

and the deer-, boar- or even bear-hunt would prepare the young man for more intrepid activities. Thus spear-bearing, bowmanship and sword-wielding would become first nature in the onslaught of danger. Military action would teach the courage and discretion to lead young men willingly onto the battlefield, and win the trust of war-hardened elders. The exercise of statecraft and diplomacy must have depended upon thorough initiations of such kinds.

The communications of south-eastern Britain with the Frankish Rhinelands had opened the Halls of the nobility to very distant and resplendent prospects. One grave in the reserved cemetery at Sutton Hoo was a man's cremation, together with his horse. The ashes were laid out with other objects on a wooden tray. His military identity was shown by a throwing-axe or *francisca*, a Frankish or Langobard weapon unusual in England. In the same grave a miniature carved limestone plaque, probably from Constantinople, showed a winged Victory raising up an Emperor or bestowing a triumph. A bronze lid found in the grave apparently belonged to an imported ewer or kettle, probably for wine, like the one found at Wheathampstead (Herts).

Bronze wares were imported from the eastern Mediterranean in some quantity to southern Britain during the late sixth century, and they were often placed in wealthier graves. They include large dishes with drop-handles and openwork foot-rings, like the Suffolk examples used for cremation vessels at Wickham Market (near the Deben), Badley (Gipping) and Chilton (upper Stour). Similar bowls occur in the high-status cemeteries at Faversham, Wingham and Sarre (Kent), and in graves in Rhenish Hesse and Baden (Germany). The Taplow burial contained a chalice of this ware. A drop-handled dish and a bottle-necked ewer were among the furnishings of the recently-discovered East Saxon chamber-grave at Prittlewell (near Southend). That ewer was fitted with a strip of stamped medallions showing a figure, apparently Christian, on horseback: was it dedicated to liturgical use?

Wickham Market: eastern Mediterranean bronze bowl. *Ipswich Borough Museums*

1 Eye: cremation urn and contents excavated in 1818. *After Akerman, Remains of Pagan Saxondom 1855*

2 West Stow: reconstructed Anglo-Saxon buildings. *St Edmundsbury Borough Council/West Stow Anglo-Saxon Village Trust. Photograph: J. Fairclough*

3 Devil's Dyke, looking south–east near Exning and Burwell. *Photograph: Author*

4 Burgh Castle: the Roman fort of Garianonum. *Photograph: Author*

5 Deben Estuary at Stonner, looking west towards Waldringfield. *Photograph: Author*

6 Lakenheath: equestrian grave excavated in 1992. *Suffolk County Council*

7 Handford, Hadleigh Road: selection of grave-goods excavated in 1906-07. *Ipswich Borough Museums.*
Photograph: D. Atfield

8 *Above left* Lakenheath: bridle fitting from the equestrian grave opposite. *The British Museum*

9 *Above right* Handford, Hadleigh Road: brooch and necklace from a woman's grave. *Ipswich Borough Museums.*
Photograph: D. Atfield

10 *Left* Sutton Hoo
ship–burial. The helmet
(Tower of London
Armouries recreation).
The British Museum

11 *Below* Sutton Hoo
ship–burial. The 'great'
gold buckle. *The British
Museum*

12 Sutton Hoo ship-burial. One of the two shoulder-clasps, its halves united by a chained pin. *The British Museum*

13 Sutton Hoo ship-burial. Clasp, detail showing interlocking boars. *The British Museum*

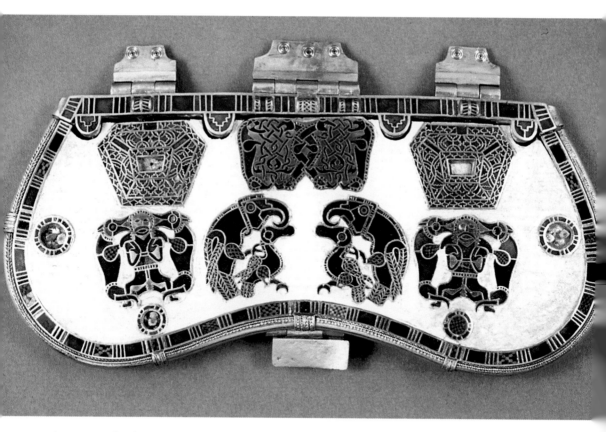

14 Sutton Hoo ship-burial. The purse lid: the jewelled panels were mounted on a base of horn

15 Sutton Hoo ship-burial. Purse lid details. *Left* Figure between wolves. *Right* Eagle with fowl

16 Above left Sutton Hoo ship-burial. The large hanging-bowl: square plaque showing a red cross motif. *The British Museum*

17 Above right Handford, Hadleigh Road. Hanging-bowl, bronze and enamel plaque. Hadleigh Road, Ipswich. *Ipswich Borough Museums*

18 Sutton Hoo ship-burial. The large hanging-bowl with champlevé enamel plaques. *The British Museum*

19 Bury St Edmunds: Abbey Precinct, aerial view from south-west. Thought to be the site of King Sigeberht's monastery of *Beodricesworth, c.635. Photograph: R. Carr*

20 Bradwell, Essex: the surviving stone nave of St Cedd's church, Peter-ad-Murum, built at Othona in *c.660. Photograph: Author*

21 Iken: promontory in the river Alde with St Botolph's church, from south-west. Thought to be the site of St Botolph's monastery of Icanho, commenced 654. *Photograph: Author*

22 Blythburgh: view north-west across the Blyth valley. Left, distance: Bulcamp, site of Anna's battle with Penda, 654. Right: Blythburgh, where Anna was buried and venerated. *Photograph: Author*

23 *Left* Brandon, Staunch Meadow: excavated ground-plan of the timber church, from the west, showing nave with eastern and western chambers. *Suffolk County Council*

24 *Below* Burrow Hill, Butley: *Insula de Burgh,* a former estuarine island occupied *c.*670–840, approached by a prehistoric causeway from the north-west. *Photograph: Author*

25 Coddenham Vale: view south-west towards the Gipping valley above Combretovium (distance, right). Buildings stood on the near slopes, burial mounds on the ridge opposite (left). *Photograph: Author*

26 Waveney valley: the Dove near its confluence with the Waveney at Oakley, in valley meadows looking south-east towards Hoxne. *Photograph: Author*

27 Bramford, Boss Hall: brooch and necklace from a woman's grave of *c*.700. *Ipswich Borough Museums*

28 Coddenham: selection of finds from the productive site. *de Saumarez/Cummings Collection*

29 Ipswich, St Stephen's Lane: the Middle Saxon road surface, looking north. Post holes show where buildings fronted onto it. *Suffolk County Council*

30 Ipswich: Buttermarket excavations (1980s) from the air, looking north, in the area of the eighth-century grid. *Suffolk County Council*

31 Ipswich: the ancient street-plan is partly preserved through 1,400 years of rebuilding. The rounded line of the tenth-century ramparts encloses the large Anglo-Saxon town. Compare with Map 1. *Suffolk County Council, 1986 Survey*

A refined import, a hammered bronze tub with friezes in punched outlines and shading, was found near the mixed cemetery at Sutton and is presumably also from a grave. The frieze shows leaping lions in combat, facing warriors with shields and bows, and a convivial Greek inscription. It is almost unique in Britain. The leaping creatures and warriors remind one of the Mediterrranean painted glassware with Greek inscriptions found in the early cemeteries at Bavenhöi, Nordrup and Varpelev (Sjælland). Suffolk also received rare glassware imports from the farther Mediterranean, as evidenced by the lugged hanging vessel, possibly a lamp, from a grave at Westgarth Gardens (Bury).

Bromeswell (Sutton): Byzantine bronze vessel, detail showing Nubian hunters. *Trustees of the Annie Tranmer Trust. Photograph: R. Carr*

Bury St Edmunds, Westgarth Gardens: eastern Mediterranean glass hanging vessel from a grave. *Suffolk County Council*

The horse and rider grave found in Mound 17 of the reserved cemetery has a different complexion. The young man in his twenties laid side-by-side with his horse, in two grave-hollows under a single mound, recalls the grave of the Lakenheath rider. The ritual confers a funerary status of horsemanship upon him. Yet in Old English there is no term such as *Ridere-sceaft*, and *cnihthad* signifies youth rather than 'knighthood'. Perhaps Germanic chivalry was considered a youthful attribute. The man was buried in a coffin with his large pattern-welded sword. Its belt carried a triangular buckle with carpeted garnet cellwork said to depict butterflies, and a pair of pyramid-shaped mounts for the scabbard. Spears and shield were also included. Vessels, including a stave bucket with iron bindings and a small bronze cauldron, perhaps contained food or drink offerings: there was a kitbag containing a cut or joint of meat.

The elaborate bridle (buried with the man's possessions) had a matched set of ornamental fittings, including cheek-pieces, strap-distributors, pendants and the complex iron bit with applied gilt castings. The decoration represents human faces, interlacing ribbons and ribbon-animals, cast out of moulds taken from models made most likely in wax. Each item was finished and gilt by the mercury process. Their interlacing patterns are managed in a very refined and controlled way. Axe-shaped pendants, similarly decorated, hung from the richly-gilt discs set at crossings of the strapwork. The discs have inset central bosses of white shell

Sutton Hoo, Mound 17: bridle-mounts from equestrian grave. *The British Museum. Photograph: Author*

or paste, into the crests of which single circular garnets are mounted. Similar roundels with applied bosses, enriched with Style II animal ornament, were found in a barrow-burial at Allington Hill, Bottisham (Cambs.) in excavations of 1860 and 1876. They perhaps belonged to a western East Anglian nobleman. Disc and pendant horse-trappings are ultimately derived from prototypes of Roman imperial military equipment, like the first-century assemblage found at Xanten on the Rhineland frontier.

Struggles and expansions of the English kingdoms

By 578 King Ceawlin of the Gewissæ (West Saxons) had extended his power far across central southern Britain. In 568 he had pushed Æthelberht back into Kent, and had slain Cnebba and Oslac at *Wibbandun*. If that was Cnebba of the Mercian tally, then the following years belong to his successor Cynewald. In 571 (when Wuffa is said to have been ruling the East Angles) Cuthwulf, a West Saxon potentate, fought the British and captured four important villages north of the Chilterns, from Eynsham, west of Oxford, across to Aylesbury, and to Limbury, east of Dunstable. The Thames valley and central Icknield Way, though perhaps under British control through the earlier sixth century, were now surrounded by English powers and must inevitably yield. Ceawlin, whom Bede calls the second supreme ruler of the southern English, scored a famous victory against the British at Dyrham, north of Bath, in 577, slew three kings, and captured Gloucester, Cirencester and Bath. Ælle held power among the Northumbrians in Deira, while the sons of Ida in Bernicia became imbroiled in lengthy wars against the British forces led by Urien and his sons.

In 584 Ceawlin of Wessex fought against the British at *Fethan leag* (Stoke Lyne, Oxon.) capturing many villages and countless booty, but departed in anger to his own lands. The next year Wendover's chronicle brings forth Credda or Creoda as the first Mercian ruler. Creoda, prominent in the Mercian tally but historically elusive, is tentatively linked by place name evidence with East Anglia, suggesting a seat of power at *Venta* (Norfolk) with royal influence in Lindsey, but extending also to the Creetings around the strategic southern junction of the Pye Road with the Gipping valley. Then his name may be traced in clusters into Hertfordshire, Nottinghamshire and Herefordshire, as if in campaigns led from East Anglia or Lindsey, or from a Midland centre. There is nothing to verify these inferences. But the later Mercian kings, who claimed to be Creoda's descendants, dominated the Middle Angles, and always sought to annexe the East Angles, never fully accepting their partition. That strongly suggests that the East Anglian state had taken shape through the secession of its rulers from an English Midland leadership which had originated in the east.

Ceawlin's angry return to Wessex signalled the beginning of Æthelberht's rise to supreme power among the southern English. In 587 the throne of the East Saxons passed to Sledda, who married Ricula, Æthelberht's sister. This alliance may continue an older role for Kent as patron or sponsor of the East Saxon throne. Æthelberht is said to have established his nephew Sæberht there as king in c.600 after Sledda's death. In Deira, Ælle died in 588 and Northumbrian power reverted to Æthelric of Bernicia, the last son of Ida. A mortal rivalry was developing: Ælle's infant heir, Eadwine, was smuggled away to safe keeping beyond the web of Bernician conspiracy.

Christian Europe: the Gregorian mission to the English

The Frankish kingdoms, having been reunited under Clothar I (Clovis' son), were partitioned for the second time in 561 between Charibert in Paris (561-67), Chilperic in Neustria (561-84), Guntram in Orleans and Burgundy (561-93) and Sigebert in Austrasia (561-75). They were again reunited in 613-28 under Clothar II, Chilperic's successor. King Æthelberht of Kent formed a dynastic marriage with Bercta, daughter of Charibert, perhaps even before 580: this important alliance was sufficient Merovingian authority for Frankish peoples settled in southern Britain. It also underlined the royal status, if not exactly equivalence, of Æthelberht himself. The marriage was agreed on condition that Bercta could maintain her Christian worship unhindered. She was assisted by a personal bishop, Luidhard, supplied by the Frankish royal house. Bercta was accustomed to pray in the church of St Martin, on a hill outside Canterbury, which had survived since Roman times and still partially remains.

Æthelberht was therefore thoroughly aware of Christianity, the religion of Rome, of Gothic and Frankish Europe, of Ireland and of the Welsh, but remained firmly enthroned within the pagan value-system which made him a living representative of Woden. He fathered a male heir, Eadbald, and a daughter Æthelburh. He possibly knew of the 12 missionaries led by the Irishman Columbanus who passed through southern England on their mission to Burgundy in around 590. He is likely to have known of St Columba, the Irish abbot who had established the island monastery of Iona within Irish Argyll, and had preached to the northern Picts, bringing a great part of the north under his pastoral care. Columba died in 597. The English kingdoms, surrounded by Christian nations, remained affirmatively pagan in the customs of their cousins and ancestors, to whom religious sentiments bound them.

Since the death of Justinian in 565, the Emperors Justin II and Tiberius Constantine had maintained the Christian East, but Italy seemed lost to them. In addition to the territories attached to Ravenna itself, the three subordinate and detached provinces of Rome, Venice and Naples remained under the rule of the Exarchate or the supervision of the East. Between these provinces now dwelt and ruled the Langobards, a migrant people from north-east Hanover who, having in the course of a century dissolved the rule of the Heruli and Gepidæ in Hungary, crossed the Julian Alps in 568 at the collapse of Gothic rule to conquer much of Italy and make their capital at Pavia. At this time they had important military alliances with Saxon armies, many of whom may afterwards have returned to north-western homelands.

After Maurice obtained the Eastern Imperial throne in 583, Gregory, a very erudite man, emerged from the noblest senatorial ranks as Præfect of Rome. His grandfather had been supreme Pontiff of the Apostolic See, Pope Felix, in 526-30. Gregory devoted his patrimony to the foundation of seven monasteries, six in Sicily and one, dedicated to St Andrew, on the Cælian Hill fronting the Palatine in Rome. During the 570s he had seen English slaves for sale in the market in Rome, and resolved on the conversion of their people to Christianity. They were Anglian youths from Deira under King Ælle's rule, possibly captured in battle and sold on by the British or the Bernicians. In 590 Gregory attained the throne of St Peter, and his plans began to take shape. In Bercta, the Christian wife of Æthelberht, he possessed the introduction he needed to the most senior of the English rulers.

In these favourable circumstances, Gregory sent the prior of his own monastery of St Andrew in Rome, Augustine, with a mission to preach to the English. Having set out they once turned back through fear; but with letters from Gregory to the Frankish rulers Theodebert II of Metz (596-612) and Theodoric II of Burgundy (596-613), and with Augustine as their abbot, they resumed late in 596 and arrived at Thanet in Kent early in 597. They had Frankish interpreters, and were soon met by Æthelberht in the open air because he feared the power of their sorcery under a roof. He permitted them to preach in Kent and to dwell in Canterbury. As they approached the city in procession bearing a silver cross and a painting of Our Saviour they sang a Gallic Rogation Day antiphon. They adopted a simple life in imitation of the Apostles, at first praying in the church of St Martin. Winning converts, they began to restore other churches and to build new ones.

In time Æthelberht himself and thousands of his people were converted and baptised. Augustine founded the monastery of St Peter and St Paul, east of Canterbury, where the chapel of St Gregory became the burial-place of kings and bishops. Augustine also rebuilt a Roman church in Canterbury and dedicated it to the Holy Saviour, on the site of the present cathedral. Pope Gregory sent him a pallium, so that he could consecrate other bishops. When a second group had arrived from Rome Augustine consecrated Mellitus to preach to the East Saxons, who were ruled by Sæberht, Æthelberht's nephew. Æthelberht built him the church of St Paul's in London for his episcopal seat. He consecrated Justus as Bishop of Rochester in Kent, where the church of St Andrew was built within an old Roman fortress overlooking the Medway. Æthelberht also gave lands and possessions to maintain the bishops' retinues. At this interesting juncture, or hereabouts, King Tyttla of the East Angles died.

RÆDWALD
KING OF EAST ANGLES 599-624
HIGH KING OF THE SOUTHERN ENGLISH, 616-624

Many have heard the name of King Rædwald, not least because of the oft-laid claim that it was he whose gold ornaments and other funeral goods were buried in the famous ship-grave at Sutton Hoo. Such renown is fitting for, despite Bede's disapproval, he emerges as a towering figure in the early pages of English history. His power issues from an Anglian, pre-Christian darkness beyond Bede's orbit of vision, and like the rumble of approaching thunder he summons attention to East Anglia for the first time. Almost immediately, in a historically decisive battle, he has won supreme royal authority among the English and his reign leaves the political scene transformed. But the foregoing darkness is so opaque that the date of his accession is barely known, and only inferred from an error made by a scribe some centuries later.

The group of annals which give us the *floruit* date for Wuffa in 571 and the accession of Tyttla in 578 fail to mention Rædwald's accession, but in two separate places they record his death, under the years 599 and 624. The *Anglo-Saxon Chronicle* is silent. This sequence of annals is incorporated by Roger of Wendover, evidently from an older source in which at some previous time the entry for 599 (and for later significant dates) has become muddled. We know from Bede that Rædwald's reign spanned the first decades of the seventh century. Even though the information given by the 599 entry is incorrect, that was clearly an important date in the sequence and most likely recorded Tyttla's death and Rædwald's accession.

Although Rædwald is the earliest and most formidable seventh-century East Anglian ruler mentioned by Bede, he does not appear in the dynastic tally of the Wuffings in the *Anglian Collection*. King Ælfwald (for whom it was apparently compiled) claimed descent from Eni, who appears next in the list after Tyttla. Eni, never described as a King, is identified by Bede as the father of King Anna (r.636-653), and presumably therefore of Anna's brothers, Kings Æthelhere and Æthelwald. Ælfwald's grandfather was Æthilric, son of Eni. Bede states that Rædwald was the son of Tyttla and grandson of Wuffa, and called him *Rex Anglorum*, King of the Angles, the fourth king who ruled over (*imperavit*) all the Angle peoples south of the river Humber. (Since the second and third were Ceawlin of Wessex and Æthelberht of Kent, this is clearly meant to include all the southern English peoples.) Hence it is taken that Rædwald and Eni were brothers, and that Eni was the younger and did not rule. The name Rædwald was also held by a moneyer, *Radoaldus*, who struck gold tremisses at *Antunnaco* (Andernach, Rhineland Pfalz) for King Theodebert II of Metz (596-612): a specimen of *c*.596-600 was found in the Sutton Hoo ship-burial.

Among the first events of Rædwald's reign must have been the funeral of his predecessor. Since the use of the Sutton Hoo cemetery field was then at its height, apparently associated with royal occupation at Rendlesham, Ufford or Kingston, we might look for Tyttla's grave there: yet some other splendid burial of that date, similar to those of Gisleham or Snape, might equally belong to the most powerful of the East Angles. We do not know what remains undiscovered, or is lost to the sea. But, anticipating for a moment the magnificence of the great Sutton Hoo ship-burial, it is argued with good reason that this burying of ships, restricted in England to two satisfactorily-known instances at Sutton and one at Snape, was most likely associated with one particular family or ruling group which controlled those exceptional cemeteries and strategic landscape points. If, as some think, the intact burial at Sutton was that of Rædwald himself, the high mound of the other (plundered) grave containing a ship may have been created there during his lifetime.

The damaged grave has unfolded its secrets to scientific investigation, and shows significant connections with the undisturbed ship-burial. Martin Carver's excavation revealed that a rectangular chamber 5m long by 2m wide had been sunk 3m into the ground and lined with planks. This corrected Basil Brown's 1938 interpretation of the chamber as a small boat. The distribution of Brown's finds was correlated with a chemical analysis of the chamber floor (the work of Phil Bethel), and provided evidence for a body in the south-western corner. Iron objects had stood at the east end, and an assemblage including a bucket and a blue glass cup stood on the median line east of centre. Precious objects were distributed nearby, including two gilt bronze discs with chip-carved animal ornament, a bronze brooch, a sword (on the south side, with the tip pointing

Sutton Hoo, Mound 2: gilt bronze disc found in 1938. *Ipswich Borough Museums*

east), and a gold-coated bronze stud from a large ornamental buckle for a waistband or sword-belt. An ornamental gilt bronze mount showing a dragon's head was part of the emblem on a large shield.

Iron rivets scattered to east and west show that a ship some 20m long was placed over the furnished chamber as its roof, and was buried when the mound was raised using earth from a circular ditch surrounding the grave. Some rivets fell into the chamber from the decaying ship. Investigators at Sutton in *c*.1860 gave many rivets to a local blacksmith to be rendered into horseshoes.

Furnished chamber-graves of this period (like those of Taplow or Prittlewell) show recurrent themes in the selection of goods and their positions around the body. These arrangements show some conformity (despite individual variations) in burials separated by long distances. Like the bronze vessels described earlier, certain valued goods recur in typical groups among them. The blue glass cup from Sutton compares closely to pairs found in chamber-graves at Prittlewell and Broomfield (Essex), at Aylsford (Kent) and singly at Cuddesdon (Oxon.). The sword fragment from this Sutton grave was forged to the same pattern as that in the undisturbed Sutton ship, probably by the same smith, and the two graves contained silver-gilt drinking-horn vandykes stamped from the same dies. Here, presumably, lay two members of the same household, despite differences in their rituals, and no more than a generation can separate them, perhaps less. The plundered grave is apparently the earlier.

Rædwald's marriage was probably contracted as a diplomatic alliance at his accession. His bride was staunchly attached to the customs of her ancestors, and although her name is unknown her character is famous. It is thought she had first married an East Saxon prince, since the name of her son Sigeberht fits the alliterative naming traditions of that dynasty. Rædwald fathered two sons of his own, Rægenhere and Eorpwald, and during their lifetimes Sigeberht was exiled in Gaul, whither he fled from Rædwald's enmity. The marriage and the production of heirs strengthened Rædwald's patriarchal authority among the East Angles. The 'R' and 'E' of his children's names follow those of Rædwald himself and his brother Eni. *Rægen-here* is an Englishing of the name *Rainier* or *Ragnar*.

Only two of Æthelberht's subject-kings received Christianity. The first was his nephew Sæberht, who assumed rule of the East Saxons on his father's death in *c*.600, and for whom Bishop Mellitus was settled in London. Rædwald was the other, and he was initiated into the Sacraments (*inbutus sacramentis*) in Kent, presumably at Canterbury under Æthelberht's sponsorship. He was, therefore, baptised and received Holy Communion: the sponsor undertook a spiritual adoption, and the candidate an affiliation. In this way Æthelberht effectively designated the succession of overlordship. This was needed to protect the Christian establishment: his own son Eadbald remained pagan, and Sæberht in Essex could hardly defend it alone. It was a bulwark against Wessex. Mercia was insufficiently consolidated and Lindsey was marginal. Rædwald was already carrying the East Angles towards leadership of the southern kingdoms in Æthelberht's lifetime. Rædwald's power, East Anglia's defensible territory and her position beyond Essex made this conversion the essential strategic advance for the Gregorian Apostles if their work was to survive. Æthelberht's sponsorship of Rædwald mandated the succession of Christian royal authority.

Material, political and spiritual transvaluations were united within the apostolic force of a royal conversion. In baptism, Rædwald was granted the remission of his sins by acknowledging the sacrifice of Jesus Christ. Thus he gained the hope of mercy in Judgement and of a Heavenly kingdom, while also joining the fraternity of Christian rulers. He therefore professed his Faith in the One God of the Holy Trinity and renounced his ancestral gods. Such were the sacred vows required of Rædwald (representative of Woden, the Guardian of Vows) before God, Augustine and King Æthelberht. Æthelberht, using the Latin alphabet diffused by the Roman missionaries, compiled the first written law-code in English. This owed something to the Salic (Frankish) system, but moderated by recompense the talionic principle of retribution and blood feud. It defined the value of money in terms of human life (or vice versa), by enumerating the payments to be made as compensation for the killing or ransom of persons of different social degrees. These classes he defined as king, earl, freeman, churl, bondman and slave. No Anglo-Saxon coins existed when this law was compiled, but Frankish gold coinage was in use among the senior classes. Requital and redemption could be expressed by the one Old English word *Edleanung*, merciful or ready compensation.

Rædwald was presumably not alone at his baptism, and other East Angles may have shared in his conversion. If his brother Eni did so, he might later have become patron of a church. Eni's son Anna made Christianity the cornerstone of his rule. Tradition places the infancy of a granddaughter of Eni at Exning, that strategic and long-established settlement near the Devil's Dyke, in *c*.631. A monastery on the Fen Isle of Soham, near to Exning, is called by William of Malmesbury a former bishop's see, echoing some ancient importance. The medieval *Liber Eliensis* preserves a story that Augustine himself founded a church near Ely at a place called *Cratendune*. Augustine died *c*.605 and was succeeded as archbishop by Laurence who had accompanied him from Rome. Christian teaching probably entered into many East Anglian households during Rædwald's lifetime, but how far is unknown.

At Æthelberht's conversion, Pope Gregory had sent him 'some small gifts, which will not be small to you, because you will receive them with the blessing of St Peter the Apostle.' Gregory died in 604. The Sutton Hoo ship-grave included two silver spoons, one inscribed 'Paulos' and the other (apparently) 'Saulos', together with a set of 10 silver bowls bearing cruciform designs. These, made near Constantinople in the late sixth century, were placed together on the right side of the king's head, opposite the famous helmet on its left. The 'Paulos' lettering is authentic for Byzantine production, but the name 'Saulos' (not the

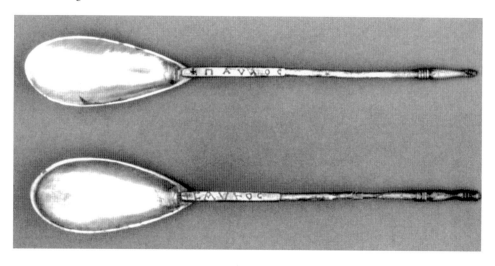

Sutton Hoo ship-burial: pair of Byzantine silver spoons marked Saulos and Paulos, placed near the 10 silver bowls. *The British Museum*

Sutton Hoo ship-burial: two of the 10 Byzantine silver bowls. *The British Museum*

name of any Apostle) was apparently inscribed later by a Frankish coin-die cutter. The spoons as a pair were therefore specially assembled to refer to the adult conversion of St Paul, originally called Saul. Brand mentions several authorities for the ancient English custom of giving apostle spoons and gilt bowls at baptism. That is evidently their meaning in the Sutton Hoo grave, probably given by a baptismal sponsor – though some scholars disagree.

Rædwald the Christian initiate returned to his kingdom, maybe in some fine vessel like the Sutton Hoo ship, accompanied by teachers or converts. His personal conversion was not accepted by all of his household. Gregory had advised Augustine that pagan temples should not be destroyed but converted to Christian use by the erection of altars within them. Rædwald's temple contained a Christian altar, but his wife and certain perverse teachers turned him away from the true spirit of his conversion. He therefore retained there another altar for 'sacrifices to devils', presumably for the sacrifice of animals to pagan gods. (A small figurine found near the excavated settlement at Carlton Colville may suggest the appearance of a seventh-century Anglo-Saxon deity.) A century later Bede wrote of this temple deploringly: Ealdwulf, Eni's grandson, in old age often told how he had seen it in boyhood. It was perhaps a square or rectangular wooden building within an external fenced enclosure, the inner sanctuaries defined by pillars. Though Canterbury could not have approved, Rædwald's public royal altar was for some time the strongest official Christian foothold north of the Thames.

It is conjectured that both the temple and the chief Hall of Rædwald's kingdom stood at Rendlesham. The use of the Sutton Hoo cemetery, linked to Rendlesham in an extended pattern of ritual landscape around the river Deben, culminated magnificently at about the time of his death and did not

Carlton Colville: silver figurine possibly representing a pagan deity. *The British Museum*

long outlast him. The historical reference to Rendlesham is later, *c.*660, but the archaeological evidence from Sutton and from Gipeswic (Ipswich), a site on the Orwell river, show that exchange with Kent, the Rhinelands and Francia were maintained in East Anglia most intensively, both commercially and at the most advantaged social levels, in the region surrounding these rivers and sites. If archaeology could demonstrate a first nucleus at Kingston with quay and market adjacent (?Woodbridge) then we might envisage that, as Gipeswic arose, the royal house removed confidently to Rendlesham to maintain strategic control of the Alde and Butley rivers as well as the Deben. That inference is compelling, and the development of this *regio* centred upon Rendlesham seems cognate with the rise of the Wuffing dynasty.

During the seventh century, estuarine trading markets or emporia (*wics*) developed around the North Sea coasts wherever ruling powers had gravitated out of the migration-age fluxions. Post-Roman London (*Lundenwic*) and York (*Eoforwic*) had hitherto served eastern Britain. In Rædwald's time the fordable headwaters of the Orwell estuary at Gipeswic, the *wic* of the *geap* or 'gap' (i.e. the valley), the highest landfall for maritime traders, became their most frequented point of arrival and departure in East Anglia. In Britain only *Hamwic* (Southampton), its West Saxon equivalent, shows similar early Anglo-Saxon origination as a town. It was apparently supervised from a royal estate on high land between Stoke and Bourne, commanding the Orwell approaches.

Some distance downstream of Handford, below the marshes where the Gipping and Orwell reconverged, the estuary widened. Before embankment it spread from near the Old Bell Inn on the Stoke side (south) to College Street on the north. The road which became College Street and Salthouse Street ran along a river embankment or quay fronted with wooden posts woven with wattle, giving draught for ship moorings. The embankment perhaps followed inlets fed by tributary streams, making docks or wharves. The river-crossing was a ford, slightly downstream of the later bridge. It linked Great Whip Street in Stoke (ultimately the road north from the Stour crossing at Manningtree) to the north bank near the west end of St Mary Quay church. The road north became Foundation Street and Cox Lane, linking to Bolton Lane and Tuddenham Road. Just north of the ford another early road (Brook Street) branched left beside a stream and formed a route northwards. The Gipeswic settlement extended from west of St Peter's Street north and east to Turret Lane. Away from the water-frontage and settlement the land rose broadly to oak-wooded and heathy uplands (Christchurch Park area). A 'corduroy' road made of logs traversed the marshy contour of the valley west to east (from Norwich Road to Spring Road, through Westgate and Carr Street).

An earthenware bottle from the Nacton foreshore, of red wheel-thrown fabric with combed decoration, heralds the arrival of Frankish and Scandinavian commercial imports into the Orwell. The first Gipeswic structures and rubbish pits are associated with local handmade pottery like the Handford wares, and with black wheel-thrown Frankish wares imported from the Rhinelands, under the control of the Merovingian rulers. Burial grounds of pagan custom lay on rising land north of the settlement. The road east from Gipeswic led towards Kingston and Sutton on the Deben only about 10 miles away, and so the Orwell became the commercial river and the Deben the royal approach. The creation of this

Above Ipswich: stakes and woven withies forming the Anglo-Saxon quay embankment. *Suffolk County Council*

Right Orwell Estuary: continental wheel-thrown bottle from Nacton foreshore. *Ipswich Borough Museums*

trading centre, presumably with tolls, tariffs and customs, seems certain to have been a deliberate foundation by the East Anglian rulers.

Rendlesham (*mansio Rendili*, the hall of Rendil) was by *c.*660 the *vicus regius* (royal vill) of a Christian Wuffing ruler, and was approached by the river Deben and by a straight road from Sutton Hoo through Eyke. Rendlesham also stands near the source of the Butley river, which rapidly becomes tidal at Chillesford and forms its own more northerly estuary and seagate. It now flows into the Ore behind the barrier of Orford Ness, but the Ness may have been shorter and the river's path to the sea more direct in early Anglo-Saxon times, subjecting the surrounding marshes to salt inundation. The oaks of Staverton, never fully cleared, gave their name to Eyke in Viking times: but the name Staverton (later an important manor) might denote stave-built structures there in early English times, as Norman Scarfe has suggested. Land routes south and north of the Butley estuary converge at Rendlesham, including those northward to Alde crossings at Iken and Glemham, both perhaps preferable to the broad fen or *snapes* where the modern road crosses Snape Bridge. Peter Warner attributes early importance to the (large) church site at Eyke and the 'castle' opposite, beside a deep lane which plunges into the valley at that point. The ancient valley-contour lanes along to Bromeswell, and between Butley and Chillesford, separate the water meadows from the rising land and are no doubt as old as the agriculture of the valley itself. The dedication of Rendlesham church to St Gregory surely belongs to the early seventh century, but whether to the time of Rædwald, or marking the site of his temple of two altars, it is impossible to say.

King Æthelfrith of Northumbria (called 'the Artful'), grandson of King Ida of Bernicia, had ruled both Northumbrian provinces since 592. During that time the Deiran prince Eadwine, Ælle's son, had grown up in exile, at first (it is said) in the British court of Cadfan, King of Gwynedd, where his childhood companion was Cædwallon, Cadfan's son. According to a Welsh tradition, the two boys dreamt they should share the Crown of Britain, if either might ever attain that elusive title. Æthelfrith, a most formidable ruler, was however extending his own Northumbrian power. He won a famous victory against the Irish of Argyll in 603, though his brother Theobald with all his army died in the same battle. Having built Bamburgh (*Bebbanburh*) for his first wife Bebba, Æthelfrith then married Eadwine's sister Acha and became the father of seven sons. He led the Northumbrian Angles to the western shores, driving a swathe between the British of Strathclyde and those of Powys, Gwynedd [and the Midlands. In his assault on Chester, *c.*613, he slew over] 2,000 British monks from the monastery of Bangor-is-Coed who had assembled there to pray for a British victory.

For this august, warlike Northumbrian, a kingdom-builder over more than 20 years, the exile's destruction would secure the inheritance of his own numerous progeny. Eadwine, driven from the protection of one king to another by the dangerous fact of his birthright, came to King Ceorl of Mercia, married his daughter Cwenburh, and fathered two sons Osfrith and Eadfrith, rightful heirs to the Deiran patrimony. But as Æthelfrith's power spread, the Humber seemed no longer to safeguard the northern frontier of Kentish influence. A Northumbrian assassin, if not an open military assault, might reach Eadwine in Mercia: the West Saxons (whom King Cynegils, great-grandson of Cynric, ruled from 611) were sympathetic to the house of Ida. Eadwine therefore turned at last to the protection of Rædwald in East Anglia. He was gladly accepted, and lived on familiar terms with the king among his retainers. In those days the Frankish Empire became consolidated under one ruler, Chlothar II of Neustria (585-628), after the deaths of Theodeberht II (of Metz) in 612 and Theodoric II (of Burgundy) in 613.

In East Anglia, possibly at Rendlesham, what now unfolded shaped the destiny not only of Eadwine, Rædwald and Æthelfrith, but also of Christian England. If the Canterbury mission and the sovereignty created by Æthelberht were to be salvaged, the hour of action was at hand. Bede, writing little more than a century later, had detailed narrative sources, some perhaps from heroic English poetry and others from monkish Latin. Learning that Eadwine was at Rædwald's court, Æthelfrith sent messengers offering large sums of money to procure Eadwine's death. At first it was to no avail (*neque aliquid profecit*): Rædwald, under whose royal promise and trust Eadwine sheltered, disdained the unworthy proposition. The Northumbrian messengers were sent a second and a third time, now offering more copious gifts of silver, but also promising war if the demands were spurned. Thus Æthelfrith, perhaps expecting West Saxon support, confronted the likely successor to Æthelberht's power. Rædwald, having solicited that power, was now obliged to defend it. The contest against the veteran of *Degsastan* seemed doomed to failure; intimidated or corrupted, Rædwald promised to kill Eadwine or to hand him over.

Eadwine's most faithful friend, who had heard of this concession to the ambassadors, came at once to his bedchamber at the palace and called him outside into the night. He offered to lead the prince away at that hour to some safe country beyond the reach of either king. Who was that friend, to know the king's secret counsels and thus to divulge them? Was he a sworn brother, perhaps the son of Rædwald himself? Did he act with Rædwald's connivance, to save the prince and to avert war? But Eadwine would not breach the king's yet unbroken trust: he would prefer death at Rædwald's hand to a renewed exile. The friend left him alone in sad and silent reflection and much anguish of spirit.

As the prince sat watchful and alone at dead of night, an unknown man in strange costume approached him and asked why he sat there. Eadwine told him to mind his own business. But then the stranger said that he knew the reason, and of the troubles which Eadwine feared should befall him. He then posed three questions. 'What reward would you give him, whoever he might be, who freed you from these troubles and persuaded Rædwald neither to harm you himself nor to betray you to your enemies to perish?' he asked. 'I would give him all I could for such a service,' replied Eadwine. 'How if he promised that with your enemies destroyed you would truly become a King, and transcend in power not only all your ancestors, but all who had been kings before you in the race of Angles?' Eadwine, encouraged, promised to show due gratitude to one who brought him such benefits. 'If the person who truly foretold these things could also give better and more useful counsel concerning your salvation and way of life than any among your parents and kinsman had ever heard, would you consent to obey him and accept that saving advice?' Eadwine avowed forthwith that he would follow in all ways the teaching of one who having saved him from such calamities could raise him to the summit of kingdom. The stranger thereupon placed his right hand on Eadwine's head, saying 'When you receive this sign, remember this conversation and fulfil the promise you are now making.' He then disappeared into the night.

Eadwine's friend returned and called him indoors joyfully, explaining that Rædwald had resolved to keep faith with him and protect him. Having secretly told his plans to the Queen she had admonished him that no reason could justify a king who sold his best friend, placed in such trouble, for gold; none could restore the loss of honour, more precious than every ornament, for the love of money. Bede seems to savour the inflexibly pagan resonance of her words, as she instructs her Christian husband in the nature of kingship. Yet there had also been a conference, and Eadwine's nocturnal stranger was, as we know from the Whitby *Life of St Gregory*, none other than Paulinus, a member of Augustine's mission at Canterbury. What he had offered to Eadwine could not have been contemplated without Rædwald's support.

The ambassadors were sent home: Rædwald rapidly gathered an army, and made his way north to meet Æthelfrith before he could assemble his whole force; and there Rædwald, with much greater numbers, slew the Northumbrian King on the east bank of the river Idle at the Mercian border. Rædwald's son Rægenhere was slain in the battle. The river Idle flows from Blyth (Notts.) past Bawtry to Heckdyke where it joins the Trent, south of the Isle of Axholme. From this event rose the proverb that 'The river Idle was polluted with the blood of the Angles' – *Amnis Idle, Anglorum sanguine sorduit*. It is not known whether Rædwald's armies reached this point by naval embarkation through the Witham to Lincoln and thence north along the Ermine Street (or the Fossdyke navigation), or indeed by a march from the south and west side of the Fen. Rædwald may have rallied his forces in southern Lincolnshire. The place names Uffington (east of Stamford) and Ufford (beside Barnack) suggest Wuffing control of the Welland in this part of the Fen Edge, for there, and in Lindsey north of the Wash, East Anglia's surrounding countries felt the immediate influence of Rædwald.

Henry of Huntingdon, a twelfth-century chronicler, preserves a circumstantial account of the battle based on unknown authority. Rædwald's army was elegantly arrayed in three battle-lines, one of which was led by Rægenhere. The lines were bristling with helmets, spears and standards (*galeis, hastis, vexillis*). Æthelfrith was contemptuous and amazed that anyone should dare to resist him and, despite having highly-experienced and chosen warriors, attacked in disorderly fashion. As if sighting his prey (*quasi praeda inventa*) he suddenly rushed into the thick of the troops, and with swords cut down Rægenhere together with the whole of his formation. Rædwald, supremely enraged (*iracundior*), held invincibly fast with his two remaining units, and, breaching the Northumbrian lines, cut down their King amid a great slaughter of his armies, which were completely routed.

How did Rædwald then mourn his warrior son? It is tempting to conjecture that Rægenhere was buried in Lindsey in the mound at Caenby (Lincs.), just east of the Ermine Street near its junction with the road from Gainsborough. This included an assemblage of circular and axe-shaped mounts of gilt bronze with central metal studs, and with chip-carved ornament, which demand comparison with the harness mounts from the horse-and-warrior grave at Sutton Hoo and with the pair from the looted ship-grave there. Lindsey, like East Anglia, yields important finds of rich weaponry, but the Caenby grave had contained a helmet made in the 'Swedish' style like the famous Sutton Hoo example, as shown by a fragmentary panel depicting dancing warriors. This is so unusual in England that it suggests a direct connection with the East Anglian ruling culture centred on the Deben. Yet Rægenhere may equally have been cremated or carried back to Sutton for burial. The discovery of magnificent gold sword-furniture in Lincolnshire encourages the view that Lindsey and East Anglia in many ways formed a single cultural area under Rædwald's influence during the early seventh century.

The outcome of the battle left Rædwald the undisputed master of the southern kingdoms, and the sponsor of the King of Northumbria. Perhaps they rode together triumphantly into York. Eadwine now became King of Deira and Bernicia. His nephew Hereric had lived in exile under King Ceretic of the British kingdom of Elmet, north of Pontefract, and there was treacherously poisoned, probably at Æthelfrith's instigation. Among Eadwine's first actions was the conquest of Elmet, probably in retaliation for this crime: Ceretic was driven out, and died in 616. The reversal of East Anglian fortune in Rægenhere's death deprived the kingdom of its expected heir, though Eorpwald his brother remained. For Rædwald, the sacrifice of his own son for the honour of Eadwine's defence made the Northumbrian king the substitute heir to his wider power, perhaps (in the promises of Paulinus) his adoptive son or godson.

King Sæberht of the East Saxons died in c.615. The Prittlewell grave, perhaps of about this date (not necessarily of a king) included miniature sheet-gold crosses at the collar of the corpse, Christian ornaments of Langoard type. Three East Saxon princes, the brothers Seaxred, Siward and Sigeberht (I) ruled together, and resumed the worship of idols. They refused baptism, but demanded that Mellitus give them Holy Communion, which he refused. Therefore they drove him and his companions out of their kingdom. In Kent, after Æthelberht's death in c.616, his son Eadbald outraged the mission by marrying his own stepmother in heathen custom. Utterly disheartened, Mellitus and Justus (Bishop of Rochester) went into Gaul to see what would happen next; Archbishop Laurence was about to follow when Eadbald relented and accepted baptism, and the bishops were recalled. Rædwald's patronage or indifference is not recorded; nor did the East Saxons return to Christianity for many years. Laurence died in 619 and was succeeded by Mellitus at Canterbury. The three East Saxon Kings were killed fighting King Cynegils of the West Saxons in 623, and in the next year Mellitus died and Justus became archbishop. He consecrated Romanus, another member of the mission, in his own place as Bishop of Rochester. Rædwald apparently died c.624-25, at the height of his power.

The mission to the English was among the great achievements of Pope Gregory, who had died in 604. The Emperor Maurice, having abdicated, was murdered with his sons at Chalcedon in 602. Pope Boniface IV persuaded Phocas, murderer and successor of Maurice, to decree that the Roman Church should preside over all Christian churches. He also acquired the Pantheon in Rome for a church. Phocas was removed in 610 by Emperor Heraclius I, son of the Exarch of Africa. But this was too late to stop the advance of the Persian, Zoroastrian monarch Chosroes II into imperial Jerusalem in 614, whence he removed the True Cross into Persia. He proceeded into Constantinople in 615 and then into Egypt, much reducing the Empire. In Rædwald's time the Christian west was holding to the precious remnants of Roman civilisation. In 622 the Prophet Mohammed made his escape from Mecca, and began to impart his message. In campaigns from 623-27 Heraclius reconquered what had been taken, drove Chosroes to Tauris (Tabriz), across the Zab to Nineveh, Dastagerd and Ctesiphon (near Baghdad), and to his death in Persia, and restored the True Cross to Jerusalem. But as the Persian Sassanid dynasty fell, the apostles of Mohammed materialised into that void of power; and though Heraclius ruled until 641, the provinces he had recovered were again lost after 633.

THE SUTTON HOO SHIP-BURIAL

The burial of a large oak ship with a richly-furnished funeral chamber deposited at Sutton Hoo in c.625 (and uncovered in 1939) is thought by many to have been the grave of Rædwald. That is uncertain, and other theories have been advanced, but this member of the ruling culture based near Rendlesham was buried with ritual and artefacts suggesting his pre-eminence in that group. The quality and nature of the goods cannot readily be explained in any other way than as having been assembled and commissioned by a ruler of Rædwald's stature. But a step of faith is still required. Poised like Rædwald himself in the half-dawn of English history, the treasure seems awakened not merely from a long slumber but from another world, as if it had migrated from a fairy tale. The ship's outline, the treasure and the ritual they evoke still haunt the seaward landscape which for so long safeguarded that trust under a high mound. Rædwald and this ship-burial are together, as history or as myth, like a huge ghostly presence in our midst which will not lie down and sleep.

Sutton Hoo ship-burial: Mound 1 before excavation in 1939, still guarding its secret. *Ipswich Borough Museums*

The ship herself was about 27m long, pointed at both ends, with a flat-topped keel-plank which developed into tall rising posts, their tops some 4m above the keel level, at the prow and stern. The clinker hull was built up with nine planks or strakes on either side of the keel, which overlapped and were fastened with many iron rivets. She was repaired, and had weathered the sixth-century seas. Her shape, 4.5m broad at the centre and 1.5m deep, was held firm by 26 wooden frames set at regular distances within, bolted to the planking below the gunwales and secured by wooden pegs. Along the gunwales were recurved wooden tholes (thorn-shaped oar rests), showing that there had been place for up to 20 oarsmen on either side. At the stern, the strengthening frames were clustered to carry a heavy steering-oar. This, together with all decking and seats (and any evidence for a mast, if there ever was one), had been removed before the ship was buried. The whole vessel, weighing perhaps 20-30 tons, was hauled up from the river Deben through a long coombe to the edge of the cemetery field, at the hill spur's crest opposite Woodbridge. There she was somehow lowered into a deep pit, leaving only the stem and stern posts rising above ground-level.

The contents of the burial
A burial-chamber was constructed at the centre by laying about 5.5m of decking, with a wooden wall at either end. The ship's sides formed the walls in the longer dimension. In this section the tholes had been removed, and the chamber was covered by a roof, probably one pitched like a hall. Although no bones were

Sutton Hoo ship-burial: impression of the 27m ship exposed by excavation in 1939. *Photograph: Payne no 8. Print: Ipswich Borough Museums*

Sutton Hoo ship-burial: ceremonial whetstone, detail of carved faces soon after excavation. *The British Museum*

discovered it is believed that there was a body, and that it was laid out on a long central wooden podium or bed-frame (or, as some think, within a large coffin) with the head at the west end and the feet to the east towards the ship's prow, which pointed inland from the river. Although only metal objects survived with any completeness, the furnishings had been very sumptuous and were arranged in groups along the east and west walls of the chamber, and around the body itself within the area defined by the wooden podium.

At the west, the head end of the funeral chamber, various precious objects were set out along the wall. A large and extraordinary whetstone, shaped like a long bar with faces carved on the sides at either end, was placed centrally. Its metal mounts included an ornamental ring at the top surmounted by a bronze figure of a stag. The assembled object resembles a sceptre of Late Antique Consular or Imperial type. The stag and the stone were probably of different origins, but both items of sacred or totemic numen. North of this was a very large shield of Swedish design, having a central boss with fine plaques of stamped animal-ornament and a central garnet-inlaid stud, and with elaborate chip-carved and sheet-silver fittings for the front and back including emblems of a predatory bird and flying dragon.

Standing north of this, or laid beside it, was a tall iron stand with a grid mounted near the top and wrought animal heads at the summit. Its function is uncertain: an iron stand (with short legs) was found in a corner of the Prittlewell burial-chamber also. South of the keel axis was an iron-bound wooden bucket. Another complex near the south end of the west wall included a bronze hanging-bowl of insular Celtic workmanship with superb enamelwork hook medallions and other plaques, including an enamelled fish sculpture mounted to rotate on a pin within the bowl. A six-stringed Anglo-Saxon lyre with decorative gold and garnet mounts was contained in a beaver-skin bag. A bronze bowl with drop-handles, of eastern Mediterranean manufacture, bore a procession of animals engraved within.

At the north-east corner (at the foot of the chamber) was a cooper-made tub of yew with iron bindings, and a similar bucket inside it. Near the centre axis was a large bronze cauldron. To the south were two smaller cauldrons of thin bronze, one globular and the other round-bottomed and concave-sided (like the examples already mentioned from Brightwell Heath and Ixworth Thorpe). All three may have hung on pegs or nails on the east wall. The large cauldron, which had wrought-iron fittings and two ring-handles, resembled one from the Taplow burial and was designed to be suspended from a chain with suspension hooks. Such an iron chain, the most elaborate of its kind with many complex links, swivels and ornamental sections lay or hung near to the cauldron. Almost 3.5m long, it had hung from a hall roof-beam some 5m high to suspend a cauldron over a central hearth. Its maker, a blacksmith of outstanding skill, belonged to a tradition of his craft unbroken since the Roman period.

The body itself is thought to have dissolved, bones and all, in a 'soup' of putrefaction within the buried chamber and later in contact with acidic sands.

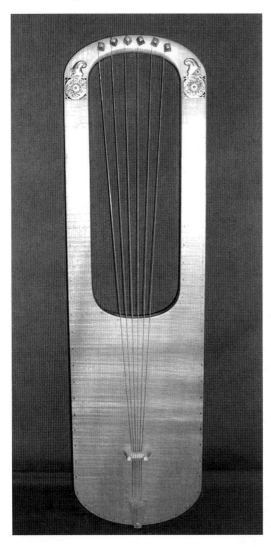

Sutton Hoo ship-burial: the six-stringed lyre, reconstruction by Arnold Dolmetsch Ltd. *Ipswich Borough Museums*

Its position was shown by personal objects on or around it, between the fifteenth and thirteenth ribs of the ship. A normal, warrior-sized body up to some 6ft tall could occupy the space, especially if laid in a sleeping posture. To the right of his head were the two baptismal spoons with a set of 10 silver bowls nested and inverted over them, products of Christian Byzantium of the years around 600. In a similar position left of his head was the iron helmet with its arresting manlike mask. Some fragments, possibly from gaming-pieces, found *above* (i.e. west of) the head position suggests a gaming board may have been placed in that area. On his right side lay the splendid pattern-welded sword in its scabbard, the hilt (with its rich ornament) uppermost. Near it was a wand with a small applied plaque representing a wolf. A large, long-bladed spear lay further to the right: beyond were five chosen spears, and three angons (with barbed heads and long metal sleeves), the tips of which had been pushed through one of the handles of the bronze bowl in the south-western corner.

More closely associated with the sword and body were the gold and garnet (cellwork) fittings, including the scabbard-bosses and pyramid-mounts, and the decorative panels, buckles and strap-distributors of the sword-belt or harness, which was either worn by the body or laid between it and the sword. In death the man was apparently dressed in his boiled-leather cuirass, a stiff Roman-style body armour made in two close-fit halves, front and back. This was fastened at the shoulders by a pair of clasps, each of two matching halves held together by a removeable pin. These are of solid gold, spectacularly carpeted by interlocking stepped cells of cut garnet and millefiori glass, and edged by garnet friezes of interlaced animals which appear inset in gold. A motif of two interlocked boars, in glass and garnet with surrounding filigree, occupied each semicircular clasp-end.

The waist belt was fastened with a large crafted-gold buckle, its plate carved with interpenetrating dragons and interwoven snakes, stamped and inlaid with niello (a black enamel) to enliven the gold surface. From the belt a leather purse hung over the right thigh, its lid of horn set in a frame and with applied panels, all of golden garnet cellwork, depicting predatory birds, manlike figures between wolves, interlacing creatures and interlocked mosaic patterns. These ornaments, the wonder of their age, were made by a master goldsmith or jeweller working in East Anglia for this patron. In the purse were 37 gold tremisses (carefully assembled since each was struck in a different Frankish mint), three blanks, and two small ingots of gold.

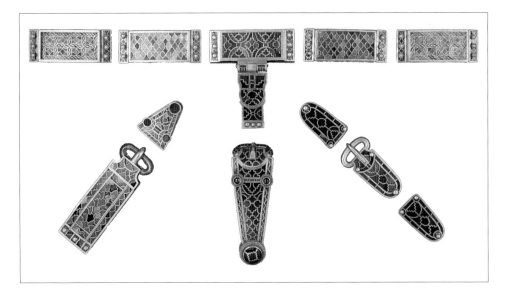

Sutton Hoo ship-burial: the cellwork sword-belt fittings. *The British Museum*

Beside the man's lower legs was a heap of textiles, a large pair of drinking-horns with gilt silver vandykes and cast gryphon-headed terminals, and a set of maplewood bottles or cups similarly mounted. The foil panels were impressed with richly-textured interlacing animal ornament. Beyond the feet, occupying the lower end of the dais were three convergent heaps of textiles and other objects. One consisted mainly of a folded coat of iron mail (probably thigh-length), a most valuable and unusual possession, worked in alternate rows of butt-jointed and copper-riveted links: beside it lay an iron axe-hammer with a long handle, probably a weapon. In other heaps were two further bronze hanging-bowls, pairs of leather shoes, and other folded textiles and leather objects. Above the mailcoat was a silver fluted bowl with drop-handles, showing the head of a woman at the centre in Roman style. Within this imported Mediterranean vessel were many smaller *personalia*, including bone-handled knives and bone combs, eight small walnut burwood cups with silver mounts, and a cylindrical ivory gaming-piece, thought to be the 'king-piece' from a set.

Over these lay a large silver platter with chased ornament at its raised rim and centre, including small roundels with seated figures representing Rome and Constantinople, and running genii embodying commerce and letters. Almost 75cm in diameter, this eastern production bears control stamps of Emperor Anastasius (491–518). Some cremated bone was placed on it in the burial. Beneath was a silver ladle with ornament of beading and gilt triangles and another small bowl,

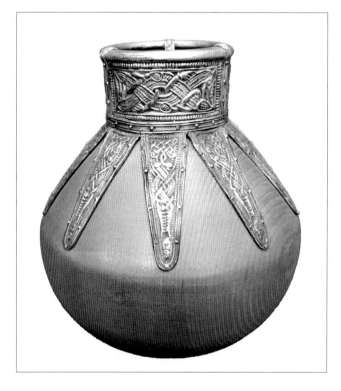

Sutton Hoo ship-burial: wooden cup with stamped gilt vandykes (reconstruction). *Ipswich Borough Museums*

also Mediterranean imports. A small wheelmade pottery bottle and an iron lamp containing beeswax were placed near the south-eastern corner of the dais, and a further iron-bound wooden bucket stood at the middle of the south side. The dais was apparently curtained around or surfaced with multi-coloured hangings with lozenge-shaped or diagonally-worked red panels backed with a twill. Using a Syrian technique, alternate weft rows were looped individually around the warps to give the cloth a rich, textured surface. Other patterned textiles lay near the drinking-horns and at either end, and thick-piled yellow or golden cloaks overlay the central area. The red and yellow textiles and the patterned hangings must have echoed the colours of the jewellery on the body.

Interpreting the burial goods
Not only were all these individual items of supreme value, but the whole assemblage represented the functions, the cultural identity and affinities, of the ruler in a magnificent way. It recalls the visual imagery of Arthurian Romance, however inappropriately. The knightly figure lay in state among his linens, coloured textiles, treasure and weaponry. It might almost be the fair bed in midst of the ship called Faith, which Sir Percivale found in the land of Logris. Behind that medieval romance lies some Britannic memory of the same ritual which the opening funeral in *Beowulf* presents in a Germanic or early Danish sense. The ship is not merely treasure-laden as if with booty, but furnished neatly in an approved hierarchy of symbolism and utility, ready to bear the sleeping warrior magically elsewhere. The dream-vision, the other-worldly richness of jewellery, coloured textiles and numinous objects, is intoxicating. We can no longer assume that the Sutton ritual was intentionally pagan, or that even this, the highest elaboration of mound-laying custom, was incompatible with Christian identity.

In addition to the baptismal spoons and bowls beside the dead man's head, the large Celtic hanging-bowl also bears explicitly Christian motifs. Its enamels are among the finest of their kind; the circular glass insets leave the red enamel field to form patterns emphasised by chequer and starburst millefiori pieces. The square ornamental escutcheons each show a large red cross with expanding arms (like the Templars' Cross). White oval inclusions, at first sight appearing merely decorative, represent the voids between the red cross-arms. The Christian meaning is inevitable. Crosses (between fish) appear in openwork on the bowl from Faversham (Kent), and other hanging-bowls have cruciform elements in their escutcheons. Accepting Haio Vierck's wisdom that hanging-bowls were made for mixing wine and water, this bowl's function may have been Eucharistic rather than merely convivial. The white and red fluids could thus signify the blood and water that issued from Christ's side on the Cross, and the Fish (which rotates on a pin inside the bowl) may be His primitive symbol.

Two patches to the vessel, made by the Sutton jeweller, suggest the deliberate display of its repair, as if the damage might have been considered sacrilegious.

Did the late sixth-century British or Irish enameler who made this refined bowl work for an Anglo-Saxon patron, or was it produced for a British patron and afterwards acquired by the Sutton potentate, living or dead? Hanging-bowls appear in Anglo-Saxon contexts throughout central and eastern Britain but not in the western, Welsh areas. Continuing, seventh-century production of the enamels is represented in Suffolk especially by the extremely fine (lost) escutcheon plates from Badley cemetery (Needham Market), and from the composite enamelwork, gilt interlace and chequered millefiori of the bowl from Handford near Gipeswic.

Some objects from the burial reflect the life of the royal Hall, most obviously the great chain and cauldron, and the coloured cloth hangings of textured weave, which had formerly curtained or decked some ornate recess. The drinking-horns had no doubt been passed or carried among the warrior household, as portrayed in the epic *Beowulf*. Their owner was presumably master of the ceremony in which the pouring out (*scencan*) and drinking of mead was token of the lord's *bestowing* role towards his companions, retainers and guests, of his wife's part in the conduct of hospitality towards them, and of their reciprocal bond of loyalty. The six-stringed lyre was the classic Germanic accompaniment for dramatic recitation, and had an important distribution in East Anglia. Lyre-bridges have been found at Oakley (a 'productive site' near the confluence of the Waveney and Dove rivers) and in graves at Snape and Bergh Apton (Norfolk). Thus it appears that poetic or lyric recitation formed a typical part of noble and royal culture in this region.

Old English heroic poetry owes a primary debt to genealogical verse extolling the deeds of ancestors. That was the necessary counterpart to the creation of the

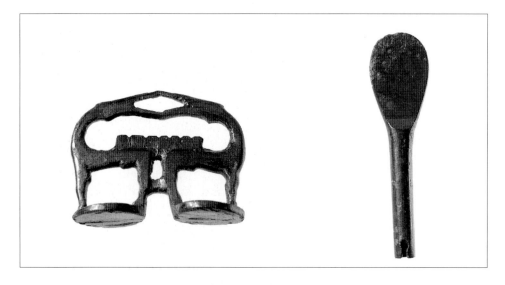

Oakley: bridge and tuning-peg from a lyre. *The British Museum. Photograph: R. Carr*

high burial-mounds, where the heroic dead and their possessions were locked away forever from human sight. The *Beowulf* poet invents a primary authenticity for the ship-funeral ritual, by attaching it to the most remote founding ancestor, the creation-myth, of the English and Danish ruling houses. The great wealth of treasure from far-off lands laid around the body of Scyld Scefing in his ship is consigned to the ocean's bosom, not buried under a mound. That ideal departure is what a burial such as Sutton Hoo figures or signifies, where the treasure is consigned to a ghostly elsewhere beyond the mythic *garsecg* or world-circling sea.

The cemeteries of the warrior knights of Vendel and Valsgärde, beside Vendel Sound and the river Fyris in eastern Sweden, show boats up to 9m in length buried with human inhumations and many animals, including horses, sacrificed with them. Their helmets and shields are of similar, sometimes closely similar, production to those of Sutton Hoo: the helmets, with beaten figural plaques, wire-inlaid *wala* or serpent-crest, and assembled castings around the eyebrows, seem like those named by the 'last survivor' in *Beowulf*, the polished battle-masks from which the beaten plates shall rust and fall away. We see them anew in Ivor Lawson's magnificent re-creations. The arched-necked creatures of the Oakley

Vendel cemetery (Uppland, Sweden): helmet from Grave 1. Recreation by Ivor Lawson. *Ivor Lawson*

lyre-bridge remind one of the helmet brow-castings of Vendel and Valsgärde, as it were linking the hero and the song. Beowulf's story culminates in his cremation and burial with treasure under a high mound on a sea-promontory. The graves of Ongentheow and Eadgils are perhaps represented by the high mounds near Old Uppsala in eastern Sweden, the seat of the sixth-century Swedish rulers. The mound named for Ottar (Ohthere) is at Husby near Vendel.

The fittings for the Sutton cups and drinking-horns share this special artistic link between Suffolk and Swedish Uppland. They feature richly impressed ribbon-beasts in the Scandinavian Style II, which has a significant development in south-eastern England. The Sutton Hoo examples bridge the evolution of the English and Scandinavian aspects of the style, perhaps for the last time before its English development became absorbed into a new insular language of ornament. Dies for the manufacture of helmet-plaques like those from the Vendel and Valsgärde helmets were discovered at Torslunda on the isle of Oland. East Anglia, however, could produce die-struck vandykes and applied cup- or horn-mounts in the interlaced animal style, for some simpler dies have been found at Icklingham and at Benhall in Suffolk. The cup- and horn-mounts from the Prittlewell grave will no doubt enlarge our understanding of the Sutton examples.

The imagery of the helmet-plaques was widely understood. The Torslunda scene of a warrior between bears, for instance, appears on harness-mounts from an equestrian grave at Eschwege (eastern Hesse) in the lower Werra valley, a tributary of the Weser. The Sutton helmet has two figure-scenes. One is of paired 'dancing' warriors with spears, swords and horned helms. The other shows a

Icklingham: bronze die for making metal cup or horn mounts. *St Edmundsbury Borough Council/ West Stow Anglo-Saxon Village Trust*

spear-bearing horseman trampling a fallen warrior who, in mortal retribution, pierces the horse's breast with his sword. The latter, classical in derivation, occurs for instance on a repoussé disc from Pliezhausen, Tübingen, in Germany. In general form these helmets resemble late Roman prototypes, but their scenic plaques include a northern mythological sequence. Processions of footsoldiers are shown wearing boar-crested and eagle-crested helms, the mounted horseman and warriors confronting monsters or flanked by them in scenes of mutual destruction. The Sutton helmet, with its neck and cheek-guards, is the most developed of all beside its Swedish counterparts, and its manufacture is distinguished by the single iron dome which forms the cranial shell. The small shield from a warrior-grave in the mixed cemetery field at Sutton Hoo displayed small dragon and eagle motifs, related to the large shield's imagery, and also a group of studs or shield-nails as depicted on shields shown on the Swedish helmet-plaques.

The famous Sutton Hoo helmet with its unique mask, and the round shield almost a metre across with its large central boss and emblazoning jewels, must immediately have identified the most important person on the battlefield, to whom the *gesiths* – the companions, bodyguard and most loyal retainers – would rally. The shield's applied gilt strips and bosses suggest the enchieved status of the bearer: the added interlocking rings on one strip resemble those sometimes found attached to swords or drinking-horns as bestowed tokens of honour. One particular craftsman seems to have made fittings for shields at Sutton and Vendel. If the dragon-head fragments from the looted Sutton Hoo ship-grave (Mound 2) really are shield-fittings, then we must envisage a second great shield; that man's drinking-horns matched those from the undisturbed ship.

These two royal graves and the new shield-warrior all reflecting the Vendel culture illustrate more than merely trade or exchange. There are, as Angela Evans expresses it, societal links. East Anglia is a patron-centre within the cultural area of the Vendel Style. From such links the related customs of large ship-burials in East Anglia and smaller boat-graves in Sweden also arise. The ruling family of East Anglia might acquire Swedish affinities by descent, marriage or other alliance. The underlying unity of the Vendel and Valsgärde 'chieftain' equipment, and the related Sutton Hoo items, suggest that these armourers were creating accessories for patrons belonging to an organised military association, and distributed them as *insignia*, not as 'commodities' available to any patron. Hence the shield-attachments and rings could express specific rankings, and the blazoned images their (somewhat totemic) emblems. The Roman features of the helmets might reflect the origin of a league or sworn company that had campaigned under late Imperial command elsewhere in Europe. Under the auspices of the ruling culture which buried at Sutton Hoo, their chief patrons in Britain, these armourers became itinerant between Sweden and East Anglia.

It was this English patron buried at Sutton (perhaps Rædwald himself) who procured a garnet-inlaid golden regalia in Imperial style as the image of his own ascendancy. He was fully conscious of his considerable power. He, perhaps, enrolled the name of Cæsar below that of Woden among those worthy or reckoned to be Rædwald's ancestors. The outfit, consisting of the sword and its fittings, the leather cuirass with its shoulder-pieces, the belt and purse (and those enigmatic coins contained within it) proclaimed the wearer's sense of approaching equivalence to the contemporary Frankish suzerain Chlothar II, representative of a dynasty which had achieved extraordinary success since the conversion of Clovis. Anastasius, whose stamps adorned the great platter in the Sutton treasury, had approved the pro-Consular authority of Clovis.

Indeed, Childeric, Clovis' predecessor, had been buried at Tournay with garnet cellwork jewellery, though not so lavish as the Sutton work. Such goldwork required Frankish bullion and access to the garnet trade fed through the Frankish Rhinelands, but sourced through Middle Eastern trade from India. 'Carpeted' garnet cellwork ornament was very widespread in early Germanic Europe. It became established in south-eastern Britain in the late sixth and seventh centuries, especially for the composite disc-brooches, the richest of which are distributed between Kent and the Thames valley. A gold disc-brooch plate combining garnet cellwork and filigree ornament was found by a ploughman at Sutton in the 1830s, who threw away the stones. But in the ship-burial ornaments (a far more elaborate and specialised application of the technique), genius prompts the manipulation, matches and cutting of the stones, and the designs they serve. Geometric stones are used to represent a tree-scroll on the rectangular sword-harness buckle. The pyramidal jewels, their faceted corner-stones glowing with doubly-admitted light, enclosing vari-coloured cellwork on each face, and with chequered millefiori apical settings, defy adequate comparison. The purse-mount and shoulder-clasp ornaments are completely unparalleled. Such work illustrates the Old English term *ge-weorthian*, meaning simultaneously to bestow adornment and honour, combining moral and material worth.

Garnets were cut with especial skill to the shapes required for interlacing animal designs on the shoulder-clasps and purse lid. They are set among cells lidded with gold to create the illusion of solid metal. The jeweller cut various unusual shapes with great control and originality for the clasps and purse lid. For the purse he chose the man and wolves scene from motifs found on the Swedish helmets, and adapted the interlaced animals from a group shown in impressed sheet metal on the Sutton shield boss. The eagles are related to the shield-blazoning. The imagery of predator and prey, or mutual destruction of man and beasts or of rider and fallen warrior, express retribution or recompense, the themes of *Edleanung* or *Edlesung* (reciprocality) associated with money, again combining moral and material values. The dissociation of material wealth and spiritual worth, the ascetic Christian revolt against worldly *value*, had not yet overthrown the pagan sense of the bestowing *virtue* of gold.

The same jeweller's work, or the continuing influence of his technique, are seen in cellwork fragments now kept at Tongres, in other pyramidal

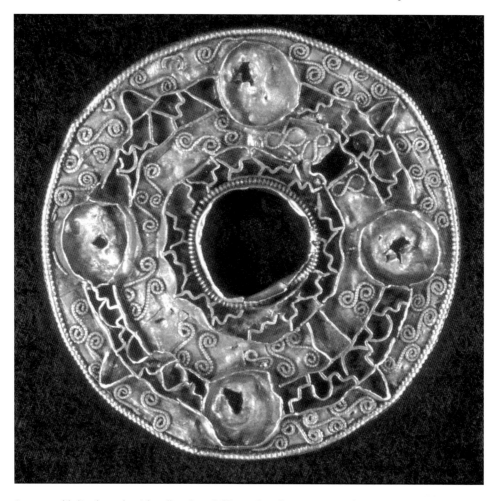

Sutton: gold disc-brooch with cellwork and filigree found in 1834. *Ipswich Borough Museums*

mounts, and in the cruciform pendants from Wilton (Norfolk) and Ixworth. The superb cellwork of a circular composite brooch set into the so-called 'Egbert' reliquary at Trier may also be the product of an East Anglian workshop. The appearance of Christian cruciform design elements in cellwork ornament may have received a strong impetus in East Anglia: some think the patterns of the Sutton Hoo scabbard-bosses are intentionally Christian.

The Sutton jeweller worked closely with his patron to bring the cellwork technique to Scandinavian motifs in the East Anglian kingly armoury. Their shared project was to create regalia which combined Roman, Franco-Germanic and Scandinavian rulership imagery as symbols of the patron's Britannic authority. No other East Anglian than Rædwald fits that profile. There were other brilliant and original goldsmiths, like those of the Faversham and Kingston Down brooches, the Crundale buckle, or the Taplow clasps. But only at Sutton

Hoo can we see the goldsmith borrowing from other sources within the patron environment to create such a connected assemblage. He transcends the traditions of form and method in which his craft is based. His use of millefiori glass unlocks the palette of cloisonné colouring and the definition of design elements, and introduces a Roman craft into the synthesis. His work attached to the king's person a refractive lustre signalling the many values of the state bound in his bestowing authority. Where the maker of the Handford bowl-escutcheon mixes insular techniques, this man fused them. He simultaneously made himself an instrument and asset of royal identity. That evolved also at the Frankish court in the work of the moneyer and goldsmith-in-chief Eligius for patrons Chlothar II and his successor Dagobert I (628-38).

The Sutton jeweller's zoomorphic cellwork is compared with a brooch-plate from Wijnaldum, Friesland, which has no lidded gold cells nor millefiori settings, however, and uses the white paste or shell bosses. Those white bosses are significantly absent from the Sutton regalia, though they appear on the lyre mounts and on the Mound 17 harness furniture, and were therefore known and contemporary. They feature in Kentish and continental cellwork, appearing (for instance) as the eyes of a pair of eagles of Gothic or Langobardic manufacture from Milan. English seventh-century circular gold necklace-pendants with filigree ornament and central settings have Langobard counterparts. As this patron joined the most elect company of western European rulers, did he acquire the jeweller for his needs from a Langobard court, from Ravenna or from the turmoil of the Eastern Empire, as it fell to Chosroes? The art of the further, Sassanian east was, with the collapse of their own Empire, about to disseminate into the west during the seventh and eighth centuries. The nearer East had for long breathed its imaginations into the Germanic empires of the Mediterranean basin including North Africa. This jeweller's technical skill was supreme, but it existed in order to serve the Mercurial power which transfigured his patron's authority and identity. This Art was creating, not describing, reality.

Within a short time, all that we have described was consigned to the darkness of the tomb, and was not seen again until 1939. As the men and women of *Estengle-lond* had paid their funeral tribute to the ideal nationhood represented by the *tracht*, so their greatest ruler procured the living ideal of the East Angle kingdom by the disposal of himself and his royal and imperial insignia within the great ship at Sutton Hoo. At his right hand were the tokens of his baptism. In the world of his ancestors he established not only Wuffing dynastic right but the sovereignty of the *baptised* heirs of Woden in the soil of East Anglia.

4

The age of conversion

EORPWALD, 625-27

When Rædwald's funeral rites were completed, and his *regalia* were buried with him in the tomb, Eorpwald, his surviving son, inherited the East Anglian kingdom. Eadwine, King of Northumbria, now emerged as the foremost ruler of the English and indeed of all the peoples of Britain, indicating that Rædwald, by his adoption of Eadwine's cause, had in some way designated the succession to his power. No Northumbrian ruler had held authority in southern Britain before. Eadwine's relations with Eadbald the Christian King of Kent, with Eorpwald in East Anglia, and with Lindsey, show their acquiescence in his ascendancy. Thus Rædwald's intentions, and the words spoken to Eadwine in exile by Paulinus, were fulfilled. It is not unlikely that Eadwine helped to arrange Rædwald's funeral. The completion of Eadwine's power was, as Bede says, 'an augury of his accepting the Faith' in fulfilment of his promises. The Christian future which Rædwald had not been able to establish in his own reign became possible through that of his successor. Bede's *Ecclesiastical History* is our principal guide through the affairs of the seventh century.

At Rædwald's death, Eadbald of Kent was the only Christian ruler among the English. Eorpwald had not accepted his father's religion, and Eadwine, though he had forsaken his idols, had not yet resolved upon baptism. He married Æthelburh, Eadbald's sister, and she and her retinue came north in 625 with Paulinus as her bishop, on the understanding that she could maintain her faith and practice. She encouraged Eadwine as perhaps her own mother had encouraged her father. Eadwine built a little wooden church for Paulinus in York, his southern capital. Since the murder of Hereric in Elmet, Eadwine had turned his face against the British rulers. A doubtful romance narrative, given at length by Robert Manning of Brunne (*c.*1338), asserts that Cadwallon, King of Gwynedd (Eadwine's childhood companion), had permitted his rule, but would not share his British sovereignty and now unsuccessfully attacked him. Cadwallon was driven out of

Eadwine's realm, but sent an agent to York to murder the royal astrologer and chief wizard, Pellith, who had foretold the movements of the British.

The supremacy of Ceawlin the West Saxon had, with his fall, transferred to Kent, and Eadwine's marital alliance added Kentish authority to the sovereignty attained with Rædwald's help. Bede's narrative of Eadwine also tells of assassins. Cwichelm, West Saxon sub-king under his father King Cynegils, sent an agent to kill the Northumbrian ruler. On Good Friday 626, as the ambassador Eumer stepped forward to deliver his pretended message he lunged at Eadwine with a poisoned dagger. Eadwine's beloved minister Lilla leapt forward and received the fatal blow. On Easter Sunday following, Æthelburh gave birth to a daughter Eanfled, whom Eadwine gave to Paulinus for baptism. He then marched against the West Saxon conspirators; having subdued them he returned home sensing that he was divinely protected, and submitted himself to Paulinus' teaching. Letters and gifts were received from Pope Boniface encouraging him to destroy the lifeless idols and their shrines and to spurn the arts of divination.

Eadwine searched his heart deeply until at last Paulinus gave the sign which the stranger had shown him in exile; then, seeing that all that was predicted had come to pass, the astonished king remembered his promise and understood his duty. He and Paulinus conferred with the pagan priests, and their leader Coifi took arms and mounted a stallion (things forbidden to his calling), rode to his temple, hurled in the spear in defilement and had it burnt down. Eadwine was baptised at York on 12 April 627 together with the Northumbrian nobility and many subjects. Among them were Eadfrith and Osfrith (his sons by his Mercian wife Cwenburh), Osfrith's baby son Yffi, and also Breguswith (Hereric's widow), with her two daughters Hereswith and Hild. Then he commenced work on a large stone church around the smaller oratory, and appointed York to be the see of Paulinus as Bishop in Northumbria. The King had a great hall and royal complex at Yeavering in Bernicia, and Paulinus once spent 36 days there, teaching and baptising in the river Glen nearby. In Deira he baptised in the river Swale near Catterick.

Without delay the leadership of the East Angles and of Lindsey cemented their alliance with Eadwine by accepting Christianity. King Eorpwald was baptised in 627, presumably by Paulinus himself and with Eadwine as his sponsor. Many East Angles received the faith, and Paulinus was soon afterwards in Lindsey, where he baptised the Governor and his family at Lincoln: hundreds were baptised in the river Trent. One who actually saw Paulinus remembered him as a tall, dark-haired man with lean Roman features and aquiline nose, with a slight stoop, at once venerable and awe-inspiring. The enactment of river-baptism sealed an apostolic bond between the river itself and the Life of the Spirit.

So we may picture the baptism of Eorpwald and the East Angles, and believe that Paulinus, in completion of his work begun in Rædwald's time, made good the consecration of Eorpwald's church; perhaps St Gregory's church at Rendlesham. But in these affairs direct Kentish communications must also have grown. As Archbishop Mellitus (who had succeeded Laurence to Canterbury in 619) died in 624, Bishop Justus took his place and elevated Romanus, another of the Canterbury missionaries, to his own bishopric of St Andrew's, Rochester, at the Roman fortress on the Medway. This was directly accessible from the Orwell or Deben by ship, and was indeed the first important port of call in Kent and the closest established bishopric to East Anglia. The Christian diplomatic alliance of Northumbria, Kent, East Anglia and Lindsey briefly formed a bulwark along the eastern seaboard.

In Mercia whatever remained of Eadwine's alliance with Ceorl (the father of his first wife) was now overshadowed by the hostility of Penda (son of Pybba, and grandson of Creoda), whose ambition took its shape from opposition to the Christian powers. The East Saxons under Sigeberht the Little remained outside the Church, and therefore their share of the trade through London could be aligned with Mercian and West Saxon interest, which was similarly distanced from Eadwine's system of power. Perhaps many in East Anglia, too, were resolved against Eadwine, for soon after his baptism Eorpwald was murdered in 627 by a heathen named Ricberht. Eorpwald was the first English king to suffer death in consequence of his Christian faith and alliances.

?RICBERHT, *c*.627-629

Since Ricberht's name was remembered, perhaps it was he who took hold of East Anglian power for the following three years, during which Christianity was abandoned. Indeed the rapidity with which Eorpwald's murder followed his baptism suggests either a violent backlash or a very prompt intervention from Mercia or Wessex. Was Ricberht the agent of a foreign power or the leader of an internal uprising? Were there rival dynasties in East Anglia? Did Rædwald's wife survive as a dowager to endorse the rule of another offspring or near kinsman grasping at the shadow of Rædwald's empire? It was not insubstantial: a central English power controlling a coastline from the Humber to the Thames, and from Oxford or Hereford to the High Peak, might successfully divorce Canterbury and York and in time subdue them both. Penda never lost sight of that vision, in which East Anglia, and especially the southern part of that kingdom (controlling the Icknield Way, the Gipping corridor and the dynastic seat near Sutton) was the key to unlocking that prize, if Northumbria could be held at bay.

SIGEBERHT, *c*.629-635 AND ÆTHILRIC, *c*.629-636

Northumbrian and Kentish influence with the new Frankish ruler Dagobert, who succeeded Chlothar II in 628, probably helped to restore Sigeberht to the East Anglian kingdom. Bede calls Sigeberht Rædwald's son, but later writers identify him as a stepson. In Gaul, fleeing from Rædwald's enmity, he had received baptism and Christian education. He was the first English king to receive them before entering upon his reign. His people afterwards recalled his success as a military leader, which suggests that he established his rule by warfare against the adherents of Ricberht. If Sigeberht was not of the Wuffing bloodline, the regalia consignment in the Sutton Hoo ship-burial might possibly represent the disposal of the symbols of Wuffing power, in the grave of a Wuffing, in this dynastic stand-off. Sigeberht shared the kingdom with Ecgric, taken to be the same person as Æthilric named in the East Anglian royal tally as a son of Eni, Rædwald's brother.

In after-times the East Anglian kingship passed in succession to three brothers of Æthilric's, suggesting that no direct descendant of Rædwald's then survived. When, in 664, the last of these brothers had died, Æthilric's son inherited the power as the rightful *paterfamilias* of the Wuffings, showing Æthilric's precedence in his generation. Æthilric married Hereswith, Eadwine's great-niece (and daughter of the murdered Hereric), who had been baptised with the Northumbrian King at Easter 627. As an estimate of her age, her younger sister Hild was born *c*.614. This diplomatic marriage was therefore undoubtedly supervised by her protector and patron Eadwine to strengthen the alliance between Northumbria and the East Angles, and bore the presumption that Æthilric was, or should become, a Christian ruler of his own people.

Bede states that the shared rule involved a partition of East Anglian territory. This might have followed the natural division of the Waveney or some quite different principle. Æthilric's brother Anna was presumably resident at Exning, in the shadow of Devil's Dyke, if one of his daughters, Æthelthryth, was born there in 631. That royal house was well placed to supervise the defences across the Icknield Way, controlling Mercian access to East Anglia. A devoutly Christian man, Anna had married a woman (possibly named Sæwara) who brought him a stepdaughter named Sæthryth. Their names suggest a relationship by marriage or blood to the East Saxon Christian king Sæberht (d. *c*.615). Anna's own daughters were Seaxburh, Æthelthryth, Æthelburh and Wihtburh, and his son Jurmin, (probably a form of the name *Eormen*).

The mission of St Felix the Burgundian

The devout Sigeberht resolved to build Christendom within his realm. His design was favoured by the mission of Felix, by whose labours the knowledge of the Gospel of Jesus Christ first came widely to the nation of East Angles. Felix, a man of Burgundy who had lived a religious life there, was called to the work of teaching and conversion among the English. Having been consecrated a missionary bishop, he came to Canterbury and explained his vocation to Archbishop Honorius, who sent him into East Anglia. In the twelfth century, William of Malmesbury wrote that Felix and Sigeberht had known each other in Gaul and came to England together, but that differs from Bede's account.

The religious life of the kingdom of Burgundy had been transformed a generation before by the example and energies of the great Irish monk Columbanus (545-c.615), who trained in the seminary for missionaries at Bangor on the south side of the Bay of Carrickfergus in north-eastern Ireland. In *c.*590 he made his way through England with 12 disciples on his way to Burgundy to preach to the heathen, among whom he counted the ignorant multitudes and their worldly bishops. There he founded the monastery at Luxeuil and established a particularly strict and ascetic rule, making his retreat in a ruinous castle in an uncultivated wilderness. It was his custom to travel on foot, reading from his bible and meditating, and exhorting those he met to receive the faith. His reforms spread through many religious houses in that region, and he afterwards went into north Italy and founded another famous monastery at Bobbio. The education of Felix was no doubt permeated by the teaching of Columbanus, perhaps directly inspired by his personal example.

Sigeberht had seen many excellent religious institutions in Gaul, and sought to imitate them. He established a school in which boys were taught to read and write in Latin, and Felix assisted him by providing masters and instructors of the kind who taught in Kent, probably in the Frankish or Roman mould. Sigeberht established for him the see of *Dommoc*, the first Bishopric of the East Angles. Felix gathered a rich harvest of souls for Christ, presumably by travelling about the kingdom to preach with companions and interpreters, and by being introduced into households where he could preach and baptise. He is said to have baptised Æthelthryth, Anna's daughter, in St Mindred's Well, a natural pool at Exning. His obedience to Archbishop Honorius placed the East Anglian Church firmly within the framework of the Roman mission at Canterbury.

The likely site of *Dommoc* or *Domnoc* was for many centuries (since the thirteenth) accepted as Dunwich, the 'splendid city' now entirely lost into the sea. The name could derive from Latin *dominicum* (church building), perhaps in an Erse form *domhnac*. Doubt arises because the bishopric disappeared entirely at the time of the Viking wars, *c.*900, and was never revived. Yet for 240 years it was the primary seat of East Anglian Christianity, the home not only of its Church but also of its first Bishop's Palace, of its ecclesiastical library, treasury and vestry. A community of priests and deacons possibly accompanied Felix to Suffolk, or at any rate must have been established by him at Dommoc in a canon community like that of Augustine's followers at Canterbury.

Dunwich possessed a natural haven with woodlands extending on a promontory to the east. The churches and schools of Dunwich were granted to the Priory of Eye in the charter of its foundation by Robert Malet, and a cell was established there. Eye thereafter acquired an early Insular gospel-book written in Lombardic majuscule and apparently with purple-stained vellum pages (the Red Book of Eye), affirmed to have belonged to Felix. Furthermore, the seal-matrix of a ninth-century Bishop of Dommoc otherwise known only from his Profession of Faith was found at Eye during the nineteenth century.

Possibly these were acquired from Dunwich, although the episcopal importance of Hoxne during the tenth century might equally have brought them into the sphere of Eye. Dommoc is sometimes called *Dommoc-ceastre*, showing it had been a Roman place, but the sea has erased all possible evidence of this at Dunwich.

Some prefer to identify Dommoc with the Roman fort and town at *Burch* (i.e. 'burgh': Walton, Felixstowe), since that claim was made in the Rochester monastic register in 1251 and in other late thirteenth-century sources. The monastery of St Felix founded at Burch in the time of William Rufus was a possession of Rochester (St Andrew), a connection probably formed early in the mission to the East Anglian court, when Felix was obtaining teachers for Sigeberht's school from Kent. Even if Burch was not Dommoc, its Roman castle, an outward symbol of the ruling culture settled on the Deben, may well have been used by Felix. That inference is reinforced by the dedication of St Felix Hallowtree, Alnesbourne (also belonging to Rochester), probably named after an early preaching-cross. The place name Felixstowe arose long after the time of Felix.

As Felix's work took root, catastrophe struck in Northumbria. In 632 Cadwallon, in league with Penda, rebelled against Eadwine and slew him in a fierce battle at Hatfield Chase near the Isle of Axholme. For a year the victors raged through Northumbria making great and indiscriminate slaughter. Eadwine's thegn Bass took charge of Paulinus, Queen Æthelburh, her children Eanflæd and Wuscfrea and grandson Yffi, and got them safely away by ship to Kent. The two boys later died in Gaul at the court of King Dagobert, where they were buried with honour. Paulinus rescued the great golden cross and chalice from the altar at York and took them to Canterbury, where Honorius (who had succeeded Justus as Archbishop) appointed him to the newly-vacant bishopric of Rochester. But James, the deacon at York, remained there and afterwards lived at Catterick, where he converted many and taught the singing of church music. Penda assumed rule in Mercia.

The historical traces of Felix are elusive, though his spiritual footprints have never been effaced. He is associated with a religious foundation at Soham (Cambs.), then a Fen Isle midway between Exning and the Isle of Ely, quite surrounded by Soham Mere, Isleham Fen and other waterways of the South Level. Had Augustine already established that foundation at *Cratendune*, as *Liber Eliensis* tells? There was no firm causeway to Soham until the tenth century, but a monastery founded there by one Lutting under Abbot Werferth was remembered, of which William of Malmesbury reported the visible remains, burnt by the Danes, in the twelfth. Felix's presence in the Cambridge area cannot be discounted, though the walled Roman town at *Grantacæstir* was *desolata* in 696. At his death in 647 Felix was buried at Dommoc, but was long afterwards translated to Soham and then to Ramsey.

The work of Felix seems discernible around the Waveney and Yare. Two places named Flixton in north-east Suffolk are thought by some to be associated with him, despite certain etymological objections. Flixton, south-west of Bungay, is one of the parishes of South Elmham: as we have seen, a large settlement evolved there in the sixth century below the long ridge overlooking the broad acreage of water meadows at that point in the Waveney valley. The settlement and its cemeteries had been centred upon conspicuous Bronze Age barrows, and upon what may have been a pre-Christian religious sanctuary enclosure. Some years ago, before all this was known, Norman Scarfe made the case that Flixton, under episcopal tenure at Domesday within the larger holding of South Elmham, might represent an original grant to Felix around which the later episcopal establishment of South Elmham grew. Its church site (St Mary), on a significant mount, was marked in the tenth or eleventh centuries by a stone tower with 'Rhenish helm' roof, faithfully rebuilt by Salvin during the 1850s.

At Flixton in Lothingland (near Lowestoft) Norman Scarfe notes that the original church was that of St Michael at Oulton. It stands on a prominent terrace above Oulton Marsh, probably then flooded by the Great Estuary: beyond the marshes to the south lay the settlement at Carlton, still flourishing. St Michael's church was an episcopal holding at Doomsday, when its endowment was already so large as to suggest that it had been a minster church. The ruins of a small church (St Andrew) at Flixton, now isolated and overgrown, are those of a building heavily restored in 1630. It was then thought to have been the mother church of the region, and had a very simple rectangular plan.

Late sources also associate Felix with Reedham (Norfolk), site of a substantial Roman stone building. It lies at the southern tip of the ridge of higher land on the north side of the Yare flowing from Caistor into its estuarine bay west of Lothingland. From Reedham the tideway flowed north-east directly to the promontory on which the Roman fortress of Burgh Castle stands, near Breydon Water. Burgh St Peter (Norfolk), a Roman site overlooking the entrance to the Waveney, is unlikely to have escaped attention in the same period.

The Irish and Ionan missions
The sons of Æthelfrith of Northumbria had been exiled among the Picts and Scots since Rædwald's victory of 616, and were instructed and baptised in the Irish church. At Eadwine's death the eldest, Eanfrith, claimed Bernicia, while Eadwine's cousin Osric, baptised by Paulinus, claimed Deira. Both reverted to paganism, but were slain by Cadwallon within the year. Then Eanfrith's brother Oswald, son of Æthelfrith by Eadwine's sister Acha, gathered a Christian army and destroyed Cadwallon in the decisive battle at Hallington near Hexham in 633. He thereby recovered supreme authority over the nations of Britain, making his principal seat at Bamburgh. Hereswith, the East Anglian queen of Æthilric, was his kinswoman. Oswald asked the Irish elders to send him a bishop. After an unsuccessful episode with the first candidate, the monk Aidan was selected and consecrated in c.635 from Columba's monastery at Iona, a man suited by his discretion and piety for the difficult task. Oswald, who spoke Irish perfectly,

settled him on the Isle of Lindisfarne, and interpreted for him as he preached the gospel to the thegns and ealdormen.

Around 633-4, probably before Aidan reached Lindisfarne, an Irish monk named Fursa came to Sigeberht with his brothers Foillan and Ultan and a company of priests. Born around 597, his father is said to have been Fintan, son of Finlog the pagan King of Munster, and his mother Gelges, Christian daughter of Aed-Finn, King of Connaught. Their child Fursa was given to Abbot Brendan, Fintan's uncle, on the island monastery of Inisquin in Lough Corrib (near Galway town), where he studied sacred books and the religious life and duty. Brendan's successor Meldan continued his training, and he retired to a hermitage near the lough shores. Later he built a monastery at Kill-arsagh where he was joined by Foillan and Ultan, and with a larger group he travelled and preached among the Irish for a year. Then he was bidden in a vision to make the *peregrinatio*, to journey forth in pilgrimage, and he did so, taking with him relics of the holy Meldan and Beoan.

Fursa came into the province of Angles through British lands, possibly through Galloway. Sigeberht gave him a pleasant wooded site near the sea in the old Roman fort of *Cnobheresburg* (usually taken to be Burgh Castle). Professor Whitelock cited a ninth-century Irish writing, *The Monastery of Tallaght*, which contains a fable about the foundation of Fursa's East Anglian monastery. It attributes the grant to the daughter of the 'King of the Eastern Country.' (There is no other record that either King had a daughter). Fursa met her on his arrival in East Anglia:

> 'What manner of man are you?' she asked.
> 'Like an old smith, with his anvil on his shoulder', came the reply.
> 'The anvil of devotion?' 'Perseverance in holiness', said he.
> 'If God gave you a block whereon your anvil could be planted, would you abide there?'
> 'That would be likely indeed', he replied.
> Then she granted him the spot where they stood.

Three sides of Burgh Castle are still standing, their thick walls with tower-like bastions faced with courses of black flint and red brick. Some 200 yards in length, it encloses more than 6 acres overlooking the expanses north and west beyond Breydon Water, then a vast domain of marshland, river and estuary. It is likely that Fursa and his company lived together around a wooden oratory in wattle-built huts, with a bell-sacristy nearby, in the Irish fashion. Charles Green's excavations at Burgh Castle appeared to show the foundations of such huts, but this interpretation is not universally accepted. The site had certainly been occupied during the sixth century, and had a cremation cemetery. The identification of Burgh Castle as *Cnobheresburg* is not certain, as Walton, Brancaster and Caistor-on-Sea are also possible, but it accords with the evidence of Felix's work in the same region.

Fursa was a mystic and an ascetic, wearing only a thin garment even in winter. He experienced illnesses accompanied by dramatic visions, which have a very early place in the history of medieval apocalyptic literature and influenced Christian notions of experience after death. He witnessed the singing of angelic choirs and the joys of the blessed. Angels conducted him above a dark valley among the fires of falsehood, covetousness, discord and injustice which were to consume the world. Devils accused him of his faults, and he held dialogues with the spirits of Meldan and Beoan. A devil hurled a burning sinner towards him, scorching his face, because Fursa had received that man's clothes when he died. These marks he actually bore for the rest of his life. He would not speak of his visions unless questioned by repentant men, and he perspired heavily as he related them. He took great care to encourage virtue by his sermons and example. Bede states that Fursa converted many people by his preaching: a ninth-century work, *Virtutes Fursei*, adds that he built monasteries and churches and established monks and virgins to the service of Christ.

Despite the differences of custom between the Celtic and Roman Churches, it is known that Felix and Archbishop Honorius had great admiration for the work of Aidan of Lindisfarne. Indeed, if Felix trained at or in the sphere of Luxeuil, the Irish example was embedded in his own training, and the use of a Roman fortress for a wilderness retreat had been the choice of Columbanus himself. Therefore Felix probably welcomed and respected Fursa and his brethren, who remained his fellow-workers in Christ for many years. Nonetheless, Felix maintained a clear attachment to Canterbury and the authority of the Roman mission. East Anglia was evangelised in the united spirit of the Roman and Irish Churches.

Sigeberht's abdication and death

By 635 King Æthilric and Queen Hereswith had an heir (Ealdwulf), and his brother Anna already had at least three daughters and a presumed association with Exning. The power of Oswald of Northumbria was feared in Kent sufficiently for Eadwine's widow to send her children to Gaul for safety. Sigeberht, perhaps believing that Æthilric was sufficiently protected by Oswald's authority, abdicated his own worldy rule as a king. This was certainly the first recorded example of such a renunciation, which was much later imitated by other English kings. Bede states that he had become so greatly a lover of the Heavenly kingdom that he relinquished the affairs of his own kingdom and commended them to his kinsman Ecgric (i.e. Æthilric), who had previously held a part of the same realm. He did this in order to enter the monastery which he had created for his own use (*quod sibi fecerat*), and receiving the tonsure to devote himself to fight rather for the Eternal kingdom. Having done this he remained there for a considerable time. The role of Felix in performing the tonsure and in the implementation of the king's plan must have been paramount.

Bede does not name the place, but in later sources it is identified as *Beodricesworth*, which afterwards became Bury St Edmunds. This identification wears the most convincing hallmarks of probability. The site is presumably that of the later medieval abbey, the rectangular precinct of which stands on the east side of the medieval town laid out in around 1066, and between that and the river Lark, which forms an eastern boundary. Northgate and Southgate Street, aligned on one axis north and south of the precinct, were originally connected by a road passing directly beside the West Front of the medieval abbey. The area west of this, which includes the Norman tower, the Gateway tower, the present Cathedral (St James) and the church of St Mary at the south-west corner, is thought to be an encroachment into the area of the town; the original curtilage probably lay between the former road and the river. Sigeberht's church may have stood near the north-east corner of the abbey church: among the medieval accumulations and confused levels, finds of Ipswich Ware pottery demonstrate occupation here between the seventh and ninth centuries.

Behind the magnificence of St Eadmund's shrine and the medieval abbey, therefore, lies the older genius, the profound spiritual example of the first English king to renounce his throne for Christ. The name *Beodricesworth* shows that it had once been the curtilage of Beodric. In later centuries a series of rulers associated both with Mercia and East Anglia possessed names with the prefix *Beo-*. The site has great amenity within the broad vale, and is usefully located high up the Lark, with access east to the sources of the Black Bourne (above Tostock), the Gipping (above Haughley) and the Brett (near Bradfield). Was this place, in fact, already a royal dwelling, the capital of a political domain or *regio* controlling the western parts of southern East Anglia? Was Beodric the sponsor of Ricberht the assassin? When Sigeberht, returning from exile, was fighting for his worldly kingdom did he reconquer this western stronghold of a rival dynasty in order to consolidate Wuffing power? At Beodricesworth, Sigeberht asserted the example of royal Christian power in his own person at the heart of his former kingdom.

Penda of Mercia, not ready to confront Oswald, attacked the East Angles in 636 having presumably heard that Sigeberht was no longer leading them. He perhaps led his armies south of the Fen and faced a defence of Devil's Dyke. Bede describes the outcome. Æthilric was sufficiently forewarned to raise a splendid force, but it was clear that the East Angles were weaker than their enemies. Therefore they asked Sigeberht to accompany them in battle in order to strengthen the army's confidence. As he was unwilling and refused their request, they conveyed him forcibly from the monastery to the battle-line, hoping that the army would be in less fear of heart and less able to contemplate flight if their former most energetic and distinguished leader were with them. Sigeberht, walking with Christ, would not bear weapons and entered the battle carrying only a staff. There he achieved martyrdom for the Way of Peace. King Æthilric was also killed and his entire army was slain or scattered in the pagan onslaught.

ANNA, 636-654

Despite this catastrophe Penda had not conquered the East Angles. Oswald, also called 'Brightblade', maintained his authority, which sufficed for Anna (Æthilric's brother) to resume Wuffing rule. Penda's warlike example drove even his former allies to realign themselves. Cynegils, King of the West Saxons since 611, had survived the retaliation incurred by his son Cwichelm's attempt to assassinate Eadwine in 626. Another son, Cenwalh, had married Penda's sister to hold the Mercians in alliance or abeyance. But Christian teaching came to Cynegils through the missionary Birinus, who sought England at the suggestion of Pope Honorius I (625-40) and was consecrated Bishop at Genoa. While Oswald was visiting the West Saxon court, Cynegils was baptised at Dorchester-on-Thames, and received by Oswald as his godson. Oswald afterwards married his daughter Cyneburh, thus confirming Northumbrian patronage through religion and kinship.

Anna must have undertaken the funerals of Sigeberht and Æthilric, but nothing is known of them. Sigeberht was presumably buried in his church at Beodricesworth, and Anna probably accorded Christian rites to his brother Æthilric. A distinguished presence is indicated to the east of Bury at Tostock, where a gold buckle set with a very large rectangular garnet was discovered. A pyramidal gold scabbard-mount richly decorated with filigree, with a garnet setting on the apex, has recently been found in that district. The cruciform garnet-cloisonné pendant found at Ixworth shows Christian activity nearby under the most senior patronage. The related pendant from Wilton (Norfolk) encloses a coin of Heraclius (associating his son, which occurred in 619), but is set to display the image of the Cross on the reverse. The setting surely alludes

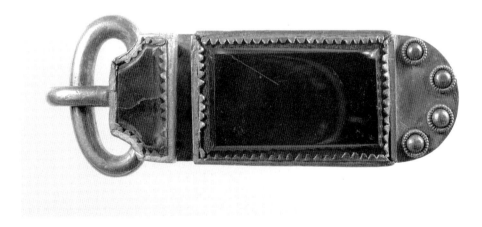

Tostock: gold buckle set with garnets. *The Ashmolean Museum, Oxford. Photograph: R. Carr*

Ixworth: gold pendant cross with cellwork. *The Ashmolean Museum, Oxford*

Wilton (Norfolk): gold pendant Cross set with a coin of Heraclius (seventh-century). *The British Museum*

to the recovery of the True Cross, which occurred in Sigeberht's time. Its loss at Wilton may suggest early royal interest in the Brandon area, where a monastery afterwards arose. The communication from Tostock through Ixworth lay along the Black Bourne vale, and proceeded towards Brandon along the Little Ouse.

The strength of Kent lay in the ecclesiastical authority of Canterbury, and in its royal Frankish alignment, since Eadbald himself was not only son of Æthelberht but grandson of Charibert. Kent espoused continental royal standards by minting gold shillings equivalent to the Frankish tremissis, with portraits based on Roman imperial prototypes. Most surviving examples derive from a single hoard (Crondall, Hants). This first known English coinage may not have survived Eadbald himself. Under Sigeberht and Anna, East Anglian royal and commercial engagement with Frankish affairs remained fundamental, as it had been to Rædwald. If they issued no East Anglian coins, new north Frankish issues continued to reach directly into Anna's kingdom. Two small, thick gold pieces marked with a double cross, found at Sudbourne and Coddenham, are of a Merovingian type also found at Crondall and at three other English sites. Dr Arent Pol notes 28 known examples, most with Netherland findspots including Wijnaldum, Wijk-bij-Duurestede, Bruchem, Winsum and Remmerden. Nine occurred in a hoard at Nietap, dated c.630-35.

Eadbald of Kent died in 640 and was buried at Canterbury. His younger son Eorconberht succeeded him in precedence to his elder brother Eormenred, and consolidated his rule by marrying Seaxburh, eldest daughter of King Anna of the East Angles. Her Latin *Life* tells that she was at first unwilling. However, this alliance profoundly strengthened both kingdoms, and Anna became a formidable patriarch.

Diplomatic alliances and religious commitments
The confrontation between Oswald and Penda could not be long delayed, and was of the most violent nature. In a great battle at Oswestry in 641 Penda's brother Eowa died fighting by his side. But Penda triumphed: Oswald himself was killed and his head and limbs were left impaled on stakes around the battlefield, a monument to Penda's fury and atavism. Then Oswald's brother Oswy shared Northumbria with Oswine, of the house of Eadwine. In Wessex, on the death of Cynegils, Cenwalh assumed rule, and although not yet a Christian he discharged his own wife, Penda's sister, and took another bride. Cenwalh's sister had been the queen of Oswald, and thus their kinship with Penda was revoked. Penda accordingly attacked Wessex and drove Cenwalh into exile in 644. So far had Anna's power increased that Cenwalh took refuge in East Anglia for three years, and was welcomed as an honoured royal guest into the Halls of the Wuffings.

As Cenwalh arrived in East Anglia, Fursa was planning to leave. After a long probation his brother Ultan went off alone to live as a hermit. In around 644 Fursa gave the monastery, its inmates, and the priests Goban and Dicuill, into

Foillan's keeping. He left to find Ultan, and passed a whole year with him in abstinence, prayer and daily manual labour. But heathen attacks, probably from Mercia, disturbed the kingdom and threatened the monasteries, so he took ship for Gaul. There he was welcomed by King Clovis II of Neustria (r.638-56) and Eorconwald, Mayor of his Palace (640-57). They gave him land at Lagny on the Marne, where he founded an abbey in c.645, and built churches to St Peter and to the Holy Saviour. Queen Balthild, wife of Clovis, also assisted Fursa. A gold seal-matrix expressing her authority and union with Clovis has recently been discovered at Postwick (Norfolk) a little east of Norwich.

Queen Hereswith, widowed when Æthilric died with Sigeberht in 636, sought the monastic life, but there was no nunnery in her kingdom. Therefore she took the veil and went to live in Gaul (according to Bede, at the Frankish royal house of Chelles near Paris). Her sister Hild, with whom she was baptised at York by Paulinus when Eadwine received the faith, felt the same calling and heard the teaching of Aidan in Northumbria. Paulinus had died in 644 at Rochester. In 647, aged 33, Hild came to East Anglia; finding that her sister had already gone into Gaul, she remained for a year preparing to follow her. Anna's daughters, all very religious girls, discovered a most interesting relative. Æthelthryth, now 16 and destined for royal marriage, affected the finery of gold and pearl-bossed necklaces: no doubt she listened admiringly to Hild's tales of the Northumbrian court.

In that important year, at Anna's instigation, Cenwalh received Christianity in East Anglia; Malmesbury states this was through instruction and baptism by Bishop Felix himself, and with King Anna his sponsor. Perhaps they were all there: Abbot Foillan and his priests, Hild, Æthelthryth and her sisters, when the exiled West Saxon dynast accepted the Faith which his successors should someday defend in the name of England. As a Christian king Cenwalh was restored to Wessex in 647 from East Anglia, probably with the military support of King Anna. His bishops Birinus and Agilberct (c.650) were appointed from the Gaulish rather than the Kentish Church. In the same year Felix died, far from his native Burgundy, having honoured his adoptive country for 17 years in the service of God.

Hild saw what had been achieved by Felix. In the 17 years of his episcopate, under two devoutly Christian rulers, churches must have been dedicated in various parts of the kingdom, particularly at centres under royal supervision including presumably Gipeswic, Sudbury, Exning, Cambridge and Blythburgh in addition to those already mentioned, though we have no immediate testimony of them. Archbishop Honorius consecrated Thomas, a deacon of Fenland nationality, as the second Bishop of Dommoc. Christianity had taken root in the Fen, perhaps under the patronage of Felix at Soham. Hild, as Aidan's pupil, must have felt affinity with Foillan at Cnobheresburg. Anna and his nobility endowed that monastery with finer buildings and other gifts. At the end of the year Aidan summoned Hild to begin a monastic life in Northumbria, and after being ordained she settled with a few companions on the north side of the river Wear. Under Aidan's close supervision she soon after became abbess of the monastery at Hart Isle (*Heruteu*), now called Hartlepool.

Two of Anna's daughters, however, did go into the religious life overseas. They found a popular destination, the double house with separate communities of monks and nuns called Faremoutiers, near Meaux, in the land of Brie. Its foundress Abbess Fara had been dedicated to the religious life by Columbanus in childhood, and was still ruling the house when Æthelburh and her half-sister Sæthryth went to live there. Their pious example, the fruit of their training by Felix or his deputies, was much admired. Their retirement removed them from the register of prospective royal brides, and therefore strengthened the independence of Anna's house. In time they were joined by their niece Eorcongota, daughter of Seaxburh and Eorconberht, who had outlawed the worship of idols and established the observance of Lent in the kingdom of Kent.

The marital choice of the Northumbrian king, Oswy, fell upon his cousin Eanflæd, Eadwine's daughter, who had remained in Kent with her mother since the disaster of 633. Oswy's first wife had been a British princess, but by this second marriage he added the Deiran right of his uncle Eadwine to the Bernician right of his father Æthelfrith, and so united them in a single line suitable to oppose the ambitions of Penda. Eanflæd was fetched from Kent by ship in 651, and arrived with a religious mentor called Romanus, charged with safeguarding her Roman observance in this land where Irish customs of Christianity prevailed. Oswy secured his rule by the murder of King Oswine of Deira, who had gone into hiding to avoid him. Aidan, who loved Oswine dearly, died soon afterwards, and Bishop Finan succeeded him at Lindisfarne.

Ely tradition dates Æthelthryth's first marriage to the same year, 651 (though a later date is also possible). She married a prince of the southern Fenland people (*Gyrwæ*) named Tondberht. The Isle of Ely was then truly an island of 600 hides surrounded by deep peaty fen, and thenceforth always remained part of the East Anglian kingdom. Between Ely and her early home at Exning lay Soham, from which, perhaps, Christian teaching had spread to Tondberht's household and had called the deacon Thomas to Dommoc. Æthelthryth remained a virgin for Christ, and Tondberht died soon afterwards. She gained a great friend in her personal minister, a man with the Welsh name of Owini.

The Mercian threat: exile, destruction and slaughter
Penda turned again upon the East Angles. In *c*.651 he attacked the monastery at Cnobheresburh, probably from the sea. Anna's force arrived in time to hold off the Mercians while Foillan rescued the church treasures and books, and escaped with his life in a ship to France. The monastery was abandoned, and Anna was driven into exile. Fursa had died at Mézerolles in Ponthieu about a year before, having set out to revisit his Suffolk brethren, and was buried at Péronne. Foillan and his friends were received there by Eorconwald, but soon afterwards expelled.

The religious women Iduberg and her daughter Gertrude welcomed them at Nivelles, however, and Foillan founded a monastery at Fosse beside the river Biesme. Near there he and three companions were murdered by bandits in around 655. Norman Scarfe suggests that Dicuill, one of the Irish presbyters in Fursa's band, became settled at Dickleburgh at the head of the Norfolk tributary of the Waveney. An Irishman of the same name later ruled a small and remote community at Bosham in Sussex.

Foillan's escape was recorded at Nivelles. Among the books he saved was doubtless the gospel-book from the altar. George Henderson allows that the Book of Durrow, the celebrated early painted gospel-book, looks to East Anglian models for aspects of its ornament, though under Irish influence. Its richly decorated carpet-pages, text initials and illustrations of the Evangelist symbols stand at the beginning of the surviving series of such books, among the great devotional works of their age. Its ornament borrows directly from East Anglian and Celtic metalwork like that represented in the Sutton Hoo burial, including the distinctive works of the East Anglian master-goldsmith. The figure of St Matthew, for instance, with its representation of lidded cells and millefiori settings, seems based upon a cloisonné shoulder-clasp, for which Sutton Hoo provides the obvious parallel, and which has animal-ornament closely related to that of the book. The spiral ornament of the first carpet-page has particular resemblances to the enamels of the lost bowl from Badley (Needham Market) with its triangular

Badley Bridge: spiral ornament from lost bowl escutcheon (reconstruction). Silvered bronze (shown black) with red enamel fill. *Drawing: Author*

stud insets. These objects were already buried when Fursa arrived in Suffolk, but similar work must have been available for use as models under royal patronage. The peregrinations of Fursa's band from Galway or through Galloway could have supplied them with Pictish images also reflected in the painting. The textual tradition of the book was derived from a Columban source. Whatever the origin of the Book of Durrow itself, the altar-book of Cnobheresburh might certainly have resembled it.

Having driven Anna from East Anglia, Penda made his son, Peada, King over the Middle Angles. Peada's sister Cyneburh was married to Oswy's son Alhfrith, and Peada now made his wooing-journey to Northumbria with his thegns and gesiths, for the hand of Alhfrith's sister Alhflæd. Oswy made the condition that Peada and his nation must receive the Christian Faith: Peada agreed, all their company and servants were baptised by Finan, and Oswy received Peada as his godson. Four priests returned with the king to preach and baptise, led by the Irishman Diuma, with the Englishmen Adda, Betti and Cedd. Then even Penda allowed their teaching in his own kingdom. Oswy, meanwhile, frequently welcomed the heathen king of the East Saxons, Sigeberht III (called 'the Good') to Northumbria, and presided at his baptism by Finan. Cedd, a disciple of Aidan's, was recalled from Mercia and sent with a priest to preach to the East Saxons, over whom he was later consecrated Bishop.

King Anna might well have turned to Wessex in exile. Perhaps thus he came to the Magonsætan, where Norman Scarfe's detective work has followed him. This people dwelt in Hereford and Shropshire west of the Severn. Their King, Merewalh, was the head of a local dynasty: Malmesbury makes him Penda's son. Merewalh received Christianity from Diuma's mission, if not before, and married Eormenburg, a daughter of King Eorconberht's brother Eormenred. A Ludlow tradition tells that Anna built a little wooden church near the Welsh border, which later became dedicated to his daughter Æthelthryth. Furthermore, 25 years after Anna's death a Suffolk monastery, founded in the year of Anna's death, owned extensive lands at Much Wenlock and close by. A record survives of their transfer back to the monastery of Wenlock under its abbess Mildburg (Merewalh's daughter). It is difficult to explain how the Suffolk house obtained them if not through diplomatic relations involving Kent, perhaps through Merewalh's marriage settlement. His wife and two saintly daughters, Mildthryth (Mildred) and Mildgyth, later became closely involved with Seaxburh in the monastic life of Kent.

In Anna's absence Bishop Thomas died in 651-2, and Archbishop Honorius consecrated Berhtgisl, called Boniface, from the kingdom of Kent to the see of Dommoc. A year later Honorius himself died, last of the Gregorian Apostles to occupy the see of Canterbury. The election of his successor was delayed for 18 months while a suitably orthodox candidate was found. Deusdedit, a West Saxon, was elected archbishop in March 655 and consecrated by Ithamar, Bishop of Rochester.

By 653 Anna was back in his own kingdom. His youngest daughter, Wihtburh, must have been born in his last years, as she reputedly lived down to the year 743 at East Dereham in Norfolk. Anna is last seen in company with his son Jurmin (?Eormen), of whom nothing else is known, at Blythburgh in Suffolk. The principal Roman roads surrounding that large haven and estuary were maintained, and led to the ancient ford at Wenhaston, a significant town in Roman times. East of Wenhaston and Blyford, among the leas of the open vale beneath the bluffs and spurs on either bank, the estuary widens rapidly towards the mount on which Blythburgh church stands, and spreads into broad tidal waters and reed beds. Seen from the Walberswick road, the estuarine Blyth valley presents evocative contours on its way to the sea at Southwold.

The name and situation of Blythburgh lead us to expect that a royal dwelling stood near this road and river junction, commanding the water highway. The pre-Conquest stone tower at Thorington may mark a site of earlier importance. The Blyth watershed partly defined the extent of the Blything Hundred, formalised in the tenth century. This was presumably an ancient department, perhaps a tribal area or *regio* centred upon the river at the haven's fordable headwaters. East of Blyford on the north bank is an open down or wold above the river, called Bulcamp. Here, in 653–54, King Anna and his son Eormen died fighting Penda and his army. It was the last battle recorded on East Anglian soil for many years afterwards. Huntingdon, who gives Penda the soubriquet *Strenuus*, states that Anna was put to the sword with his entire army, so that hardly any remained alive. Whether (as one historian suggests) Anna, returning, was surprised by Penda awaiting him, or whether the Mercians made an unexpected incursion upon the Blyth valley, we cannot certainly decide. Presumably the royal bodies were borne sorrowfully from the battlefield to Blythburgh, where (according to *Liber Eliensis*) they were entombed and afterwards venerated.

ÆTHELHERE, 654

Penda, having ensured that the East Angles could not threaten the rearguard, was now ready to attack Northumbria. Within months of the brutal assault at Blythburgh, Anna's brother and successor King Æthelhere had accumulated a fighting force and bodyguard, which he led into alliance with Penda in the northern expedition. For this reason Bede, who could have told us more, calls him the cause of the war which followed. But Æthelhere's motive for changing sides is plain enough. Penda's continuing wars showed his ambition to supreme authority in the name of pagan Anglian kingship. This was Penda's final chance. Æthelhere deflected him from the inevitable destruction of East Anglia by joining him.

In an immense company of 30 legions, led by the noblest and most war-trained ealdormen under Penda's command, they gathered in the north-west together with the armies of the British near *Loidis* (Leeds), site of a Northumbrian royal dwelling. Oswy, besieged there with his son Alhfrith, had only one legion, and his nine-year-old son Ecgfrith was held hostage in Mercia by Queen Cynewise. He offered a huge treasure to buy off his attackers, everything at his immediate disposal. Bede says Penda refused it, but the Welsh chronicler that he took all the riches of the place (called *Iudeu*), distributed them among the British kings, and still determined to destroy the Northumbrians. Oswy prayed, promising his infant daughter to God, and 12 estates to be given as monasteries, if he might prevail.

In the night of 14 November 654, Cadafæl, King of Gwynedd (who had come with Penda), rose up and withdrew with his army. The next day Oswy went out with his little force at a place called Caius' Field beside the river Winwæd. His nephew, Oswald's son, was there to support Penda, but stood aside to await the result. Through the Northumbrians' faith, valour and desperation the British and Mercian armies were cut down or put to flight. Nearly all the 30 royal generals died. King Æthelhere of the East Angles saw all his forces and his personal bodyguard slaughtered around him before he also was killed. Heavy rains had put the river in spate, flooding over the land: many men were drowned fleeing through its torrents, more even than were put to the sword in the battle. King Penda himself was slain, making death and glory the terms of his personal victory. Thus (says the Archdeacon of Huntingdon) came about the saying, that the slaying of Anna, of Sigebert and Ecgric, and of Oswald and Eadwine, *in Winwed amne vindicata est.*

Oswy fulfilled his promise to God: Ælfflæd his daughter was sent to abbess Hild at Hartlepool under vows of perpetual virginity, and later went with her to the new monastery built by Hild at Whitby.

ÆTHELWALD, 654-664

One nephew of Rædwald's, Æthelwald, the fourth son of Eni, was yet living, and in this dawn of hope the peace of the East Angles was entrusted to his kingship. He continued or renewed his family's residence at Rendlesham. Its situation gave ready access to the growing harbour at Gipeswic, to the East Saxons, and (above all) to the Kentish court, to Rochester, Canterbury and London. Under Bishop Berhtgisl Boniface the ecclesiastical bonds to Kent were assured. Queen Seaxburh had borne a family to Eorconberht, the sons Ecgberht and Hlothhere (i.e. *Lothair*), and daughters Eorcongota and Eormenhild. Through Kent also lay the route into Gaul, where Sæthryth and Æthelburh were conducting lives of exemplary piety. Seaxburh no doubt maintained links with her sisters there, particularly when, after the death of Fara in *c.* 655, Æthelburh succeeded her as abbess of that famous house.

St Botolph of Iken

In the year of King Anna's death, the *Anglo-Saxon Chronicle* records that Botolph began to build a monastery at *Icanho*, that is, at Iken Hoo, on the south bank of the river Alde. Botolph and his monastery became very famous during his lifetime. The two principal sources, a *Life* written by Abbot Folcard of Thorney, and some notices in the *Breviary* of Slesvig, were both compiled in the later eleventh century. By that time, tradition or inference supplied what history had neglected to record. Botolph's cult was renewed with the translation of his relics, in the later tenth century to Grundisburgh, and in Edward the Confessor's time to Bury St Edmunds.

The Alde estuary opened north of Blaxhall through 'dismal swamps' into a wide basin edged by salt marsh and reed beds. A bourne rising near Tunstall, its slight vale fringed by Bronze Age tumuli, skirted the Great Wood at Sudbourne, and emerged into the Alde through water meadows at Iken. The island promontory was approached by a causeway at low tide where a stony track can be traced in the field east of Church Lane. From the island a ford also crossed the river northwards to the burial grounds of Snape, where pagan burial rituals were still practised in the years before Botolph's arrival. The riverside environment is described authentically, but differently, by Folcard and the Slesvig author, who may have visited Iken or have drawn upon older descriptions.

Folcard tells that Botolph first raised up the sign of the Cross and drove out various devils, who howled as they went. Some imagine the indignant British fisher-folk expelled from their marsh-fastnesses. Wild places were favoured for monastic life, especially in the Irish tradition, to purify them and dispel popular beliefs that they were infested by demons. When Cedd, Aidan's disciple, founded the house at Lastingham (Yorks.) soon after Botolph came to Iken, he and his brother Cynebill first spent the whole of Lent in prayer and fasting to cleanse and consecrate the site. Cedd told King Oswy this was the custom of those from whom he had learned the discipline of the Monastic Rule. A source which Folcard probably knew says the same about Guthlac, the Crowland hermit of *c.*699-714.

This estuarine spot was a short ride or an hour's walk from the royal mansion of Rendlesham, and closely within its domain or *regio*: its patronage lay immediately within King Æthelwald's sphere. The Slesvig narrative claims that Botolph was of Irish royal descent (a confusion with Fursa?). Folcard contradicts this (*de Saxonica gente*), but states that Botolph sought an untilled place, and one that should not dispossess existing owners. That was the formula of Columbanus himself, and implies a continental-Irish source. Folcard has some story that Botolph, at a continental monastery, was chaplain to the sisters of a king of the South Angles named Æthelmund, whose mother, Sæwara Sywara, had kinsmen named Æthelhere and Æthelwold. The Slesvig source makes him wait seven years before receiving his grant of land, during which time he dedicated a church to St Martin elsewhere. It is tempting to suppose that Botolph met Sæthryth and

Æthelburh in around 646-7 at Faremoutiers, that Sæwara was Sæthryth's mother (as her name suggests), and that Æthelmund was either the full name of Anna himself or that of an otherwise unrecorded sub-king in East Anglia. That is the tenor of the legend.

Anna's legacy: Christian marriages and sponsorships

Whatever funeral Æthelhere had arranged for his brother Anna, Æthelwald had the better opportunity to consecrate his martyred brother's memory. Early in his reign Hild founded the monastery at Whitby, which became the burial-place of the martyr Eadwine. Such a royal enshrinement may have recommended itself at Blythburgh in an existing church (if there was really a royal dwelling here), perhaps near the parish church site, or by the building of a new one. The relics of Anna and Jurmin were afterwards venerated there, and the saintly fame of his daughters enhanced the cult. From the discovery of certain pottery, and an ornamental whalebone tablet for writing in wax, it appears that an early literate community lived just north-east of the church, where the medieval priory afterwards arose. Probably the tablet was one leaf of a diptych, as Michael Lapidge suggested, on which the names of those to be commemorated in prayer were inscribed for use at the High Mass. The fragmentary texts scratched onto it appear to be written in Latin, but using the runic alphabet.

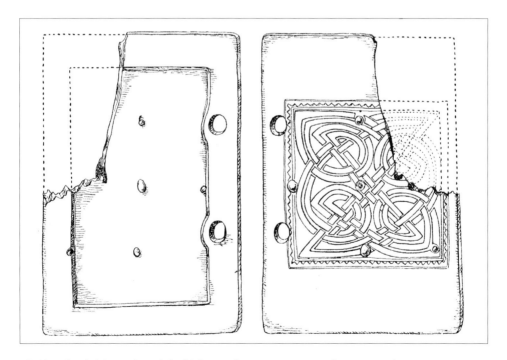

Blythburgh: whalebone diptych leaf. *The British Museum. Drawing after R.A. Smith 1923*

Diuma, the Irish missionary to the Mercians, was consecrated their Bishop by Finan of Lindisfarne. King Peada presumably created churches and granted endowments, fulfilling his marital promise before being poisoned by his wife Alhflæd on Easter Day 656. The great monastery at Peterborough, then called *Medeshamstede*, was probably established by his brother Wulfhere in *c*.661-4, perhaps (as *pseudo*-Ingulf suggests) using an original grant by Peada. Its foundation on a western Fen Edge promontory asserted an eastern extent of Mercian authority at the Fen opening of the river Nene, just as Ely had become East Anglian territory. The founding abbot ('constructor') of Medeshamstede, Seaxwulf, cannot have been educated in Middle Anglia where the mission was yet new, but must rather have been trained in Kent or East Anglia. The relation of his name to Seaxburh (and to the founder of Saxmundham, on a tributary of the Alde) is suggestive of, but insufficient to show, a connection with the Wuffing house. Early foundations from Medeshamstede include Brixworth (Northants.), where the stone church reflects Kentish architectural fashion.

After Peada's death, which left Alhfrith of Northumbria overseeing Mercia, his brother Wulfhere emerged as his successor. He was converted and married Eormenhild, Seaxburh's daughter. (Perhaps it was thus, and on her behalf, that Seaxwulf was sent to Medeshamstede.) This diplomatic marriage promised to be less fatal than a Northumbrian one, and at once cemented a Christian alliance between the families of Kent, East Anglia and Mercia. At much the same time, in 660, Northumbria embraced East Anglia as Æthelthryth, aged about 30, married Ecgfrith, Oswy's 15-year-old son. Even so the boy could not deflect her virginal resolve. Her minister Owini accompanied her north, where her marriage settlement apparently included estates at Hexham.

Cedd, now Bishop of the East Saxons, established monasteries at Tilbury, not far from London, and at the Roman shore fort of *Othona* (Bradwell-on-Sea), then called *Ythancæstir*. Part of a stone church built on the Kentish pattern may still be seen at the latter site, on the extreme northern promontory south of the Blackwater estuary, even today a remote place. It stands at the western entrance to the fort, perhaps adapted from a Roman gatehouse structure. The apsidal chancel lay within the precinct, but the nave and west porch outside it. Equal arches separated the nave from the chancel inside: the north porticus was entered from the chancel and the southern one from the nave. If the fort walls abutted the church, they created a physical separation between the monks living in the precinct and lay persons attending the Mass. There is no evidence that the East Angles built in stone at this time, but this arrangement might reflect what Cedd had seen in Suffolk. He taught the East Saxons to observe the discipline of a Rule, says Bede, so far as those rough people were able to understand it.

Cedd certainly had the opportunity to see Walton Castle. After the death of King Sigeberht the Good, murdered in *c*.655 by two of his own East Saxon thegns, King Suithhelm succeeded him, who was still heathen. Under Cedd's teaching he agreed to accept the Faith. King Æthelwald therefore invited them to Rendlesham in around 660, where Bishop Cedd baptised his king, and Æthelwald received him as his son in Christ as he emerged from the saving waters. A baptistery and royal chapel at Rendlesham had evidently superseded Rædwald's temple of two altars. The ceremony, which confirmed or renewed ties of friendship and duty between the two kingdoms, was no doubt attended by Bishop Berhtgisl, Abbot Botolph and many gesiths and thegns of both royal households. Did the exercise of hospitality and Hall festivities at Rendlesham resonate in East Saxon hearts as they took ship for home, leaving the fort at Walton as their last sight of the Deben?

St Wilfrid: The Irish mission submits to Rome
The mysticism, austerity, and pilgrim spirit of Irish Christianity had reached into the heart of Suffolk, though the Dommoc bishopric looked to the first authority of Canterbury. Few outside Kent and East Anglia did so. By 660 King Cenwalh in Wessex had grown so weary of Bishop Agilberct's speech, which no one could understand, that he divided the see of Dorchester and appointed Wini, an Englishman consecrated in Gaul, to the new see of Winchester. Agilberct went off in disgust to Northumbria, and became friendly with King Alhfrith, Oswy's son. He, like his stepmother Eanflæd and sister-in-law Æthelthryth, was a firm believer in the Roman Church. They found a fellow-worker named Wilfrid, a young man newly returned from training in Rome and Gaul.

From the age of 14, *c.*648, Wilfrid had lived with the monks at Lindisfarne. The studious boy had become impatient of Irish teaching and longed to go to Rome, so Eanflæd sent him to the Kentish court to observe the work of Archbishop Honorius. There he met Benedict Biscop, another Northumbrian, and they set off for Rome together. After studying in Rome, Wilfrid returned to Lyons, where he stayed for three years under the tutelage of Count Dalfinus and his brother, Archbishop Annemund. At the end of this time he witnessed the execution of his patron at the command of Queen Balthild, and he returned to Britain filled with learning and determination.

Alhfrith gave him land at Stamford, and Agilberct ordained him priest. Soon afterwards Alhfrith made him Abbot of his newly-founded monastery at Ripon, expelling Eata (Aidan's disciple) whom he had first put in charge of it. When the Irishman Colman succeeded Finan as Bishop of Lindisfarne, Alhfrith resolved to persuade King Oswy to establish Roman custom throughout the English Church. At their Council in 663 at Hild's monastery of Whitby, the Irish cause was argued by Colman, supported by Hild and Cedd, who acted as Anglo-Irish interpreter. Alhfrith, Agilberct, Wilfrid, Romanus, James the Deacon and others formed the Roman faction. Oswy decided for the Roman cause; those who, like Colman, would not accept the change left England and returned to Iona or Ireland. The Irish Church withdrew to prepare itself for a mightier spiritual enterprise in which Kent and Northumbria were to play an essential part.

Even as they held their Council a great plague was sweeping through England. Archbishop Deusdedit lay dying in Canterbury, and both he and King Eorconberht of Kent died on 14 July 664. Seaxburh found some retreat as her elder son Ecgberht assumed the Kentish throne. The plague killed Cedd at Lastingham: his East Saxon monks travelled there to be near the grave of their beloved father abbot, and most of them died. King Æthelwald of the East Angles died in the same year, and so ended the 35 years in which the four nephews of Rædwald had ruled the kingdom.

EALDWULF, 664-713

Twenty-eight years had passed since Æthilric and Sigeberht had died in battle against Penda, and Ealdwulf, Æthilric's son, was perhaps about 35 when he inherited East Anglian rule in 664. A *paterfamilial* system of inheritance is implied by the reversion of title to the son of the eldest brother. His reign lasted 49 years, the longest of any Anglo-Saxon king after Æthelberht of Kent. In childhood he had actually seen Rædwald's temple of two altars, and he used to tell the story (*testabatur*) as a remarkable fact when he was old. It is certain that Ealdwulf married and had at least two children, a son Ælfwald and a daughter Ecgburh, and he was undoubtedly a ruler of very considerable influence: but almost nothing is known of him personally.

The Church without an Archbishop, 664-669
The death of Archbishop Deusdedit left Berhtgisl of Dommoc as the only bishop remaining in England who had been consecrated canonically by the Roman Church of Canterbury. Agilberct became Bishop of Paris, and King Alhfrith sent Wilfrid to him to be consecrated as his Northumbrian bishop. This took place at Compiègne, but Wilfrid delayed there. Cedd having died, his brother Chad came from his studies in Ireland to supervise Cedd's monastery at Lastingham (Yorks.), and King Oswy sent him to Canterbury to be made Bishop of York. Of course the archbishop was dead, and Chad was consecrated by Bishop Wine in Wessex. Wilfrid, returning to find Chad at York, had to settle for a bishopric based at Ripon.

In Essex King Suithhelm died, and the kingdom was divided between his sons Sebbi and Sigheard, the former of whom remained Christian, but the latter reverted to idols in the hope of escaping the plague. King Wulfhere of Mercia deployed his bishop, Jaruman, to draw them back into the fold. Then Berhtgils at Dommoc died. King Oswy and King Ecgberht of Kent sent a candidate to Rome to be elevated to Canterbury, but he and all his companions died there of the plague. Pope Vitalian (657-72) himself therefore undertook to find a suitable replacement. England was without an archbishop for its new universal Roman Church for the first five years. In Brie, Abbess Æthelburh died in *c.* 665, perhaps of the same cause. Sæthryth succeeded her half-sister as abbess. Eorcongota, who joined her aunts there, also sickened and died in this or a later plague after nursing others in the infirmary.

East Anglian life had other dangers. Folcard relates that Botolph was bitten by a snake in *c.667*. Large adders can still be seen on Snape Common. Having spent some time convalescing, he visited a remote estate granted by his original patron. In a valley fed by a stream, far away from the sea, in a vast solitude approached through dense spinneys, he built two churches both dedicated to Sts Peter and Paul. It is not possible to identify the place meant by Folcard, but Thorndon or the Thornhams were apparently *spinosa loca* like those through which Botolph made his way. Among other places Hoxne and Eye on the Dove bear these dedications, and the island or *Heia* of Eye among its surrounding marshes might certainly have interested the resident of Icanho, or a patron of such sites. That conjecture aside, Botolph may certainly have come to Botesdale, which took his name as *Botolvesdale*.

Botolph was at Iken in *c.669*. Bishop Wilfrid sent a newly-ordained man named Ceolfrith from Ripon to study for a year in Kent and with Botolph himself. According to his anonymous *Life* (but a fact omitted by Bede), Ceolfrith 'wished to see the institutes of Abbot Botolph, who was spoken of everywhere as a man of exceptional life and teachings, and full of the grace of the Spirit. Ceolfrith returned home well instructed, as briefly as he was able; no one at that time could be found more learned than him either in ecclesiastic or monastic rules.' On his return north, Ceolfrith, who worked in the monastic bakery, was introduced to Benedict Biscop; after making a journey to Rome with him, he assisted at the founding of Wearmouth monastery. Later, in *c.681*, Ceolfrith founded the sister house of Jarrow with 22 monks and the eight-year-old Bede, who was to pass his entire life there as the abbot's devoted pupil. Bede makes no mention of Botolph, though Ceolfrith's visit is not in doubt. He therefore cannot confirm the statement in the *Slesvig Breviary* that Botolph made a journey to Rome.

Wilfrid's approval of Botolph, sufficient to entrust a pupil to him, is a testimony to Botolph's excellence. Wilfrid had enjoyed Seaxburh's hospitality in Kent before 653, and his Suffolk connections were reinforced through his friend and patroness Æthelthryth, Ecgfrith's queen: Botolph had started building at Iken six years before she left East Anglia. Wilfrid's biographer Eddius tells that she gave Wilfrid her estate at Hexham, where he built a stone monastery thought finer than any north of the Alps. King Alhfrith, Wilfrid's former patron, rebelled against his father King Oswy and is heard of no more. Alhfrith's wife Cyneburh, Penda's daughter, settled with her sister Cyneswith in a monastery, built according to Malmesbury by King Wulfhere and his brother, at Castor (Roman *Durobrivæ*) near Peterborough: Wilfrid built another nearby at Oundle. These foundations clustered near Abbot Seaxwulf's flourishing house at *Medeshamstede*, with water access to Ely and East Anglia. Chad built at Barrow in Lindsey, east of the Ancholme river and the Humber terminal of the Ermine Street.

Pope Vitalian selected Theodore, a very learned man of Tarsus, to be the new archbishop, and he arrived at Canterbury in 669 with his assistant Hadrian, who had declined to accept that dignity for himself. They set about the reform of the English church and the creation of a magnificent centre of learning and scholarship at Canterbury, the influence of which spread throughout England. In his general visitation, Theodore consecrated Bisi to the see of Dommoc, recently vacant through Berhtgisl's death. Wilfrid was made Bishop of all Northumbria, and Chad, after retiring to Lastingham, was sent to Mercia as Bishop of Lichfield until his death in c.672. In 670 King Oswy died; he was buried near Eadwine in Hild's monastery at Whitby, and Queen Eanfled, the daughter of Eadwine, retired there to live with her own daughter, the ever-virgin Ælfflæd, whom Oswy had promised to God before the battle of Winwæd.

Æthelthryth at Ely and Seaxburh at Sheppey

Æthelthryth never consummated her marriage to Ecgfrith, who now became King of Northumbria. Wilfrid, despite the King's requests that he should persuade her to give him an heir, instead helped her to enter the monastery at Coldingham (near Berwick) in 672 and take the veil. She may have found her new home rather lax, for the nuns were given to gossiping in the cells, and to weaving fancy clothes. A year later she made her dramatic escape from Northumbria and set herself beyond her husband's reach. The legend of her escape tells that Ecgfrith's soldiers pursued her as far as St Abb's Head, an isle attached to the mainland only at low tide. There she sat out a storm for three days, and the king's henchmen, unable to reach her, at last went off realising that God favoured her enterprise. Then she took flight down the coast, perhaps by way of West Halton (near Flixborough in north-west Lindsey) where her dedication occurs, not far from Chad's monastery beside the Humber. At last she came to her own estate of Ely in 673, and founded there a double monastery which soon acquired great renown.

The Latin *Lives* or *Passions* of Kentish royal saints suggest equally dramatic events in that kingdom. King Ecgberht, Seaxburh's elder son, had taken in charge his two cousins Æthelred and Æthelberht, the sons of Eormenred, at his Hall of Eastry near Sandwich. A retainer, seeking to ingratiate himself by strengthening Ecgberht's succession, had the two Christian youths murdered and their bodies hidden beneath the royal seat. When the crime was revealed Ecgberht, filled with remorse, attempted to bury them at Canterbury, but by miraculous admonition they were instead taken to Wakering near Prittlewell (Essex), and were buried at an existing monastery there. A fragment of sculpture recently excavated at Wakering may derive from a shrine later erected over them. Ecgberht's brother Hlothhere ridiculed the idea of their sanctity, says Malmesbury. Ecgberht also established a double monastery at Minster-in-Thanet for the sister of the murdered princes, the wife of Merewalh, and another at Eastry. She left her west Mercian estates to become abbess in Kent. In 669 Ecgberht furthermore gave the Roman enclosure at Reculver for monastic purposes to a priest named Bass. Possibly he feared retribution from Mercia for the crime, but averted it by these endowments.

Seaxburh herself held the estate of Sheppey, on the north coast of Kent directly south of Wakering, and at Minster-in-Sheppey constructed the double monastery to which she retired. There is a theory that before doing so she married King Cenwalh (her father's godson), who was still ruling in Wessex. His queen, named Seaxburh, ruled the West Saxons alone for a year after his death in 672 before being driven out. In any case, Seaxburh of Kent was Abbess at Sheppey by 673, when her son King Ecgberht died and his sceptical brother Hlothhere succeeded him. He incurred retribution from Mercia, for Wulfhere's death in *c*.674 removed the protection afforded by Eormenhild's marriage: Wulfhere's brother Æthelred ravaged Kent in 676 and ransacked the church at Rochester.

Soon after Ecgberht's death, with the monasteries of Ely and Kent firmly under matriarchal governance, Archbishop Theodore held the first Council of the reorganised English Church at Hertford, in the presence of King Ecgfrith of Northumbria. Bishop Bisi of Dommoc was present, and the bishops of Rochester, Mercia and the West Saxons: Wilfrid sent his proctors. After various decrees regularising the duty and authority of bishops, the final chapter, most carefully dictated by Theodore to the notary Tytill, recorded the Church's position with regard to divorce and remarriage. This clearly indicated to the 28-year-old Ecgfrith, who had no heir, that he could not remarry as a Christian within Æthelthryth's lifetime.

Foundation of the See of Helmham

Although Bishop Bisi attended the Council, he was in seriously failing health and could no longer discharge his duties. Shortly afterwards, although the Council had not agreed the procedure, Theodore appointed two bishops in his place, Æcci and Baduwine, while Bisi was yet living. Thus the East Anglian diocese was divided between the southern see of Dommoc and a northern one based at a place called *Helmham* (Elmham). Theodore proceeded to divide others: he expelled Winfrith from Lichfield and raised Abbot Seaxwulf in his place, and established Eorconwald as Bishop of London for the East Saxons, who had recently founded monasteries at Barking and Chertsey. Wilfrid was driven out in 677 by King Ecgfrith, who took another wife. Theodore accepted this and created three bishops in Northumbria, with sees at York, Lindisfarne and in Lindsey. Wilfrid, not among them, reputedly spent some time at Ely before going to Rome, where he remained until 680.

Both South Elmham in Suffolk and North Elmham in Norfolk have been claimed as the site of *Helmham*. There are large remains of early stone churches at both places. Some foundations, with an apsidal eastern feature, at North Elmham are possibly of the eighth century. The 'Old Minster' at South Elmham is certainly later and probably post-Conquest, though with some early features, and containing part of a tenth-century grave-slab in the fabric. Neither is a seventh-century structure. South Elmham has the unusual distinction of embracing nine separate parishes ('The Saints', including Homersfield and Flixton), west of the Stone Street between Halesworth and Bungay and bordered to the north-west by the Waveney. To their east are the several parishes of Ilketshall, to which Ulfcytel lent his name in the tenth century. The origins of their multiple compartments are not fully understood.

If (as Norman Scarfe proposed) Flixton was the subject of an early land-grant to Felix, it may naturally have formed the core around which Helmham developed as the kingdom's second bishopric, at South Elmham. Field-walking suggests an ecclesiastical site on the ridge overlooking the Old Minster and the feeder-stream of Sconch Beck, on a platform-like elevation in Ash Field, probably the Elden Hall of John Ridgard's researches. Here Mike Hardy's discovery of grozed Anglo-Saxon window glass in context with Middle Saxon sherds provides convincing evidence of an early church. Another important site nearby yields pottery of fifth- to eleventh-century types. There is nothing comparable at North Elmham. Nearer to Frog Hall and the drive of South Elmham Hall, a gold shilling of the 650s-60s of the 'Two Emperors' type, struck in Kent, was found in 1988 and sold. The coinage, imitating a fourth-century imperial solidus, was produced in considerable numbers and gained circulation in East Anglia, but specimens are rare. Findspots of this Kentish issue include Reculver and Lymne, both important minster sites. The discovery shows a contemporary wealthy presence at *this* Elmham at the time of the Helmham foundation. Perhaps, then, it was here that Archbishop Theodore established a bishopric for Baduwine in 673. A community of priests and deacons was no doubt attached to his episcopal church.

Botolph, old and infirm, died on 17 June 674 in the presence of the brethren in his monastery (says Folcard), and was buried there. Abbot Æthelheah, who suceeded him, perhaps arranged for his enshrinement at Iken. It was Æthelheah who not long afterwards attested the return of landed endowments in western Mercia to the double monastery at Much Wenlock where Mildburg, one of Merewalh's daughters, was abbess. Iken then received other estates in exchange; this is the transaction mentioned above, by which the claim is developed that earlier relations existed between King Anna and the family of Merewalh, probably during the years 651-54. Mildburg's sister Mildred later succeeded their mother as abbess of Minster-in-Thanet; the third sister, Mildgyth, was reputedly abbess at Eastry.

Bede, who wrote a hymn in her praise, supplies details of Æthelthryth. At Ely she led a life of simplicity and devotion, remaining at prayer in the church from the service of mattins until dawn. She wore only woollen clothes, never linen, ate once a day, and took her turn among the sisters at bathing times. A stone cross found near Ely inscribed with a prayer for Owini suggests that her old minister eventually rejoined her. A practical man, he had entered Lastingham monastery, and went to Lichfield when Chad became bishop. While working in the garden outside the oratory there, he witnessed the visitation of angels who announced to Chad his coming death in 672. Owini probably came to Ely soon afterwards.

Æthelthryth died at Ely in 679 of a plague tumour on her throat which she attributed to the childhood vanity of her gold necklaces. She was buried according to her wishes in a wooden coffin in the cemetery, taking her place alongside the other nuns. Seaxburh took leave of her nuns at Sheppey, placing them in the care of her daughter Eormenhild, and returned as Abbess of Ely to the land of her childhood. In the same year Abbess Hild died at Whitby, and was buried there: 33 years had passed since Aidan had called her back from East Anglia to begin her religious life.

Theodore held his second general Council at Hatfield in 679 attended by an emissary from Rome and in the presence of King Ecgfrith. It was held on an open plain, the parties bringing their tents and attendants. A declaration of orthodoxy was made against the Monothelyte Heresy. Rome had also determined that 12 bishops should be sufficient for the English province. The Council decided to meet in future twice yearly at a place called *Clofesho*: many famous gatherings occurred there during the eighth and early ninth centuries, at which various transactions were ratified. Claude Morley's suggestion that *Clofesho* was at Mildenhall cannot be sustained.

Wilfrid attested the Council's confession at Rome in 680, and returned to Britain bringing confirmation from Pope Agatho of his rights to Hexham and Ripon. (In later centuries the monasteries of Medeshamstede and Ely claimed that he had then obtained Privileges for them, but the earliest sources are silent as to this.) However, Ecgfrith threw him into prison in Northumbria and, after a brief stay in Middle Anglia and Wessex, he was received among the South Saxons, whom he converted over the next five years from Selsey. Meanwhile King Æthelred of Mercia had taken possession of the kingdom of Lindsey, and in Mercian hands it remained. Penda's sons, though they had become Christian and had married into the houses of Kent and Northumbria, had not lost their vision of a Greater Anglia.

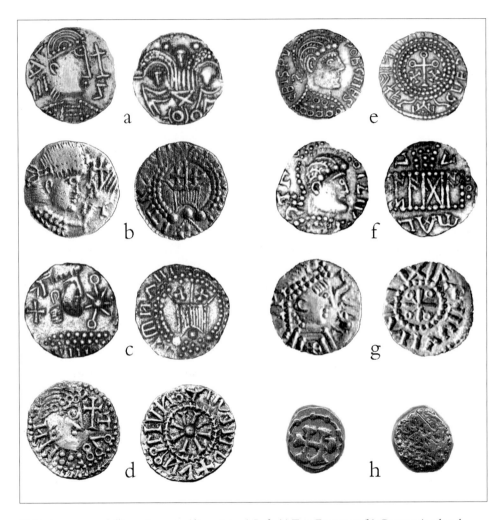

Gold thrymsas or shillings, 650s-70s. (diam. 1.4cm) Left: (a) Two Emperors (b) Constantine hand and cross (c) star type (d) unique 'wheel rosette'. Right: (e) Crispus 'Desaiona' (f) Pada, runic reverse (g) Pada, rosette reverse (h) Merovingian tremissis of Nietap type, c.635-640 . a-g, Coddenham – de Saumarez/Cummings; h, Sudbourne – Alan Calver

5

The long East Anglian peace

In 679 the Northumbrians and Mercians fought near the river Trent, and a junior King Ælfwine, brother of Ecgfrith and of the Mercian queen Osthryth, was killed. That was the Mercian reconquest of Lindsey, which Ecgfrith had wrested from Wulfhere soon after 673. A blood feud was threatened, but the Mercian King Æthelred, advised by Archbishop Theodore, paid compensation or *wergild* to prevent this. After the same battle, Imma, a Northumbrian military retainer captured by a Mercian gesith, was sold to a Frisian in London (probably a slave-trader), but was afterwards redeemed by King Hlothhere of Kent because he had been a thegn of Queen Æthelthryth's (Hlothhere's aunt). At this time Hlothhere was revising his great-grandfather's codes in which the man-prices had been specified. The story illustrates how money, the authorised issue of measured gold currency, unlocked the obligations of mortal retribution, much as Imma's fetters were, in his story, loosed by the power of prayer. Money made possible the transfer or untying of bonds.

The importance of money
Although no East Anglian law-code survives, nor any early charter to show (by its exemptions) the nature of early duties, we may infer similarities to Kentish and Mercian principles. The hideages of ploughland and other resources attached to a free man's household in time became the basis of taxation assessments: the *Tribal Hideage*, a Mercian document, lists small early administrative regions within which they were parcelled. In early times a food rent (*feorm*) was exacted annually from each group of settlements enough to maintain the king and his retinue when travelling to his various halls and estates. Adjustments owing to local variations, and other forms of common justice, were probably carried out by popular councils or folk-moots. Legal penalties and customs also generated fines and tolls, and the king might transfer these benefits as endowments to religious houses for their

maintenance, or to nobles charged with administrative authority. Districts were required to yield a given number of fighting men for the *fyrd* or levy. The repair of bridges and defensive fortresses, provision for royal hospitality, or perhaps work on the king's buildings or cartage of his goods, might also be universal exactions.

During the seventh century, cemeteries dedicated to pre-Christian customs fell into disuse and many settlements were relocated. At West Stow the halls and workrooms successively rebuilt over 200 years were abandoned and a new settlement arose some distance away. Quantities of pottery from Gipeswic had reached them before they moved. New organisation of resources, industry, exchange and service emerged under the institutions of Christian royal patronage and its lay, ecclesiastical or monastic lordship. North Sea traffic, controlled by the Frisians but providing constant engagement with the Christian Frankish world, fed this economy as it shaped the Christian kingdom. The international travel which it brought to Gipeswic no doubt assisted the spread of plagues (like those of 663-7 and 679-80), which in Essex turned King Sigheard and his people in desperation to idolatry. East Anglia's Christian institutions were more securely rooted.

The 'Two Emperors' type of pale gold shillings (like the South Elmham example) were struck in Kent during the 650s-70s. Various types were then issued in Kent, in London and in East Anglia, and mixed in circulation. They effect a transition from pale gold to silver, following the decline in Merovingian gold coinage standard. Some English types carry runic inscriptions, for instance those naming the moneyer *Pada*. One East Anglian series bears a well-executed portrait in imperial style, the raised open hand with a cross before it. Whether this represents the elevation of the Cross or the vow of faith, it is an overtly Christian symbol associated with the coinage itself. A subsequent issue replaces the hand and cross with a star-like device (examples from Billockby, Norfolk, and Coddenham, Suffolk). The reverse shows a motif perhaps intended for a hanging banner with crosslets above, and a surrounding inscription. Such coins were circulating during the earlier part of the reign of Ealdwulf, though the extent of royal concern in their issue is not decided. Independent or ecclesiastical mints may have been involved.

The pale gold coinage became reduced to silver, and issues of the little silver coins called 'sceattas' emerged during the last quarter of the seventh century. These are apparently the first English *pennies*, a term which occurs in legal contexts at this time. The earliest overlap with the later shillings (thrymsas), and are issued in the south-east, especially in Kent and in East Saxon territory. There are various types, and their distributions are studied intensively because constant new discoveries make this a fast-growing field of historical inquiry. Many of the shillings, and some of the earliest groups of sceattas, have an obverse displaying a head or bust. One series attributed to the East Saxon sphere, but found very widely in Suffolk, shows a classical head with a surrounding inscription, and a bird perched over a cross on the reverse (Type B). The beaded ring surrounding the central motif contains one forked element, like a serpent's head, so that the ring becomes a snake devouring its own tail.

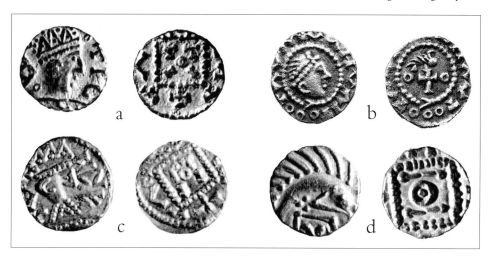

Some early sceattas: (diam. 1.2cm) (a) Kent, ?reign of Hlothhere *c*.673-685 (A, 'TIC'): (b) Essex or East Anglia, *c*.680s-700s (B): (c) East Anglia from 705 (Late C/R, 'EPA'): (d) Franco-Frisian 'Porcupine', Rhine mouths area (E). *a,c,d, Coddenham − de Saumarez/Cummings; b, Sudbourne − Alan Calver*

Some of the earliest Kentish pennies (Type A) show royal heads with three-pointed crowns or radiate diadems with the letters 'TIC', possibly associated with Hlothhere's reign 673-685. They replace the gold 'PADA' coinage. Others marked 'ÆPA' in runes (Type C) provided models for an East Anglian coinage marked 'EPA', more barbarous in design (Type R), which commences *c*.705. The inscriptions may refer to moneyers. Many similar coins were struck around the lower Rhine, notably the 'porcupine' sceattas (Series E) which were in use at Dorestad and Domberg, a frontier coinage issued probably under Frankish authority but within the Frisian sphere and with Frisian imitators. A mint on the coast south of Domburg, or in the Meuse valley, has been suggested for some continental runic types imitating English coins. During the late seventh century English and continental coins were mixing extensively in circulation in East Anglia (especially at coastal or estuarine sites) and in all the English kingdoms. Sceattas were certainly issued in East Anglia during Ealdwulf's reign: research increasingly suggests earlier dates and a greater diversity of types for East Anglia than had previously been recognised.

The growth of Gipeswic (Map 1)
The harbour and quay of Gipeswic formed the centre of East Anglia's commercial relations with the Continent and Kent, developed under Wuffing patronage. It occupied an important place in the trade which linked coastal markets of the Baltic and North Sea states, so that the various controlling powers participated in a shared franchise. This great enterprise stimulated the construction of the first new towns since the collapse of the Western Empire. Gipeswic was in the forefront of them. East Anglia's trading capital, with York and London, presented the face of eastern England to the seafaring merchants of Scandinavia, the northern continent and the Rhine.

The quayside development on the north bank spread over rising land from the marshes skirted by Greyfriars Road around St Peter's Street, Turret Lane and Foundation Street to the north and east. St Peter's, richly-endowed before Domesday, was surely dedicated by Felix as the mother church of Gipeswic in Sigeberht's or Anna's time, for then the settlement and street-plan took shape around it. On the south bank, Stoke had spread around Great Whip Street some distance inland and west along the riverfront. The dedication of St Augustine (south of Stoke, now lost) and St Mary's on its prominent site overlooking the harbour both probably arose before 700. Recent excavation suggests that the quay itself was formed of many separate jetties reaching into the river, as at Dorestad.

The north side embankment to create draught for moorings necessitated moving the crossing upstream. Probably by c.700, the first Stoke Bridge was constructed, linking a westerly diversion of the Wherstead Road on the south side to what became St Peter's Street on the north. The latter continued north on the line of St Nicholas' Street and Queen Street to join the corduroy road (Westgate and Tavern Street) near the present Corn Hill. On this hillside between Foundation Street and Queen Street, south of the corduroy road, lay the Gipeswic burial grounds. Parts have been excavated: they remained in use until the close of the seventh century. Of over 50 graves found, nearly half contained objects such as knives or occasional ornaments. There were no cremations. Many were not richly furnished: those customs weakened among an artisan population building commercial values under Christian influence. Circular ditches surrounded some graves indicating that a small barrow had been raised. The richest was of a man buried in a coffin with a sword, two spears, a shield and a pair of glass cups. The style of his belt-fittings suggests that he was an important Frankish visitor from the Upper Rhinelands.

Excavations near St Peter's Street and Greyfriars produced large amounts of seventh-century pottery, both native handmade wares and fragments of wheel-thrown vessels imported from the Frankish Rhinelands and from Merovingian Gaul. Gaulish trade came primarily out of the ancient port of *Quentovic* at the mouth of the Canche, a little south of Boulogne: Wilfrid returned thence from his first Roman expedition in c.660. The important centre of Domburg on the island of Walcheren stood on the south side of the Rhine mouth (in the course it then took), and about 80 miles upstream, below Utrecht, stood Dorestad. These faced Gipeswic across the North Sea, over which both the Frankish Rhinelands and the pagan Frisians to the north had maintained steady communication with Britain since the migrations. Frisian control of sea-trade was the motor and balance of North Sea development. North of the Rhine the Frisian kingdom extended to the river Yssel and beyond, and remained distinctly pagan in custom and belief. Wilfrid, on his way to Rome in 677, was received by King Aldgisl of the Frisians and baptised many, but appears not to have left a lasting impression.

Early in Ealdwulf's reign (if not before) the technique of throwing pots, and of kiln-firing them, was established on the north-east side of early Gipeswic. A Potter's Quarter grew up, where the road from the ford reached the boggy ground and track around Carr Street and Cox Lane. Over the next two centuries Gipeswic remained the only English centre to produce such wares, which were distributed throughout the English Midlands and even to Wessex and Northumbria. They were recognised and described by Stanley West and the late John Hurst. They resemble Rhenish pottery, and it is thought the potters either learnt from Frisians, or that a colony migrated here to set up the industry. Their products varied from the simplest mass-produced cooking-jars (probably the work of trainees) to more adept works such as large pitchers with handles and spouts. The clay was dug locally. The internal shape, the walls and rim, were thrown on a slow wheel; after drying, the lower sides and base were formed by paring away the leather-hard clay manually with a sharp tool. These pots typically have a sagging base and a globular profile. The half-round bases were effective on uneven surfaces such as an earth floor, among straw, or actually in a fire. Small bowls were also made, and lamps thrown in one piece, with a flat base, column and flared bowl for the lamp-fat.

Ipswich Ware: cooking jar, spouted pitcher and lamp. *Ipswich Borough Museums*

Some finer products were decorated. Large pitchers, and globular bottles with collared necks and flared rims, have triangular patterns grooved or combed from the neck across the shoulders of the pots, imitating the metal vandykes or mounts which fastened the ornamental rim onto wooden vessels or drinking-horns. Stamped patterns of stars or grids were impressed with notched wooden or antler implements. These decorative techniques were carried over from indigenous sixth-century potting traditions. A richly-patterned vase from Bramford shows the development in transition. One Ipswich sherd is stamped with a human face motif, an echo of that fashion in earlier English art. A complete excavated kiln is of later date, but even the early sherds show the definite innovation of hard-firing.

Ipswich Ware: fragments showing vandyke decoration. *Ipswich Borough Museums*

Ipswich Ware: sherd with human mask stamps. *Ipswich Borough Museums*

The kiln was shaped like an igloo: a circular clay-lined pit was sunk, with a tunnel from one side into an ash-pit. A clay shelf supported by a pillar was built over it, with piercings for the heat to rise through. Pots were piled on top and encased by a dome, leaving a hole to draw up the draught. The fire was then kindled in the tunnel and lower chamber, and the ash was scraped out and fresh wood introduced for several hours to reach the necessary heat. As this was achieved, the kiln roof was smothered to exclude air, making the pots turn black and become less porous. Many deformed kiln-wasters show the problems of controlling temperatures. Woodlands on the higher ground (now Christchurch Park) might provide their fuel, as well as timber for house construction, suggesting a managed environment of mixed oak standards, coppice and underwood. The wares began to achieve wide distribution by 700, and production had started some decades earlier.

The Gipeswic settlement near the quay included a number of trade specialists, including blacksmiths, ship-builders or repairers, leather-workers, antler-workers and basket-makers. We may infer others such as glass-workers, but on less firm evidence. Their timber houses and yards spread around the church and along the radial lanes leading from it as an industrial community serving the trading quay. This, in turn, required a provision-market to serve the inhabitants. Twill textiles from East Anglian looms were a principal export, and whatever slaves were received from East Anglia by Frisian merchants probably left through Gipeswic. Society at various levels, townsmen and travellers, merchants, craftsmen and provisioners, religious, officials and seafarers were to be found there.

The Wicklaw and the Rendlesham Estate

Adjacent to Gipeswic on its north side, and extending north from the Orwell to the river Alde and beyond, and north-west to the upper Deben, lay the extensive lands drained by that group of rivers, and served by their estuaries, which centred upon the royal dwelling at Rendlesham. During the 940s, after the end of the period described in this book, this entire province was administered from Sudbourne (beside Iken) by a Danish earl. It was then known as the Wick-law (*Uicchelaue*), a name suggesting an administrative relationship between the province and the wic of Gipeswic. It was defined by the five-and-a-half Hundreds of Colneis, Carlford, Plomesgate, Loes, Wilford, and Thredling ('third-ling'), and included Saxmundham, Framlingham and Debenham. However, it is inferred that this province had originated as a *regio*, effectively a sub-kingdom, presumably during the sixth century when the East Anglian kingdom was yet forming. The central position of Rendlesham and Sutton Hoo in relation to it suggests that this was in fact the sphere in which the Wuffinga dynasty had originally centred its power.

As Gipeswic was growing into an urban commercial centre of the first importance in the decades around 700, the monastery of Ely, a stronghold within the peaty Fen on the west side of the kingdom, became an East Anglian dynastic seat under the rule of a succession of royal women. While Wilfrid was in Rome, around 680, his friend abbess Æthelthryth died; if, as *Liber Eliensis* claims, he truly brought back a papal Privilege for Ely, he must have delivered it to Seaxburh, her sister and successor. Medeshamstede similarly became an extremely important eastern citadel of the Mercian Middle Angles under royal patronage, as it developed from Seaxwulf's time.

When Æthelwold, Bishop of Winchester, refounded the monastery of Ely after 970 he made the Wicklaw its largest endowment, adding the estate of Stoke at Gipeswic (separately purchased) and many others. Historians suggest (but cannot prove) that this was a restitution of Ely's original possessions. Was the franchise of that province in fact brought by Æthelthryth to her (first) marriage to Tondberht, as some think, and never thereafter dissociated from the estate of Ely? Recent discoveries at Sudbourne include the early coins illustrated above from high land north of the Butley river reed beds. The wealth of Rendlesham extended easily and immediately from the Deben to the Alde in Ealdwulf's time. Yet if Rendlesham remained a foremost royal dwelling, the dedication of the franchise of its immediate province to Ely can never have been intended as an *alienation* of those rights, but rather as the establishment of a perpetual tie, consolidating Wuffing patrimony across the southern part of the kingdom. Ely's papal Privilege, if it had one, would have afforded singular lustre, perhaps even the inviolability of papal sanction, to the royal seat in the east.

The occupation of the Rendlesham and Sudbourne area certainly continued to develop. An important new settlement was established during the later seventh century on a classic defensive hilltop site within the estuary of the Butley river, which divides Butley from Sudbourne. Staverton's oak woodlands spread towards Butley from Rendlesham, and shelter the rising Butley Run which then flows through freshwater meadows to Chillesford, where it opens into a tidal channel and turns toward the sea. Burrow Hill is a large natural gravel-capped mount which stands among low-lying fields on the south-west side of the tidal river, where it flows towards the Ore like a long silvery serpent. Before embankment the surrounding ploughland was marsh, traversed by a magnificent prehistoric causeway called 'The Thrift' and fed by the tributary river Tang. Valerie Fenwick's patient work to recover archaeological information from a site severely damaged by gravel-extraction has yielded extraordinary results and information.

During the later seventh century, defences were created at the riverward end of the hilltop in the form of sharply-cut, deep and parallel curving ditches, from which the upcast no doubt formed ramparts not now visible. Also at that end was a cemetery of male burials, some apparently laid in small boats or boat-shaped coffins, suggesting an economy using river and sea resources. Clearly the defensive requirement faded, for the ditches were soon being filled with domestic rubbish including food, and occasional daub refuse. Buildings of timber and wattle-and-daub once spread over the hillcrest. Loomweights, combs, iron tools and metalworking debris show that the community included craftsmen of various kinds. Use of horses was shown by an iron bit. The inhabitants fished in the sea with long lines; in addition to fish, including cod, they had venison, fowl from the marsh, and they tended and ate swine, cattle and sheep. Oysters provided a staple diet, and their discarded shells remain as witness to many enviable feasts.. These furnished a sequence of horizons from the later seventh to the earlier ninth centuries.

A large wrought iron cauldron-chain with decorative links showed that an important hall stood here, and a sherd of dark red window-glass strongly suggests a church as well. This was no mere village, but a central household with service community. Was it, in fact, a private royal *burgh* or fortified bower away from the formality of the royal palace? So near to Rendlesham, and in this strategic lookout position, no one can doubt that Burrow Hill was under immediate royal supervision. It was a necessary outpost on that northern estuary, capable of bringing early news of an approach from the sea. We have to understand Rendlesham as the centre of a large and integral domain. The Snape cemetery, Iken monastery, the Sudbourne estate, Burrow Hill and the Butley river, Staverton, Rendlesham itself, Ufford, Eyke, Sutton Hoo, Woodbridge and Kingston, and the Deben to its mouth and to Walton Castle, together formed the immediate surroundings of the royal dwelling. The later use of Sutton Hoo as a gallows site, conspicuous on high land overlooking a river-crossing, has a parallel at Gedgrave Hall, where a gallows formerly stood on the high land opposite Burrow Hill. A ferry operated here until the Second War.

The security afforded by the East Anglian position, well distanced from Kent, with its own trade depot for Rhineland communication and its strong Fenland citadel in the west, became apparent as military disputes broke out in other kingdoms. In Northumbria, Æthelthryth's former husband King Ecgfrith died without heir in 685, ambushed during a rash expedition against the Picts, and was succeeded by his illegitimate brother Aldfrith. In Kent, Eadric (Ecgberht's son) attacked his uncle King Hlothhere with an army of South Saxons. A legendary account makes Hlothhere associate his own son, named 'Richard', to his throne: if doubt surrounds the *name*, there seems some truth to the *person* of Hlothhere's heir, who found exile in Wessex. Hlothhere died near the battlefield as his wounds were being dressed. Eadric ruled just over a year, when Kent was invaded by the West Saxon king, Cædwallan, assisted by his brother Mul. Cædwallan withdrew, but in 687 Mul and his 12 companions were captured and burnt to death by the men of Kent. Cædwallan invaded again, but in the following year abdicated his throne to Ine, whose grandfather Ceolwald was brother of King Cynegils. Cædwallan went to Rome where, in 689, he was baptised and died shortly afterwards.

Kent was reunited in 690 under Wihtred, Eadric's brother. As the century turned, Ealdwulf in East Anglia, Wihtred in Kent, Æthelred in Mercia, Aldfrith in Northumbria and Ine in Wessex were all ruling in considerable strength: Æthelred and Ine were dominant. After Archbishop Theodore died in 690, Abbot

Berhtwold of Reculver was consecrated his successor in 692 in Gaul; Pope Sergius wrote jointly to Æthelred, Aldfrith and Ealdwulf as kings of the Angles urging them to accept him. Ine's power was felt in legislature, warfare and taxation. In 693-4 he obliged Kent to pay 7,500 shillings (30,000 silver pieces), a king's ransom or *wergild*, for the burning of Mul. William of Malmesbury adds that the East Angles, also, experienced Ine's hereditary hatred, and that their nobility were first banished and then put to flight in battle. If the record contains truth, that hatred was rooted in the age of Rædwald and Eadwine, perhaps earlier.

Beginnings of the mission to Frisia
East Anglia's relations with the Continent continued to strengthen and protect its independence from other English powers. Pippin of Heristal, Mayor of the Austrasian Palace, became supreme among the Franks after the battle of Tertry in 687. For the next 10 years he set about the conquest of his Frisian neighbours between the Rhine and the Yssel. At that time Ecgberht (639-729), a very devout Englishman in Ireland, planned to convert the nations from whom the English derived their origins. The Englishman Wihtberht preached to the Frisians for two years shortly before 690, but returned to Ireland. Then Ecgberht gathered a band of 12, of whom Wilfrid consecrated Swithberht bishop and leader. Swithberht became established at Wijk-bi-Duurestade (Dorestad), but after setbacks while preaching in the Ruhr he retired to the Rhine. In 695 Pippin sent another Northumbrian, Willibrord (658-739), to Rome where he was made Archbishop of the Frisians and was charged with their ecclesiastical development. He preached to King Radbod of the Frisians and baptised in the holy spring of Heligoland. By 697 the Franks obtained control of land south of the Yssel, and in that security Utrecht became the seat of the Archbishopric in Frisia.

Ecgberht had many associates in Mercia and Lindsey. He and Chad prayed, fasted and studied scripture together at *Rathmelsigi* in Ireland. He promised God to live always an exile there, when his dear companion Æthelhun of Lindsey lay dying of plague. Æthelhun was brother of Æthelwine, Bishop of Lindsey (680-92), of Ealdwine, Abbot of Partney and of Æthelhild, abbess of a monastery nearby. Abbot Higebald of Lindsey was Ecgberht's visitor, sharing stories of Chad's last days at Lichfield: Chad's successor Winfrith was his disciple. Willibrord studied with him, after his novitiate at Ripon, and witnessed in Ireland a miraculous cure through relics of King Oswald. These were kept at Bardney, a royal monastery near Lincoln, where Queen Osthryth had them taken: Æthelhun's sister saw them arrive. Bede greatly admired Ecgberht, and gained details of Lindsey from Abbot Duda of Partney. Bardney and Partney were closely accessible to Ely and the Fen by the river Witham.

Folcard, researching Iken, heard that a certain Adolph (*Eadwulf*) died and was buried there after being active in the English mission at Utrecht. An East Anglian presence in the mission seems inevitable. Willibrord appointed assistant bishops for his work: St Botolph's cult may first have reached Slesvig by such a path. In the Frisian mission Pope Sergius consciously imitated the Gregorian mission to Canterbury, and made it a cornerstone of Frankish dominion. Any Frisian or Rhineland cargo coming into Gipeswic might bring news or passengers from Domburg or Dorestad, or convey religious travellers – perhaps some who had followed Willibrord to preach there. At Oundle (where he died in 709), Wilfrid remained close to the royal Fenland houses: in the early 700s he travelled to Rome via Utrecht and visited Willibrord among the Frisians.

In 696 Seaxburh decided to move Æthelthryth's remains into Ely monastery church, and sent a boat party to the deserted town of Cambridge to find a suitable stone from which to make a receptacle. A tent was raised over the grave as the nuns and brethren stood by singing, and the abbess entered to remove her sister's bones. Suddenly she cried out, 'Glory be to the Name of the Lord!' Æthelthryth's body was perfectly uncorrupt and its linen wrappings whole and fresh. It was removed and laid on a bed, and Cynefrith the physician found that the tumour he had opened on her throat had healed leaving only a slight scar. The monks returned from Cambridge with a white marble sarcophagus and its lid, perfectly suited to receive the virginal body. Seaxburh herself died at Ely in 699 and was buried there. Her daughter Eormenhild, King Wulfhere's widow, left Sheppey to succeed her as abbess at Ely. Not long before, King Sebbi of the East Saxons died and was buried in a stone coffin at London, whither he had gone into a monastery, handing his kingdom to his sons. His example of religious abdication soon found imitators.

Aristocratic occupation and burial in the Gipping valley

Æthelthryth had renounced the necklaces of gold and pearl she had worn as a child, and blamed her tumour upon the vanity of having worn them. Different values attended a woman buried near Gipeswic in around 700, a little upstream in the Gipping valley. At Chapel Field, Boss Hall (Bramford), near a significant river-crossing, a graveyard of pagan custom had evolved during the sixth century containing at least one small barrow overlying a plank-lined chamber-grave, with urned cremations later placed around it. After being disused for many years, while Christian institutions transformed many aspects of life, an aristocratic woman was buried there with her jewellery placed near her head in a linen bag. The ornaments included a large composite brooch carpeted with garnet cellwork, clustered but not interlocked, set around five white paste bosses in a cruciform arrangement, emphasised by triangular gold plates with applied filigree. There was a necklace of gold pendants, including four with applied filigree and central garnet or glass settings (three in cruciform designs), another made from a Merovingian coin (a *solidus* of King Sigebert III of Austrasia (638-56)), and two larger garnets in gold settings. These had been strung with biconical silver and polychrome glass beads. There was also a set of silver toilet implements assembled on a chain or chatelaine of fine silver wire rings. A penny of *c.*690-710 had been dropped or thrown into the grave.

Norman Scarfe drew attention to Boss (or *Bordshaw*) Hall as an outlying berewick of Bramford, an important royal manor at the time of Domesday. Some 1,500 acres, then personally held by the king, suggested a tenure inherited from the early East Anglian rulers. Within Bramford a chapel of St Albright, at a place called Albrighteston, commemorated the East Anglian royal martyr Æthelberht (d.794). If a royal dwelling existed here in the eighth century, this wealthy woman's grave indicated at least an aristocratic one during the seventh, near an older cemetery of the sixth. The varied appearance of the pendants (a type found widely in seventh-century England) suggests they were gathered from miscellaneous sources. The brooch lacks the sophistication and delicacy of the earlier Kentish composite brooches, but its ponderous mass of dark garnets must once have glittered richly around the pearly white bosses and the wire-work of the expanding-armed gold cross.

The funerary disposal of this jewellery does not indicate any formal pagan belief on the part of its owner. Its deposition in a bag rather than being worn by the corpse is an essential distinction, and moreover the brooch is a Christian ornament. Although the old custom of burial in folk-costume with ornaments of ethnic, tribal or national difference died out in the seventh century, furnished burial continued in Christian contexts from Sutton Hoo onwards into the early eighth century as homage to ancestral traditions. A gold pendant with applied filigree and central cabochon garnet from Freston, on the Orwell below Gipeswic, probably came from a burial. Coin-pendants remained fashionable. A tremissis of Bishop Adibert II of Clermont-Ferrand (d.*c*.674) was found recently at Bawdsey, with a loop added: perhaps a visitor brought it from the famous shrine of St Julien at Brioude. In Kent, Wihtred's laws show that heathenism was still a force to be opposed: but the wealthy were not ashamed of funeral display.

Among the most dramatic of these late furnished burials was one uncovered in a barrow-cemetery on the southern ridge of the tributary valley from Gosbeck (i.e. *goose-brook*) and Hemingstone into the Gipping valley. Issuing near the point where the Pye Road started north to *Venta* from *Combretovium*, this broad vale is sheltered by hills on the south side and heralded by Beacon Hill on the north. Among about 50 graves explored here, two included males buried with short-sword, spear, shield, and bronze bowls of Merovingian type. In a woman's grave, a large bedstead with four iron bar supports and iron headboard-bindings had been lowered into the ground. The bars, which ran longitudinally beneath the recumbent body, show that the bed was raised off the ground on legs and framing structures, presumably of wood. The circular headboard bindings secured a wooden assemblage perhaps of ornamental openwork. The skeleton lying slightly turned aside, the hands over the breast, spoke eloquently of the sleeping posture of the lady amid her textiles or quilts, and of the devotion of the burial party. A casket lay at her knees with small bronze latches, and among her valuables was a gold cross-pendant enclosing a rare coin of King Dagobert I of the Franks (628-38). A silver penny dropped into the grave shows that she was buried in around 700.

Workmen extracting gravel here spoke of structural foundations nearby, now lost without record. But this noblewoman was apparently connected with an important household on the opposite, northern slopes of the valley. Here, in the field immediately below a wooded hangar and a track along its lower contour, a wooden hall 35ft long and 23ft wide stood aligned with the valley. It had solid timber footings to its planked walls, and additional pillars formed the portals midway along the north and south sides. At an opening in the ridge, a path runs down through the woods to this point and perhaps did so then. The south doors, when opened, would have revealed the prospect of the mounds on the ridge opposite. She who was afterwards buried in the sumptuous bed may often have looked across when she was the Christian mistress of that distinguished hall, or of another nearby. Outbuildings with thatched rooves and sunken floors, probably boarded, clustered around, and had done so on this spot for at least a century before she died.

Someone connected with this household left fragments of many precious objects to be recovered over years of patient collecting by David Cummings, Peter Murrell and their team. Gold items, including a fine large finger-ring with beaded zones, a miniature scoop with a tiny human head at its handle-end, a fragment of a superb cross-shaped pendant with stepped garnet cellwork (from which the garnets had been deliberately prised) and other delicate ornaments were hoarded and lost here. Ornamental mounts from shields, helmets and scabbards, gilt bronze harness-ornaments, brooches and Roman objects apparently scavenged from older sites nearby, were all accumulated to some unknown purpose. Broken portions of hanging-bowl escutcheons and an Irish enamelled stud show how wide-ranging the available materials were. Many small garter-hooks were dropped, and others were made by cutting and punching sheet bronze: a wealth of small fasteners and buckles has been found nearby. Hobnails or crude studs were hammered from thick folded bronze. A small pair of folding scales shows that metal was weighed.

Very likely all this hoarding reflects metalworking activity in which older objects were reused as raw materials or for decorative fittings. They were gathered from a wide range of sources. Metalworkers or other artists might adapt elements from such models without reverting to the archaic style of the originals. It is not unusual to find signs of repairs or reuse on early metalwork, which may often have remained in use for a long time. Objects like the gilt disc with animal-ornament from Akenham or the fine harness-pendant with gryphons from Coddenham, although reflecting late sixth- or early seventh-century styles, perhaps remained in circulation in the first decades of the eighth. A triangular plaque from Trimley, probably from a hanging bowl, shows three large spirals developing so-called 'trumpet-spiral' details at the outside edges, and with chequerboard millefiori settings within. The hanging-bowl buried in the

Akenham: gilt bronze disc with Style II animal ornament. *Ipswich Borough Museums*

Coddenham: gilt bronze harness pendant with fish and gryphons. *de Saumarez/Cummings Collection*

Trimley: bronze bowl mount with spiral ornament. *Suffolk County Council*

cemetery at Badley, now lost, also showed elaborate spiral work in enamel. Were these Insular works of East Anglian production, or were they, like some of the Coddenham pieces, circulated from farther afield, perhaps down the coast from Northumbrian or Pictish sources, to reach Suffolk's estuarine hinterlands?

The late seventh-century Kentish and East Anglian gold shillings found at Coddenham form a uniquely important assemblage. Of more than 14 examples, two are of the runic 'Desaiona' type with portraits of Crispus; two of the East Anglian type with the raised hand and cross; another (related) of the East Anglian star-type; and a 'Two Emperors' shilling. Four bearing the runic name Pada comprise two pairs of different types, among which one coin is holed for suspension. A unique type with portrait, seriffed cross and circumscribed reverse has newly appeared. The finder suspects that a mint operated here, but the collected range of types is perplexing. The pairings indicate deliberate collection of the group, possibly associated with the nearby find of a magnificent gold ring with beaded rows and inner sleeve, a most impressive personal ornament. Continental tremisses include a Visigothic coin of Justinian I (527-65), a Merovingian example of Justin II (575-85) and a quarter cut from another of *c*.620-50. There is also an example of the small gold type with double cross like the Sudbourne and Crondall specimens, of *c*.635-40. Late Roman bronze coins, often worn and holed, suggest scavenging in deserted sites nearby. Silver pennies (sceattas) show this activity continuing into the early eighth century, but probably not much beyond the first quarter: the latest types of sceatta are not present.

Coddenham: gold finger-ring. *de Saumarez/Cummings Collection*

John Newman suggested this might have been a seasonal market close to important water and land routes, a rural emporium by which Gipeswic trade filtered into its hinterlands. Monasteries with royal connections, or other aristocratic households or vills, are likely to have developed seasonal trading venues nearby. Yet the metal finds are not necessarily typical of market activity, but rather suggest a craft industry and perhaps a nearby patron controlling production in more private or autonomous ways than by open commerce. The seventh-century archaeology foreshadows a complex later history of patronage in Coddenham. The buildings, coins, artefacts and burials, their topographical relations and possible market, reveal the complexities of a noble East Anglian household in this generation. In every century this neighbourhood of *Combretovium* seems to have renewed its central importance to the region as a whole. A similar site producing a related range of materials, but continuing through the eighth century and into the ninth, lies beside the next tributary valley of the Gipping towards Gipeswic, on a hillbrow in Barham.

Another useful position for the control of the Gipping valley probably accounts for the precursor of Stowmarket, where the tributary streams converge. The name *Tot-hill*, meaning a high lookout point, is given to a mount with long vistas down the upper valley. Domesday Book shows that Thorney had a market on the feast of St Peter (to whom Stowmarket church was dedicated). It is suggested, on the evidence of its later tenures, that Thorney near Stowmarket had a royal dwelling controlling a *regio* later represented by the Stow Hundred. The Gipping valley, intensely active in Anglo-Saxon times, thus has this important series of contemporary sites stretching from Stowmarket down past the Pye Road intersection at Coddenham to Gipeswic at the opening into the Orwell.

East Anglian and Mercian politics in the Fen
King Ealdwulf, eldest and most venerable of English rulers at his death in 713, in his last years witnessed the approaching collapse of the Mercian dynasty of Penda's descendants. In 699, as Eormenhild (Wulfhere's widow and Seaxburh's daughter) became abbess of Ely, a Mercian prince named Guthlac laid aside his military career and built a hermitage dedicated to St Bartholomew at Crowland, an isle in the north-western Fen. 'The secret spot, empty and deserted, uninhabited, stood in God's Mind: it awaited the coming of a better guardian,' wrote Guthlac's English biographer. The site, among vaporous swamps not far from the Mercian Fenside citadel of Medeshamstede, was suggested by one Tatwine, who with a few others joined Guthlac to live there as a hermit. Norman Scarfe suggested that one of their number, Beccel, perhaps derived from the *Beccelings* associated with the Blyth valley in Suffolk. Guthlac was an Iceling, a descendant of the house of Icel (ancestor of Creoda and Penda), and therefore of royal blood. Guthlac's ordination and the consecration of his church were carried out by Hædda, Bishop of Mercia and the Middle Angles.

Mercian and East Anglian interests in the Fen were carefully counterposed. In 704, the year in which Bishop Seaxwulf died, King Æthelred abdicated and entered the monastery of Bardney near Lincoln, where queen Osthryth had developed the cult of King Oswald's relics. Osthryth was murdered by the Mercian people in 697. The East Saxons were increasingly under Æthelred's influence. His successor Coenred (704-09) was the son of Wulfhere and Eormenhild, and in his time land-grants in London had become subject to Mercian confirmation. The East Saxon ruler, Offa, was a friend of both Kent and Mercia: his sister had married Hlothhere of Kent. One legend makes Offa seek to marry Cyneburh, Penda's daughter (and Alhfrith's widow) in her retirement at Castor near Medeshamstede, he in handsome youth and she in advanced age. The tale might contain dynastic sense. She declined, but persuaded him instead to abdicate and make a pilgrimage to Rome.

Such was their mind, Offa and Coenred both renounced their thrones in 709 and together went off to Rome, where they became monks and soon afterwards died. In Northumbria, King Aldfrith had died in 705 and was succeeded by his eight-year-old son Osred, a most unsatisfactory youth. In Coenred's place came his cousin Ceolred, Æthelred's son. In the void of East Saxon power, Ceolred had East Anglia surrounded, for he controlled London, the East Saxons, the Middle Angles and Lindsey (where his father held Bardney). Ealdwulf's heir, Ælfwald, no doubt foresaw the dangers of Ceolred's ambition, and it was in the Fen, at Crowland, that a counter-claimant to the Mercian throne found protection. Æthelbald, grandson of Eowa (who had died fighting at his brother Penda's side when Oswald was slain in 641), often took refuge with Guthlac when pursued by Ceolred's agents, and there won the respect of the East Anglian ealdorman Hwætred. This protection gained permanence in 713, when Ealdwulf died and his son Ælfwald became King in succession to him.

ÆLFWALD, 713-749

At Ealdwulf's death, only Ine in Wessex and Wihtred in Kent had long experience and authority, and both ruled well into the 720s. The 85 years spanned by the reigns of Ealdwulf and Ælfwald, father and son, from the Council of Whitby to the middle of the eighth century, gave an unparalleled continuity. East Anglia was controlling its economy, courting its international commerce, planning and building its town, promoting literate and religious education, supporting its schools and monasteries, and ready to send forth its light into the world. Penda's wars were 60 years and more in the past, but Wihtburh, youngest daughter of King Anna, was still living at East Dereham. Frankish power was expanding across the lower Rhine, while Saracen influence was spreading through the Mediterranean ports of southern Gaul. English missionary Christianity was becoming the partner of Frankish military enterprise in Germanic conquests, which were shaping a new Western Empire. The Frankish Mayors (Pippin of Heristal and his descendants) were eclipsing the decayed posterity of Clovis, the Merovingian kings. Celto-Saxon Christianity, its character, learning and reforms, breathed a new Anglicised confidence and gospel into the heart of Europe. Ælfwald was a statesman and a scholar, and his reign began favourably with East Anglian tokens of encouragement to the exile Æthelbald at Crowland.

Ælfwald and Eadburgh, Winfrith and Richard

Guthlac died in 714, and abbess Ecgburh, Ælfwald's sister, provided a coffin for his burial. The dissolute Ceolred, having taken control of Mercia, had plundered its monasteries and broken their privileges, giving splendid feasts for his companions on the proceeds. For two more years Æthelbald had only Ælfwald's favour and Guthlac's name to protect him from the last of Penda's ruling heirs. After some campaigning, Ceolred was defeated in battle by Ine at Alton Priors in 715 and died insane a year later, blaspheming and communing with the devil. Then Æthelbald emerged as King of Mercia, and in gratitude to Guthlac's memory he endowed a new church at Crowland on the site of the royal hermit's wooden oratory. But the first *Life of Guthlac* was commissioned by Ælfwald and written in Latin by a monk named Felix. Felix addressed the work *To my Lord, before other grades of royal leaders the Best-beloved King Ælfwald, ruling rightly* (i.e. by right) *over the governances of the East Angles.* (The honorific *dilectissimo* is not personalised, as Professor Whitelock renders it.) Although Æthelbald was to become the more powerful king, this work preserved a dramatic image of his exile, and of the debt he owed to East Anglia. Bishop Æcci of Dommoc had been succeeded by Æscwulf, and then by Eardred, who attended a great Council at Clofesho called by Æthelbald in 716. Nothberht had succeeded Baduwine at Elmham.

King Ælfwald's sister abbess Ecgburh is mentioned in the *Life of Guthlac*. Her supposed connection with the Mercian house of Repton (Derbys.) may arise from a misreading. She is very probably the same person as the more famous Eadburgh, a religious woman of great importance in the early eighth century. (Such an interchange of 'Ead-' and 'Ecg-' forms is admitted in certain other cases.) During the thirteenth century a hermitage chapel dedicated to St Eadburga stood at the border of Thornham Magna and possessed 40 acres in Thornham Parva, at a place called Eadburga Tree. This discovery, made by John Fairclough and Mike Hardy in the Eye Cartulary (where it is mentioned several times), seems to place Eadburgh herself in Suffolk at a place where finds of Ipswich Ware indicate eighth- to ninth-century occupation. Suffolk's medieval rood-screens or murals furnish no medieval context for her cult. If she established a foundation or cell there, that would strengthen an existing theory, advanced by Professor Whitelock and others, that she was connected with – was perhaps sometime abbess of – the royal house at Ely.

Early in the eighth century Eadburgh came under the spell of an eloquent and charismatic West Saxon teacher named Winfrith. Richard (the exiled heir of Hlothhere), whose aunt Eormenhild governed the Ely monastery after her mother Seaxburh, married a near kinswoman of the same man. Winfrith was born in Crediton (Devon) in *c*.675, and was placed in the monastery at Exeter in childhood. That area, still newly under Saxon dominion, retained a strongly British population. There he drank deeply of the teaching and complex Latin style of Aldhelm, Abbot of Malmesbury (and Bishop of Sherborne 704-09), one of the most outstanding scholars and churchmen of his age, who had studied in the Canterbury school. Winfrith progressed to the monastery at Nursling near Southampton, became an impressive teacher and acquired many disciples, including a large circle of learned nuns whose friendship he maintained by correspondence throughout his life. Eadburgh was one of Winfrith's most devoted friends and disciples. The three children of Richard, the sons Willibald and Wynbald and their sister Waldburg, became deeply involved in Winfrith's missionary work.

As Ælfwald and Æthelbald came to power, the mission in Utrecht faced a crisis. Pippin of Heristal died in 714, and King Radbod of the independent Frisians (who had refused baptism) temporarily recovered lands south of the Yssel. Frankish dominion was overthrown, and Christianity fell under persecution. Winfrith, much favoured by King Ine, went to Friesland to commence missionary work in 716, but had to return in the following year. He was elected abbot of Nursling, but undeterred he travelled to Rome and received a papal commission to preach to the Gentiles. Pope Gregory II (715-31) conferred on him the name Bonifatius, a sign of the entirely Roman character of his mission and work. Pippin's son Charles (called Charles Martel, 'the Hammer') reconquered southern Friesland: Boniface began his work in Thuringia but, hearing in 719 of Radbod's death, joined Willibrord at Utrecht until 722. Then he returned to Rome where he was consecrated Bishop of the Germans and, with papal letters of commendation to Charles Martel, for the next 10 years he worked in Hesse and Thuringia. Many English missionaries now came to assist him.

In 720 Willibald and Wynbald left Wessex with their father from the river Hamble (beside Hamwih, the great West Saxon *wic*). Willibald had studied in the monastery of Bishop's Waltham. Richard died at Lucca in Tuscany in 722, where his tomb gloriously proclaims him *Rex Anglorum*, though (as Rapin says) '*il ne fut tout au plus que Roi de Kent en Angleterre.*' The sons proceeded to Rome: Wynbald remained there, but Willibald went on with two companions to make a famous journey through the Mediterranean and Near East. Passing through Sicily to Samos, he travelled along the coast of Asia Minor and by Cyprus to Syria, where he remained for two years. Obliged to leave Tyre, he reached Constantinople and remained two years more before returning to Rome in 730. Then for a decade he lived at Monte Cassino, St Benedict's monastery, reformed since its destruction by the perfidious Langobards long before. Wynbald worked with Boniface in Thuringia, and Waldburg joined them there from England.

Bede and the literary resources of East Anglia

During the 720s the Venerable Bede completed the collections for his great work, *Historia Ecclesiastica Gentis Anglorum* – 'The Ecclesiastical History of the English People'. It was finished in 731, four years before his death at Jarrow (his home since childhood). His principal adviser was Albin, Hadrian's successor as abbot of St Peter and St Paul monastery outside Canterbury. The priest Nothhelm of London, who became bishop of part of Wessex in 705, researched archives at Canterbury and Rome to discover how Roman Christianity came to the various kingdoms. Information about Cedd and Chad was obtained from Lastingham, and about Lindsey from Bishop Cyneberht and Abbot Duda of Partney (among others). Bede adds: 'I found out the ecclesiastical events in the province of the Eastern Angles partly from the writings or the tradition of men of the past, and partly from the relation of the most reverend Abbot Esi.' Nothing more is known of Esi, but he earned the acknowledgement and attention of Bede, presumably ruling an East Anglian monastery in or shortly before 731.

Bede, after all, admired the library of Bishop Cuthwine, who had presided over the church of Dommoc in (or perhaps since) Abbot Esi's time. Cuthwine had journeyed to Rome and brought back a richly-illustrated volume of the *Life and Labours of St Paul*. Bede himself saw it, and mentioned it in a work addressed to his friend Nothhelm. Cuthwine's library also included the *Epigrammata* of Prosper Tiro, and probably also the *Carmen Paschale* of Sedulius, a fifth-century work about Easter written both in prose and verse. An early ninth-century continental copy of these writings, long kept at St James in Liège, reproduces a series of Late Antique illustrations which owe important details to iconography current in fifth-century Ravenna, as George Henderson shows. These had been transmitted faithfully through copies made in England: the text of the *Epigrammata* includes an Ex-Libris note incorporated and transcribed from the end of Cuthwine's original. The illustrated *Carmen Paschale* was probably also his, like the *St Paul* brought from his Italian tour.

Thus we can just glimpse a candlelit corner of Bishop Cuthwine's bookshelf, when the light of the Ely, Dommoc and Elmham libraries, and those of Iken, Beodricesworth and every other East Anglian monastery has been extinguished, leaving not so much as a charter. In addition to the Church Fathers, English scholars had access to works of Tacitus, Livy, Pliny, Virgil, Vitruvius, Boethius, Ammianus Marcellinus, and many other primary classical texts. The Lindisfarne Gospels contain an outstandingly important textual version. Anglo-Saxon manuscripts or copies derived from them often preserve the best or even the only surviving texts of great earlier writers. In the same way their literate poets and historians transformed and recorded their oral traditions from recitation. It is difficult to realise the extraordinary energy and breadth of early English scholarship. Bede's was grounded in the wealth of books with which travellers such as Wilfrid, Benedict Biscop, Ceolfrith and Acca filled the Northumbrian monastic libraries from their travels in Italy, and in the teachings by example or instruction which he had received from each of them. Felix the monk knew works of Athanasius, Jerome, Gregory, Bede (*Lives of Cuthberht*) and Aldhelm (*Praise of Virginity*), and a *Life* of Fursa.

Among his East Anglian materials Bede apparently used a genealogical tally like the one compiled for Ælfwald during the 720s. Bede's researchers no doubt stimulated regional interest in historical traditions and archives, just when Felix was mentioning Guthlac's Iceling descent. An Old English heroic poem of *Guthlac*, which draws on Felix, presumes an audience receptive to a Christian heroic recitation with lyre accompaniment – perhaps a royal, monastic audience. Cædmon, the first English vernacular Christian poet, was discovered by Hild (great-aunt of Ælfwald) at Whitby, where his peers must have been singing secular words. Eadwine's experiences at Rædwald's court were noted in a Whitby *Life of Gregory the Great*. Perhaps a heroic poem preserved part of the narrative of Rædwald and Eadwine, and was among the 'traditions of former men' from which Bede learned his East Anglian history. James Campbell notes that a fashion for personal names derived from heroic literature arose in Mercia during the eighth century. Such was the name of Hathulac, Bishop of Elmham in 731 (though not of his Dommoc contemporary, Bishop Aldberht). Both the Christian poetry of that age and the personal names betray their awareness of literature like the source-material of *Beowulf*, even though most has not survived.

The political counterpoise of Mercian and East Anglian interests in the Fen extended and evolved in various different ways through those kingdoms and beyond. Both Ely and Medeshamstede long afterwards claimed the papal Privileges reputedly brought by Wilfrid in 680. Although Ely began with Æthelthryth's ownership and perhaps with Cratendune, Seaxburh's and Eormenhild's abbacy had linked it to Sheppey and the Kentish houses, especially to Thanet, Mildthryth's house, where Eadburgh became abbess soon after 732. Wihtred's sons ruled in Kent after his death in 725: Ine of Wessex abdicated in 727, and Æthelbald's power grew in earnest. Werburgh, the daughter of Eormenhild and Wulfhere, was abbess of houses at Hanbury (Staffs.), Threckingham (Kesteven) and Ely. Her bailiff Alnoth is linked to the foundation at Stowe-Nine-Churches in Northamptonshire. The connection with Mildthryth's family went back as far as the early days of Iken and Much Wenlock, and to the time of Anna himself. Medeshamstede later portrayed itself as the former head of a system of colonies, asserting its primary foundation by Wulfhere and Seaxwulf. That network included the wealthy houses at Bardney in Lindsey, at Brixworth (Northants.), Breedon-on-the-Hill (Leics.) and possibly Repton (Derbys.), and another group in the Wrekin area. In 731 Tatwine, author of a book of riddles, progressed from Breedon to succeed Archbishop Berhtwald at Canterbury. Many paths or traditions of patronage converged in the Fen.

A year after completing his History, Bede amended it to record an event of international importance. In 710-13 the Moslem armies or Saracens had achieved the conquest of Spain, and thereafter established their northern outpost at Narbonne. In 732 they progressed into Gaul along a vast frontier, and were confronted and driven back by Charles Martel. In this battle of Tours Charles is said to have carried the Holy Lance for the Divine protection and supervision of the Christian armies. Thus that sacred relic renewed its symbolic association with the military service of Christendom. Bede does not mention this, but records the bloodthirsty assault and the victory as foreshadowed by celestial portents and comets. In 735 both Bede and Archbishop Tatwine went to their rest, and Nothhelm succeeded to the see of Canterbury. It was in the same year that the Archbishopric of York at last gained full establishment when Ecgberht, the first since Paulinus, received the pallium. Thus Pope Gregory III (731-41) consciously fulfilled the intention of Gregory I for the reconstruction of the ancient Roman authority of the see of York.

Economy and the expansion of Ipswich

At, or soon after, the beginning of Ælfwald's reign, East Anglian mints began to supplement the English coins in circulation. D.M. Metcalf refers to the pronounced north-west/south-east axis in the monetary affairs of East Anglia. The so-called 'Q' series sceattas, of which there are several types, show a distribution focused along the west side of Norfolk, as far north as the Wash and south to Cambridge, but with a much smaller circulation in the south-east around Gipeswic. These were issued for about 30 years during the reign of Ælfwald, though not necessarily under direct royal prerogative. One group depicts human subjects including busts and figures holding crosses, while others show more generally a range of variants depicting a four-legged beast on one side and a bird on the other. For these, one or more mints in west Norfolk are proposed. They have a small distribution in Northumbria and may owe something to Northumbrian prototypes, some of which were royal issues. Even more conservative was the type (Series 'R') found especially in central and south-eastern East Anglia, which remained in circulation from around 705 right down into the 750s and formed the principal coinage of the kingdom. These show a bust on the obverse and a standard (a beaded square enclosing central motifs, with crosses emerging from its sides towards the margin) on the reverse. They were struck in imitation of the earlier, primary runic sceattas, and their distribution points to the principal mint having been in or near Gipeswic.

Their 12 different types suggest to some a number of different mints, and to others a frequent programme of reform. There might have been mints at Thetford, at Norwich or at Burgh Castle. John Newman makes us think of a minting authority centred at Ely. The corridor of the Gipping valley, the north-west route to Hunstanton, the focus near the Great Estuary, all correspond to key settlement and occupation within the kingdom. The first large series includes the inscription EPA in runic letters beside the diademed bust. It is unlikely that some which appear as GEPA refer to the port of Gipeswic. Over a period they

Late runic sceattas, *c.*730s–750s.
(diam. 1.3cm) Above: moneyer
Wigraed (possibly in Gipeswic).
Below: moneyer Tilberht (North
Suffolk or Norfolk?). *The British
Museum*

sank from a very high silver standard and weight around 1.20 grammes to below
0.9 grammes and barely half silver. A continuing series, with other short runic
inscriptions, were struck to the low weight but with further-reduced silver.
These culminate in the strikes of Wigræd and Tilberht – moneyers named in
runes. Wigræd, apparently located in south-east Suffolk, issued silver at below
15 per cent, while Tilberht, whose coins are more concentrated above central
Suffolk, around Thetford, dropped his standard below 10 per cent. Differences
of design show that their dies were cut separately, and their strikes were still
circulating in around 760 when several were deposited in the Middle Harling
hoard.

Through Gipeswic, East Anglia retained its distinct identity and role towards
Europe during the age of Boniface. So important was Gipeswic that Ælfwald
added to it an entirely new town laid out on a rectangular grid, the plan of which
still forms the centre of modern Ipswich. From the Stoke crossing constructed
around 700 the road from St Peter's ran north (Queen Street) to the Corn Hill.
This open area seems to have been the town's administrative centre from an early
date. A new east–west concourse (Buttermarket) was created south of Tavern
Street (the corduroy road), linking the Corn Hill and Brook Street (one of the
two branches of the northward road from the original ford). The new concourse
ran west through Arcade Street and beyond, probably into Handford Road and
towards the Handford crossing, but the western town sector is obscured by
medieval alterations. The main north–south intersector was the continuation of
Turret Lane through the Cattle Market and up St Stephen's Lane and Dial Lane
to Tavern Street.

The grid so created (which in time extended beyond Brook Street towards the Cox Lane potteries) was subdivided into insulæ or rectangular lots. The north-eastern quadrant was divided by St Lawrence's Lane, and the south-western one by Gaol Lane, its route still preserved within the Buttermarket Centre. In the south-eastern quadrant the division was east to west, from St Stephen's Lane through to Brook Street beside the church. Falcon Street, Old Cattlemarket and Dog's Head Street form the southern side of the grid, and probably marked the northern edge of the town in Ealdwulf's time. From this point there was a development eastwards along Tacket Street across Foundation Street and Cox Lane, and the pottery quarter itself was developing north-east into the area of Spring Road. The potteries were in full production and achieving distribution throughout midland England in the mid-eighth century. The new town was built directly over the burial grounds of the seventh century. Perhaps a changing and growing population had little sentimental attachment there, or commercial advantage or necessity outweighed it. Christian burial grounds were now presumably developed around the churches.

Keith Wade's excavations revealed the original metalled surface of St Stephen's Lane at some depth directly beneath the modern road. On its west side, the oldest houses were built close together with a frontage directly onto the road. This had been a busy lane, through which cattle were driven (presumably to and from market), and the buildings probably served both as dwellings and workshops or commercial premises. They were constructed of posts with timber cladding, and had yards and outbuildings of the type built over sunken pit floors. Wells were dug and lined with old barrels, which were lowered in succession as the shaft was sunk. Stave-built barrels made from both English and German timber indicate a continental trade in wine into Gipeswic.

Comb manufacture required the hard properties of antler for its raw material. During the eighth century, Gipeswic combs acquired the form with one set of teeth under a long arching bar cut from matching halves of a bowed tine. These were incised with cross-hatching (often empanelled) and with drilled ring-and-dot ornament. Large quantities of sawn antler-tine have been recorded from excavations in central Ipswich since the early investigations of Dr J.E. Taylor in 1880-1, and of Miss Nina Layard in 1898-1903.

Combs were used principally for grooming. Pierced bone 'cards' were probably used in the making of ornamental belts or bands, with hemp or linen warp-threads under tension, or for making warp headers for looms. Annular baked clay weights show that weaving was carried out in Gipeswic. Needles and thread-pickers of bone, sometimes decorated, have the fine polish produced by abrasion of woollen and flaxen yarns. Weaving perhaps became increasingly a male activity in this town environment as division of labour grew. Some needles derive from the manufacture of shoes, garments and saddlery: leather offcuts are preserved in waterlogged areas near the Quay. Some very large antler offcuts may suggest the import of raw material from the more extensive continental forests, though local habitats probably supplied the regular industry.

A high proportion of the numerous coins excavated in Ipswich are sceattas, from the age of the town's expansion from the late seventh to mid-eighth century. Wood and metalworking of all kinds, ship-building, cart construction and various domestic industries, including osier-work from the riverside resources, can be envisaged. Various types of Rhenish pottery, and dressed lava quernstones for handmills from Andernach and elsewhere were routinely imported. Fine hone-stones were brought from Norway. In this rapidly growing town environment, provision and hostelry required increasing organisation. Among the finds from eighth-century Gipeswic are a pair of whistle-like bone objects with matching finger-holes. Although found in separate contexts, Graeme Lawson recognised them as parts of the same instrument, the chants for an early set of bagpipes on the scale of the German or Northumbrian pipes. They show that music had a place in the town's life, perhaps with dance or group singing and other convivial affairs.

The new grid reflects planning by a royal patron, as the dedication of a church or minster to St Mildred at Ipswich Corn Hill may suggest. The medieval church, now vanished, later became the town's Moot Hall and stood on the site of the present Town Hall, occupying the south-western corner of the Corn Hill. The ancient Shambles and later Corn Exchanges occupied the equivalent south-eastern side. The body of Mildred, the former abbess of Minster-in-Thanet, gained saintly repute when it was translated by her successor Eadburgh during the early 740s into a new church of St Peter and St Paul at Minster. If Eadburgh was indeed King Ælfwald's sister, the link between the developing town and royal interest in St Mildred might readily be explained.

Two Mildred dedications also appear in the core of ancient London, both lost churches. St Mildred-in-the-Poultry (burial-place of Thomas Tusser) stood

Ipswich, Foundation Street: comb. *Ian Riddler*

between Cheapside and Cornhill and near St Stephen Walbrook. Actually within St Paul's churchyard was St Mildred's Bread-street, a Wren church destroyed by the Luftwaffe. A continental dedication, possibly unique, exists at Utrecht. This distribution at such important centres may well reflect mid-eighth-century royal relations between Kent, East Anglia and the continent in the patronage of trade or provision. Veneration of Mildred was renewed after *c.*1033 when her remains were translated to St Augustine's, Canterbury.

During Ælfwald's reign the collecting activities near the hall in Coddenham Vale cease, but those at Barham continue. Their miscellaneous artefacts and coins might, obliquely, reflect fiscal activity at Gipeswic: both places have produced good series of sceattas. Perhaps the Gipeswic administrators had residences further up the Gipping valley to oversee the river and Pye Road intersection. Domesday records that in the Confessor's time Brun (i.e. *Brown*), the *Præpositus* (Reeve) of Gipeswic, lived at Baylham and held 60 acres at Stonham. Brun was perhaps related to Bruninc and Brunman, two of the Confessor's principal moneyers in Gipeswic. There may have been a more ancient link of economy and command between these two positions controlling the river. (Incidentally, Brunnings were nearby at Helmingham in 1844 when Harriet married John Brown of Wetheringsett: their grandson Basil found the Sutton Hoo ship.)

East Anglia's contacts with St Boniface

Gipeswic, the most important estuary township between London and York, presented the face of East Anglian culture and commerce directly to the Rhine mouths, to Domburg, Dorestad and Utrecht. Boniface received the Archbishop's pallium in 732, and in 738 began to establish diocesan organisation in Germany. In the following year, when Willibrord died and was buried at his monastery of Echternach, Boniface divided Bavaria into the sees of Salzburg, Regensburg, Freising and Passau. Soon afterwards Willibald was sent from Monte Cassini to assist him and, after the death of Charles Martel in 741, was appointed to a fifth Bavarian see at Eichstätt. Boniface proceeded to found the sees of Wurtaburg, Buraburg (near Fritzlar) and Erfurt. An eighth-century English gilt bronze comb with animal-head finials, a central circular cross and interlace ornament, attached to a reliquary at Fritzlar, is attributed credibly to Boniface's ownership. At this time he appointed many other Englishmen as preaching-bishops (*chorepiscopi*) to assist him.

Under Charles Martel's successor, Carloman, Boniface began the general reform of the Frankish Church and became its leading figure. After the Synod of Soissons in 744 he entrusted the minster of Fulda to his German followers, and continued to establish English Christian teaching on all sides. In consequence papal influence over the Frankish Church was also greatly extended. In 747 Carloman retired, and his power was adopted by Pippin the Short. The Merovingian kings, in a long succession from Chlothar III (656-70) and Theodoric III (670-91) down to Childeric III (742-52), had become mere ciphers to the descendants of Pippin of Heristal; but the maintenance of their line had been the policy of Charles Martel, who designated Chlothar IV in 717.

Eadburgh's friendship with Boniface was maintained through correspondence in later years. As abbess of Thanet she was the teacher of his dearest female companion Leobgyth (Leoba), who joined him in Germany and with whom he wished to be buried. Earlier, he directs Leoba to seek advice on metrical writing from Eadburgh, whose poetical training or skills he therefore knew as we cannot. With her Thornham connections, Eadburgh presumably communicated with her kinswoman Wihtburh, King Anna's youngest daughter, who died at East Dereham in 743 aged about 90. Her relations with Ely must have been much more immediate. If we accept her to be King Ælfwald's sister, she embodied East Anglian royal culture in north-east Kent. Her education and that of Ælfwald were probably of a similar quality. His own direct communication with Boniface, a surviving letter, reveals a scholarly, fluent command of Latin, a subtle understanding of theological debate and the perfect manners of a King. Boniface has written asking his support for certain reforms to the English Church. These were to be debated or ratified at a great Council at Clofesho in 747 in the presence of King Æthelbald, a meeting which Bishop Eardwulf of Dommoc attended.

Replying on behalf of the East Anglian Church, Ælfwald mentions two points which appear as the fifteenth and thirtieth canons of the Council, namely (a) that the seven canonical hours of daily and nightly prayer shall be observed with chant and psalmody, using the same forms everywhere, and no readings except those allowed by Scripture or by custom of the Roman Church; and (b) that prayers shall be offered for kings and dukes (ealdormen), as well as for all religious people, constantly asking divine guidance for them so that all may live in peace and tranquillity under their rule. Ælfwald, a beneficiary of these prayers, remarks that Boniface's name ought to be enrolled in the services of the seven canonical hours of the East Anglian monasteries, because perfect men are often designated by the number seven. This word enrolled (*censeri*) implies the existence of an East Anglian *Liber Vitæ* or 'Book of Life', a book in which the names of the dead and those entering the Universal Way may literally be written, as occasions arise, so as to receive the continuous prayers of the monastic congregations. *Vivete*, writes the elderly king to the elderly archbishop, *felicibus finem clausuri calcibus*: 'Live, coming to your close with happy footsteps.' In fact Boniface outlived him by five years.

The phrase *in septenis monasteriorum nostrorum sinaxis* has occasionally been taken to signify the *seven monasteries*, or *conventicles*, of East Anglia, when in fact Ælfwald refers only to *our monasteries*, and the *seven canonical hours*. This does not tell us that there were seven East Anglian monasteries extant in 747. King Wihtred's Old English Constitutions were set forth in 695 and confirmed at Clofesho in 747. A continuation of them (Spelman p206-07) explains the Seven Canonical Hours: 'Sevenfold are the gifts of the Holy Spirit ... and seven are the grades of Ecclesiastical ordination and of holy duty; and seven times shall God's servants praise God daily in the church and eagerly pray for all Christian folk ... and whoever shall injure it with word or with work shall make sevenfold retribution ....' Ælfwald is evidently aware of such formulations: he has read the Clofesho agenda. He thanks Boniface ('Your Benignity') for proposing the ordinance of prayer on behalf of the King ('Our Mediocrity'), and in every way invites his superior counsels. Precautions have been taken about the servant carrying the letter, so that Boniface shall be sure to have a true report of the King's message. In all likelihood, that servant left East Anglia by ship from Gipeswic.

Ælfwald's kingdom boasted one of the largest trading entrepots on the margins of the North Sea, a magnificent new urban centre with its pottery quarter and industry, a minting organisation and monetary economy, several monasteries and two important bishoprics firmly established under royal patronage. What he did not have was an heir capable of holding it under his own sole rule. At Clofesho the reforming motion was carried. When Ælfwald died in 749, the monasteries of East Anglia were praying for him and for his ealdormen seven times a day. Soon they would be praying for a different king.

6

Under Mercian rule

HUN, BEONNA AND ÆTHELBERHT I, 749
BEONNA RULING ALONE 760

When Ælfwald died in 749 'Hunbeanna and Alberht divided the kingdom of the East Angles between themselves' – so Byrhtferth of Ramsey in the late *Historia Regum* informs us. No contemporary document mentions these rulers; but coins naming Beonna or Benna Rex – until recently just a handful of stray finds, but now well over 100 small silver pennies – prove some truth in the late record. The medieval scribe (who knew nothing of these people) perhaps ran two names, Hun and Beonna, into one. Sigeberht and Æthilric had once before divided East Anglia, in 629, at a time of dynastic crisis. Ælfwald's genealogical tally ends with his name. Unlike all his predecessors back to Æthilric, Beonna's name does not begin with a vowel. Alberht (i.e. Æthelberht), on the other hand, might be a Wuffing heir. Was Beonna regent in Alberht's minority or did he take power in some other way? Nothing more is known of the inscrutable Hun. Florence of Worcester's Chronicle states that in 760 (the annal given as 758) Beonna (*Beornus*) was ruling the East Angles.

As King of the East Angles Beonna introduced the first connected and developing series of English silver pennies bearing the King's name (sometimes with the style 'Rex' or a runic equivalent 'Ress') and the moneyer's name on the reverse. Two groups found in recent years greatly increased the numbers known and confirm understanding of their date and types. They show that Beonna, primarily, controlled the minting organisation of East Anglia during this time of division. A dispersed hoard found at Middle Harling (Norfolk) in 1980-3 (on the Thet above Thetford close to the Norfolk-Suffolk border) contained 53 pennies of Beonna, nine earlier sceattas and two blanks. Meanwhile a much smaller series was excavated by Valerie Fenwick from stratified layers at Burrow Hill, Butley, close to Rendlesham. There Beonna's coins appeared in sequence with earlier types and later rulers. Mrs Fenwick also found a unique runic sceatta

Two coins of Beonna
(749-*c*.760). Above:
Runic type *Benna*,
moneyer Wilred.
(diam. 1.2cm) Below:
Latin type *Beonna
Rex*, moneyer Efe.
The British Museum

Runic sceatta of
Ethelberht I (r.749-?),
moneyer Tiaelred.
(diam. 1.5cm) *The
British Museum*

naming Æthelberht. This gave the first tangible reality to *Alberht*, (that is) King Æthelberht I of East Anglia.

In south-east Suffolk Beonna's coins appear in numbers in Gipeswic, and an example from Dorestad reflects their continuing continental exchange. A domestic settlement excavated at White House, about a mile upstream from Gipeswic on the ridge above the valley's east side, produced one. Three from the productive Barham site show its occupants busy in Beonna's time, but none occur upstream at Coddenham. Coins from Hacheston, and from Debenham on the Deben, suggest river communication above Rendlesham. Debenham (which yields Ipswich Ware pottery) was thus already active in the Thredling corner of the province later named Wicklaw. The tenth-century patrons, for whom Debenham's large and important stone church tower was built, endowed a place which had been frequented, distinguished perhaps, in Beonna's time. (Framlingham's fortified site, occupied in the eighth century, similarly overlooked the upper Ore. A handsome bronze key shows possessions worth securing there.) We see continuity of a moneyed community at Butley through Beonna's reign, when the ditch-ramparts were used as rubbish-pits rather than as defences: they must have been feeling fairly secure. It has been conjectured that Benhall (just south-west of Saxmundham) might signify *Beonna's* hall or bower. Beonna's money had currency in the heartland of Wuffing patrimony, perhaps Ely's endowment, at Gipeswic and in its surroundings.

Both the Harling hoard and individual finds of Beonna's coins from Quidenham (Norfolk) on the Thet accent the early importance of Thetford shown by its sceatta finds. On the Little Ouse below Thetford there is one from Brandon, where a nuclear community established in the seventh century there on a sand island was gaining signs of wealth. Specimens from Exning and from its neighbour Freckenham, beside the Fen, are among various small finds (some of quality), which show these sites active at high status through the seventh and eighth centuries. Others made their way to the ancient market at Royston

Suffolk: bronze openwork keys (above: Framlingham). *Ipswich Borough Museums*

(Herts.) and to Whithorn in Galloway (there perhaps through ecclesiastical contact). All these finds, with Norfolk examples from Fakenham, Bowthorpe and Caistor St Edmunds, and (in Suffolk) from Hacheston, Debenham, Barham and Gipeswic, were struck to a 50% silver standard by a moneyer named Efe. With more than 70 of the known total (including 37 at Harling and 11 at Burrow Hill), and several variant reverse dies, Efe was Beonna's most prolific moneyer. The reverse showed a beaded square with the letters of Efe's name in surrounding quadrants: this, and the small module (later enlarged), show development from the East Anglian R-Series sceattas of the previous reign.

Royally-named sceattas had been issued by the Northumbrian Kings Aldfrith (c.700) and Eadberht (737-58). Beonna's obverses resemble them, with his name and title in runic or Roman letters around a small central motif. His first moneyer was probably Werferth (Harling 3, Barham 1), who struck to a high (75%) silver standard. To judge from style and distribution, Werferth and Efe both probably operated from the Thetford region, or perhaps Beodricesworth. Marion Archibald shows that Euston, east of Thetford where the Black Bourne joins the Little Ouse, might (as *Eofs-ton* or *Efes-tun*) represent manorial occupation by a thegnly person called Efe. As a male name 'Efe' is unique, but the female name *Eafe* (Eve) certainly existed.

Efe's large lower-silver output could represent an issue for military purposes over a fairly short period. Beonna perhaps consolidated his authority thus after the the death of King Æthelbald of Mercia in 757. Another type, found at Pakenham and Bardwell (Black Bourne valley), and 4 from Harling, has no named moneyer but an interlace pattern reverse: the Dorestad example is of this kind. These resemble Frankish or Frisian deniers issued around Maastricht in the 750s, so Beonna engaged actively in North Sea commerce. His last moneyer Wilred, using all-runic legends, reduced his silver to 25%. The Harling hoard contained 12; Burrow Hill, Barham and Gipeswic each produced 3, and the market site at Bawsey (Norfolk) one. Wilred's mint, like Wigræd's before him, was probably based around Gipeswic.

Similarly Æthelberht's moneyer *Tiælred*, Tilred, might be related to the sceatta moneyer Tilberht. His coin (about 42% silver) has entirely runic lettering, but with pellets resembling Efe's work at the northern mint. On the larger flan, and with increased weight, it was probably struck after the Efe series. The use of fully runic texts in the late Beonna period may show a distinctively East Anglian preference. Under Beonna and Æthelberht, Thetford continued as a royal centre of the first importance.

These deductions confirm that for more than a decade after Ælfwald's death Beonna established his authority, and maintained regional and overseas commerce through new regally-styled coinage which was frequently revised. His moneyers were important figures of his administration based in the south-east and north-west of Suffolk, and their issues travelled well beyond East Anglia. Æthelberht I also ruled in his time, apparently approving the issue of runic coins though in far smaller numbers. Hun remains completely elusive, but it is not an unusual element in eighth-century names. Hunston, which apparently had a stone tower before the Norman Conquest, is near Bardwell and Pakenham.

Beonna's Reign: new continental powers
The events and upheavals of that decade were momentous, and undoubtedly influenced the course of East Anglian policy. With Childeric III as titular Merovingian ruler of the Franks after 742, Pippin the Short succeeded Carloman in 747. That was the year of the great Council at Clofesho when Boniface, seeking to establish uniform observances, maintained close contact with the English kings. His letter to Æthelbald of Mercia deplores the pagan example of his adulterous marriage, reminding him of the German women who still cast themselves into their husbands' funeral pyres. (Æthelbald took steps to reform his Church.) Boniface thus makes kingship the sacred example and defence of Christian society. In Bavaria, Bishop Willibald of Eichstätt placed his brother Wynbald and sister Waldburg in joint charge of the monastery at Heidenheim in 750. A year later, papal approval was won to transfer the regnal title of the Franks to their effective rulers. Boniface consecrated Pippin King of the Franks, and the Merovingian dynasty was officially disempowered.

Taking charge of the efforts towards conversion in Thuringia and Hesse, Boniface was obliged to restore over 30 churches destroyed by Saxons in a pagan backlash in 752. In 754 he went into northern Frisia beyond the river Yssel. After a successful start his mission met disaster or beatitude at Dokkum near the Frisian coast, where he and more than 50 other bishops and followers (including Eoba, English Bishop of Utrecht) were massacred by Frisian pagans. Boniface (aged over 80) died enjoining his followers not to resist their martyrdom: he was buried at Fulda. A bone from his throat is preserved at Brixworth (Northants.). A *Life* of Boniface was afterwards written by Willibald, scion of the Kentish, East Saxon and East Anglian royal houses and of Boniface's kin, who remained Bishop of Eichstätt until his death in 786. Boniface was succeeded as Archbishop by Chrodegang of Metz, who established there a great tradition of Roman liturgical song, and composed rules for the communal life of cathedral clergy which were later taken up at York and Canterbury. As King Pippin had promised to Boniface, the Englishman Lull succeeded him at Mainz. Boniface's Frankish pupil Gregory maintained the diocese of Utrecht into the 770s.

In England Cuthred, King of Wessex since 740, revolted against Æthelbald and established his right against him in battle at Burford Bridge in 752. According to Henry of Huntingdon the East Angles were with Æthelbald there. After Cuthred's death four years later the West Saxons fell into internal strife. For reasons unknown Canterbury was burnt down. In Northumbria King Eadberht abdicated and took the tonsure, and Oswulf his son was murdered a year later by members of his own household. Various kingdoms were therefore in crisis when, in 757, King Æthelbald himself was murdered by his own bodyguard at Seckington. He was buried in a stone-built mausoleum at Repton in Derbyshire, parts of which are pointed out in the ancient crypt beneath Repton church.

This blow struck down the most powerful English ruler and indicates the high ambition of his enemies. His successor Beornred is apparently of a rival dynasty not descended from Eowa but possessing a Mercian claim. Beornred ruled for a short time and unhappily. Some think he was none other than Beonna, King of the East Angles, for the name Beonna is a familiar, shortened form. Even if the two were not identical they might be kinsmen from a dynasty which could stake its claim in both Mercia and East Anglia. Had Beonna taken power in 749 as an aspirant to east Mercian rather than East Anglian dynastic right? Did his family have an ancient East Anglian claim? Offa, the son of Thingfrith, drove Beornred from the seat of Mercian power later in 757. Late chroniclers identify Beornred with the ealdorman Beorn who, after burning Catterick in 779, was himself burnt to death by the Northumbrian high-reeves.

Whoever Beonna was, numismatists place the close of his coinage in around 760 or soon after. A Beonna is named (*sub anno* 777) as abbot of Medeshamstede (Peterborough) in a forged medieval charter which may nonetheless contain authentic features. Could King Beonna have made a religious abdication in deference to Offa, retiring with his consent to Medeshamstede? Did he instead develop the hegemony of Medeshamstede over the East Mercian or Middle Anglian houses to which these reconstituted charters refer? Medeshamstede certainly enjoyed royal patronage and was the focus of a large network of Mercian estates. But the truth is that we do not really know where King Beonna came from, or why his reign ended.

?ÆTHELRED, 760s-80s
OFFA, KING OF MERCIA 757-96
OVERLORD OF EAST ANGLIA *c.*765-96

Offa, who drove out Beornred from Mercia, derived his claim from Eowa, and therefore from Creoda, Icel, Offa of Angeln, and Woden, and was disposed to assert his hereditary right. Æthelbald was his grandfather's cousin. He learnt from the Venerable Bede's *History* of the statecraft of his predecessors. In his later reign his stature on the European stage dominated by Charlemagne surpassed that of all former English kings. His authority lay in the control of wealth and commerce, legal administration, public works and endowments, diplomatic marriage, papal authorisation and the outward display of power. English culture remained highly influential in Frankish circles, and Offa's consolidation of English power after the death of Æthelbald is called, by Sir Frank Stenton, the central fact of later eighth-century English history.

Through much of his rule the East Anglian record is intensely obscure. William of Malmesbury (*de gestis Regum*, Book I) lists the East Anglian King Æthelred, father of Æthelberht II. He is mentioned immediately after Beonna: *...Aldulpho & Elwaldo; his Beorna; huic quoque Ethelredus successit: huius filius fuit sanctus Ethelbirthus...'* This regnal list, perhaps compiled with reference to a *Passio* of Æthelberht II, also prefaces John of Worcester's *Chronicle*. It is very likely that Æthelberht I had an East Anglian successor during Offa's reign. His kinsman or son might well be named Æthelred, who in turn could have named his own son Æthelberht. But King Æthelred has no coinage, and if he really existed he was submerged under Mercian rule. Beonna's moneyer Wilred, seemingly based in the south-east in the Gipeswic sphere, was adopted by King Offa for whom he struck fine-metal broad flan pennies.

So as Æthelred remains darkly intangible, in fact tenebrous, we must view East Anglian affairs through the national strategies of Offa, in which they were increasingly involved and at times completely absorbed. Offa carried Mercian power to a new pinnacle of international importance. The Icel inheritance was doubtless perfectly known to him, as to Æthelbald and Guthlac: the prize of a Mercian East Anglia fulfilled an ancient claim while satisfying present ambition and opportunity. Perhaps his own origins were east Mercian, Middle Anglian: he was reputedly buried at Elstow near Bedford.

Pippin had introduced important coin reforms in Gaul in 755, setting a new, very high, silver standard. Under Charles (i.e. Charlemagne), who acceded in 768, Frankish dominion grew rapidly not only in the north but also into Italy and Spain, in the famous adventures to which the *Chanson de Roland* is the epic literary testimony. These events called forth the need for a strong independent English rulership, but Offa's rise to power was by no means immediate. Æthelbald's death ended Mercian authority in Wessex; there King Cynewulf inherited and held power until 786, though he ceded land north of the Thames to Offa after the battle of Benson (Oxon.) in 779.

In Kent Wihtred's sons, Æthelberht and Eadberht, and grandson Eardulf, ruled together at least until 762, when Æthelberht died. They were succeeded by kings named Heaberht and Ecgberht, whose dynastic claims are unknown. Offa, already controlling Sussex west of Pevensey, gained authority in Kent from 764. At this time, the Kentish kings began their coinage reform at Canterbury, producing a new type of silver penny which was larger and thinner than their previous 'sceatta' series. Offa adopted this, using the Canterbury mint and its Kentish moneyers. But a battle at Otford in 776 between the Mercians and Kentishmen had reduced Offa's influence there, and it was not fully reasserted until 784-5. By then, in 784, Ealhmund, a king of West Saxon royal descent, was attempting to grant land there independently to the abbot of Reculver.

Gipeswic developed apace around its newly laid-out centre and established harbour, its potteries flourished and distributed widely, its industrial production was unabated, and Offa doubtless prized it as both a strategic and an economic gain. The harbour at Norwich held a similar potential as yet less developed. The old claim that the moated site at Offton was a residence of Offa's is very dubious, and one cannot tell how early King's Field above Christchurch Park served royal supervision of the town. But Offa may well have developed strongholds in the region separate from the family halls of the Wuffing nobility. Eighth-century presences at Framlingham or Haughley could reflect fortification interests of his time. As Thetford, Thorney, Sudbury and Brandon gained importance alongside other royal, ecclesiastic and commercial centres, they still owed their development to regional patrons: if they prospered, still they were East Anglian.

Brandon, and the development of monastic arts

The wealth of religious paintings and artefacts brought into England from the seventh century onwards poured their inspirations into the English arts, especially in book-painting, precious metalwork and ivory, and in the imported craft of stone-sculpture. Much artistic production was centred upon the religious houses, to the wealthiest of which scriptoria and other workshops were attached. Their patrons and governors, frequently of royal kin like the saints and founders enshrined within them, maintained their endowment and embellishment. Intricacies of ornament, of radiant colour and precious metal, and of sumptuous display books, filled their places of worship with an other-worldly spell, a mesmerising reverberation of sacred archetypes which also reinforced and reflected brilliantly the wealth, taste and Christian authority of the patrons.

During the eighth century, Syrian and Byzantine works, including textiles, lent lively images of vine-scroll foliage, exotic animals, birds, horsemen and hunters to the more geometric or linear world of Celto-Saxon ornament. These arts further converged and mingled to create a distinctive English style of the period. Southern or midland English scriptoria produced noble painted books (like the Gospels now in Stockholm and Rome, or the 'Vespasian' Psalter) in which such ornament evolved alongside figures painted with increasingly classical volumes. These developing styles were carried by Englishmen into many continental centres and imitated or continued there. If Canterbury and York had the most famous scriptoria, Mercia was also prolific, and East Anglia cannot have been negligible. Both Ely and Medeshamstede, like twin citadels linking the interests of East Anglia and Mercia, stood advantageously open to east coast communications with Canterbury, Lincoln and Flixborough, York and beyond.

The religious and literate community at Brandon achieved conspicuous wealth in Offa's time. The excavated settlement, occupying a sand island beside the Little Ouse, was laid out (at first during the seventh century) to emphasise the situation of a church and its cemetery, a group of important buildings adjacent, and access to them from domestic dwellings nearby with less formal enclosures. All the buildings were constructed of wood, and the most important of them, including the church, were well and solidly built, probably during the earlier eighth century. The church itself was like a hall, with vertical wall-planking and with portals on the north and south sides, creating an east–west axial space, with an additional chancel structure at the east end and also a western chamber. There were windows glazed with blue, blue-green and olive-coloured glass. A fine bronze key was found here. One area of the settlement was given over to cloth-processing. The cruciform pendant from Wilton (Norfolk) shows early patrons nearby connected with the Wuffing goldsmith. Royal interest from Ely, Beodricesworth or Thetford may have overseen its development.

The particular age of Brandon's prosperity, illustrated by fine glass and metalwork finds, was during the later eighth and early ninth centuries. Brandon shared the material culture of several royal and ecclesiastical centres near the eastern seaways. It was of course adjacent to the busy water-routes connecting Ely and Medeshamstede with Cambridge and the Wash. The distinguished glassware used (and broken) there included a delicate jar of red marbled glass with a rolled lip and trailed white glass decoration, and a brown glass jar with finely-patterned rods applied around the foot. These English productions resemble coloured vessels from wealthy sites such as York Minster, Whitby, Jarrow, and Barking Abbey. Brandon also has fragments in blue and green which show that English production of claw-beakers (fancy drinking-vessels with drawn pendant glass 'claws'), fashionable from the fifth to seventh centuries, continued into the eighth: formerly such late examples were known only in Swedish sites with English associations. Valuable ceramics, including a large wine-jar of Tating Ware from the Rhinelands, were used at Brandon. This luxury pottery was ornamented with applied strips and lozenges of metal foil, and is found rarely in England and only at wealthy sites. Fragments from Gipeswic suggest a route by which such wares were imported.

Brandon excavation: fragments of a Tating Ware amphora. *Suffolk County Council*

Literacy at Brandon was both runic and Latin. Sixteen letters of the *futharc* (the Anglo-Saxon runic alphabet) were scratched on the head of a long dress-pin, and the name 'Aldred' was expertly engraved in runes on a pair of silver tweezers. (Aldred is a well-known Suffolk surname.) Styli were in use. But the impeccable credentials of Brandon's early literacy are shown by a gold plaque, a little over 3cm square, depicting the symbol of the Evangelist St John. He is shown as a frontal clothed human bust holding a book and pen, but with the profile head of an eagle with a nimbus. The lost companion-pieces would represent Matthew as man or angel, Mark as lion and Luke as calf. The symbols, as animals, were commonly used in Anglo-Saxon book-painting prefacing the gospels, or heading columns listing concordances of the gospels. The zoo-anthropomorphic symbol, both human and creature, finds a rare parallel in the famous Celtic gospel-book, the Book of Kells.

The miniature Brandon figure is masterfully delineated and incised, and filled with niello. It bears the identifying inscription 'SCS IOHANNIS EVANGELISTA' in squared capitals resembling Northumbrian display script, with serifs. It is identified as part of an ornamental cover for a gospel-book presumably illustrated with painting of similarly refined quality, or perhaps as

Brandon: gold plaque depicting St John. *The British Museum. Photograph: R. Carr*

a detail from a gold altar-cross. Brandon's Evangelist has a hieratic formality and power, with its great upward-seeing eye and its book and pen. It has some general likeness to the art of the Book of Cerne, a prayer-book painted in Mercia in the early ninth century, but there are important differences. The fine glassware and ceramics, personal ornaments and splendid gospel-book, show distinguished patrons and literate residents at Brandon in Offa's time and beyond.

The dress-pins found at Brandon illustrate developing East Anglian metalwork ornament of the later eighth century. As we have seen at Coddenham, outward interactions brought many kinds of metalwork into the region. Anglian jewellers or ornamental metalworkers absorbed and resynthesised the art of former times into new fashions. There were external influences: superb animal and spiral ornament were juxtaposed in gilt chip-carving on an Irish-made shrine or reliquary boss which reached Steeple Bumpstead (Essex), just at the south-west corner of Suffolk. In more English terms, a silver sword-pommel from Chelmondiston has modelled *wyrm*-like heads, an enmeshed animal and a spiralled plant-scroll in panels. That controlled, richly compact style gives way to freer depictions of imaginary animals and faces crowding the ornamental spaces, seen upon one dress-pin from Brandon.

The fusion of insular ribbon-like lizards with the more naturalistic animals seen in imported Syrian vinescrolls or medallions produced a new creature in English art, with two front legs, a long interlacing tail and tongue, often a pointed wing, and occasionally a residual hind leg. The chip-carving technique suited the meshing and spiralling of the threads which surround the creatures. They adopt 'heraldic' poses with their heads raised or turned back, often in

Chelmondiston: sword pommel with animal ornament. *Suffolk County Council*

Brandon excavation: gilt silver dress pin (detail). *Suffolk County Council*

Near Wickham Market: gilt silver pin-head. *Suffolk County Council*

Brandon excavation: silver dress pin (detail). *Suffolk County Council*

balanced pairs. Two pin-heads from Brandon, one showing paired animal heads, and another with spiralled and meshed animals, illustrate the later eighth-century developments. A complete pin probably from a linked group with gilt disc heads is engraved with facing bipeds with woven extremities. A gilt silver pinhead from near Wickham Market, shows fine work of this kind.

These animals underwent various stylistic developments in later eighth-century manuscript painting (for instance the Anglo-Saxon gospel-books in the Vatican (Barberini) and St Petersburg Libraries), and in metalwork book-mounts and other precious fittings. Through the monastic workshops the art of the painters, metalworkers, sculptors and others developed in overlapping ways. A miniature ivory box (probably a container for the chrism or Eucharist), thought to have been made at Medeshamstede, late in Offa's time, is richly carved with animals and trimmed with decorative metal mounts. It was long kept at Gandersheim monastery near Brunswick, indicating direct Middle Anglian relations with the Continent. East Anglian books might have looked like this.

The well-known group of three pins with disc heads from Fiskerton (near Lincoln) exemplify the metalwork style with its meshed animals, and the ecclesiastical site of Flixborough has very similar work. Two important Suffolk examples were found at Ixworth: one is a complete disc, apparently a brooch, with stippled singleton creatures in quadrants. A fragment of another disc shows a crowded panel (from a circular cruciform arrangement) enclosing tightly spiralled foliate scrolls. A disc from Bolnhurst (Beds.) has paired creatures in the

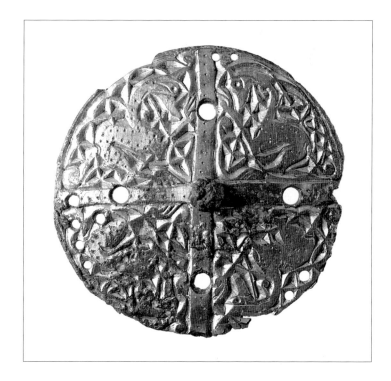

Ixworth: gilt silver disc-brooch. *The British Museum. Photograph: R. Carr*

?Ixworth: fragment of gilt silver disc-brooch. *The Ashmolean Museum, Oxford*

quadrants. Many related pieces of English metalwork travelled to Norway in ancient times. A cruciform pendant from Kaupang (Vestfold) and a superb chip-carved plaque from a woman's grave at Bjørke (Møre og Romsdal) show work in this style at two important Norwegian trading centres. A mount from Fure (Sogn og Fjordane) and a disc showing leaping beasts in foliage from Hillesøy (Troms) also have distinct similarities to the east Midland ornament. They are apparently eastern English objects, rather than specifically Northumbrian as Egil Bakka first proposed. A new example from Lackford shows whorled heads.

Metalwork finds from the productive site at Freckenham, near Exning and Soham, include work of this kind. A gilt book-mount, another mount with spiral foliate carving, and a glass stud decorated with pecking birds, indicate a literate and wealthy presence at Freckenham during the later eighth century. Although an Alfredian charter referring to Ffrekeham Castel is spurious, a later reference of the Conqueror's time, when the Church of Rochester claimed Freckenham, Falkenham (on the Deben) and Stoke Denniton as property taken away from it in the Danish Wars, seems authentic. Freckenham has produced a number of early coins, including several sceattas: a silver 'St Andrew' penny of Rochester for Ecgberht of Wessex (802-39) was recently found there. Close to the presumed royal centre of Exning and in the immediate sphere of Soham and Ely, therefore, stood some aristocratic house on this naturally fortified fenside site.

Offa consolidates the power of Mercia

The Church of York made a new investment in the continental missions. Alcuin, later a foremost scholar and theologian in Charlemagne's empire (and called its spiritual ruler), studied in the cathedral church at York. In the late 760s Alubert was selected by the Northumbrians to continue the mission to the Old Saxons, and Liudger, a Frisian pupil of Gregory of Utrecht, twice studied in York with him while Alcuin was teaching there. In around 770 a new English missionary, Willehad, was sent for the conversion of heathen Friesland near Dokkum, and further south in Drenthe, with the approval of King Ealhred and a Northumbrian synod. Ealhred sought the assistance of Lull of Mainz in maintaining friendship with Charlemagne. At that time an English priest, Leofwine, was preaching in the Frankish and Saxon borderlands near the river Yssel and around Deventer. In 780 Charlemagne sent Willehad to preach to the Saxons in the old homeland area between the lower Weser and Elbe. He did so for two years before many of his followers were killed in an insurrection. After visiting Rome he stayed at Echternach, where his Northumbrian cousin Beornred, Alcuin's disciple, was abbot. In 785 he was able to resume his mission and restore the destroyed churches, and in 787 was consecrated Bishop of the Saxon and Frisian provinces, fixing his seat at Bremen. He died in 789. Meanwhile Alcuin, closely acquainted with all of these men, became the master of Charlemagne's court school in 782.

In around 784-5, as Offa reasserted his hold over Kent, Charlemagne prompted Pope Hadrian I to reaffirm papal influence in England. Three years previously, Hadrian had anointed Charlemagne's sons into Frankish kingship under their father. He now sent a Legation under Bishops George of Ostia and Theophylact of Todi (extremely distinguished churchmen) first to Canterbury, and afterwards to Offa's court, to receive assent to 20 points of ecclesiastical and lay obedience. These were ratified at their Legatine Council of 786, which Alcuin attended. Offa's authority was hampered because the senior English spiritual power lay under Archbishop Jænberht at Canterbury in the rebellious land of Kent. Now, therefore, he sought papal approval to found a new Archbishopric at Lichfield near the heart of his own kingdom. He won the English clergy's consent to the division at a turbulent Council at Chelsea in 787. Late in the following year the Bishop of Lichfield, Hygeberht, received a pallium from Rome to denote his consecration: the seniority of Canterbury was nonetheless maintained. Bishop Heardred of Dommoc attended the Legatine Council and the long series of Councils from Brentford in 781 to Chelsea in 789 in which these matters were debated and decided. He had succeeded Bishop Heardwulf, who attended the famous Council of 747. East Anglia, until now the least recalcitrant of Offa's external dominions, was apparently annexed to the see of Lichfield.

Having established his second coinage at Canterbury, Offa proceeded there and in London to issue a series of pence bearing portraits of himself or of his wife Cynethryth. He also commenced an East Anglian issue (without portraits) using the moneyers Botred, Wihtred, and another whose name can only be read Hun..c, perhaps Hunlac or even Huninc (son of Hun). Offa's East Anglian moneyers regularly used runic letters for their own names. In 787 (following Charlemagne's example), Offa's son Ecgfrith was anointed as his successor. In the previous year King Cynewulf of Wessex had been treacherously slain, and Offa supported his successor Beorhtric, in 789 giving him his daughter in marriage. Beorhtric produced the first West Saxon regnal coinage. Charlemagne, recognising Offa's growing importance, then proposed that his son Charles should marry one of Offa's daughters. Offa made it his condition that Ecgfrith should marry Charlemagne's daughter, Bertha. Charlemagne thereupon closed the ports of Gaul to English trade, and they were still closed at the end of 790.

Relations worsened because Charlemagne provided refuge for exiles from Offa. They included Ecgberht, son of that King Ealhmund ruling in Kent in 784, before Offa regained his power there. When King Æthelred of Northumbria reclaimed his throne in 792 Offa also gave him a daughter in marriage, extending his patriarchy in the north. Now the Northumbrians commenced a regnal coinage, copper 'stycas' not unlike the simplest issues of Beonna. The Frisian trade, the most important for Gipeswic, may not have been unduly affected by Charlemagne's embargo. In any case, archaeology is unlikely to produce evidence of a single year's suspension of trading. Imported vessels from the Rhinelands included the new wares produced at Badorf, large fast-thrown wine-jars decorated with strips of clay with stamped impressions. A famous letter survives in which Charlemagne refers to the cloaks exported by the English (now regrettably shorter than they had formerly been), and to the black stones exported from his kingdoms, often taken as a reference to lava mill-stones from the Rhinelands. These are found plentifully in Gipeswic and elsewhere.

Ipswich: fragment of Rhenish Badorf Ware amphora. *Ipswich Borough Museums*

ÆTHELBERHT II, BEFORE 794

Here steps forth the princely figure of Æthelberht, in whose breast arose as one the expectation of personal destiny and the noble sentiment of patriotism. In *Lives* of Æthelberht, some containing plain invention, his father King Æthelred appears based at Beodricesworth. Perhaps that was where Malmesbury found Æthelred, to list him after *Beorna*: but equally the 'biographer' might dress his fable in patches of truth. We should probably allow that the East Angles maintained some regional leadership through Offa's reign. The duration of Æthelberht's power before his recorded appearance is unknown. Bishop Heardred having died soon after 790, he was succeeded at Dommoc by Alfhun. Archbishop Jænberht, the Kentish thorn in Offa's side, also died in 792, and Offa obtained the succession of Æthelheard, previously Abbot of Louth in Lindsey, who was sympathetic to his authority. On Alcuin's advice, Æthelheard was consecrated by Hygeberht of Lichfield. Offa again reformed his coinage in Kent, some of which was minted by the archbishops through an ancient Canterbury privilege. In East Anglia Wihtred, and a new moneyer named Lul, began to produce coins for Offa in the style of his latest Kentish series. These show a three-line arrangement of the legend 'M OFFA REX' on the obverse, and no portrait. Other East Angles, Æthelwald, Ecgbald, Eadnoth and Earwerht, were also minting for Offa.

Startling events in Northumbria in 793-94 no doubt forced the East Angles to seek firm local leadership. Coastal trade and communications merged inseparably into the northern advance of Frankish imperial conquest. As Frisian control of the seaways declined, and as English power was centralised, coasts were exposed to less sympathetic visitors. In particular, disunity in Norway caused many to cross in ships and to make at least temporary encampments in the northern and western Scottish islands and in Ireland. In 793 Lindisfarne was looted from the

Penny of Offa, moneyer Eadnoth (runic letters). (diam. 1.6cm) *The Fitzwilliam Museum, Cambridge*

sea by northern pirates, and a year later Jarrow was also attacked. Three ships of Norwegians from Hardanger Fjord arrived at Portland and slew the reeve of Dorchester. England, finding herself vulnerable, no doubt hurried to strengthen her regional defence commands. In representing East Anglia's right towards Mercia, Æthelberht presumably allied himself to a Wuffing dynastic claim.

In *c*.792 Lul the moneyer issued a silver penny on which he and Æthelberht are named above a portrait head (obverse), and the title REX stands above a framed image of Romulus and Remus suckling the she-wolf. That allusion to the foundation-legend of Rome was borrowed by Lul, perhaps at Æthelberht's suggestion, from the fourth-century *Urbs Roma* type of the Imperial coinage. Hitherto only Beonna, during the 750s, had issued coins naming the independent East Anglian ruler as *Rex*. Æthelberht's coin, long known only from a single example, was an ambitious production. It suggests that he did claim to be one of the Wuffings, whose tally showed their descent from Cæsar (after Woden), and to whom the image of wolf-children may have held totemic family resonance. Its *Romanitas* echoed the imperial intentions of Charlemagne, who was guided in English affairs and in many other matters by Alcuin.

This theory has taken a new turn, for a unique coin of King Offa also struck by Lul, and showing the suckling twins, has been found at Needham Market. Lul again uses runic letters for his own name, which appears on the reverse where REX is inscribed on Æthelberht's issue. Latin characters are employed for Offa's name and title, which surround a portrait bust. The findspot seems to bring the dealings between Æthelberht and Offa into the Gipping valley, where both had strong interests in the affairs and communications of Gipeswic. Perhaps Offton's claim that Offa sometimes resided there is not unrealistic: from such a vantage he might have overseen Gipeswic and the behaviour of Æthelberht.

Penny of Æthelberht II, *c*.792, moneyer Lul. (diam.1.6cm) *The British Museum*

Penny of King Offa, *c*.792, moneyer Lul. *The Fitzwilliam Museum, Cambridge*

The *Anglo-Saxon Chronicle* records that in 794 Offa ordered Æthelberht's head to be struck off. The reputed scene, a royal dwelling at Sutton Walls near Hereford, became home to a patron-cult of St Æthelberht. A late thirteenth-century latten inlay from the tomb of St Thomas Cantelupe at Hereford Cathedral depicts him seated holding his crowned head above his lap. The deliberate execution of one king by another (as opposed to death in battle) is very unusual. At Sutton Hoo, groups of secondary burials (excavated as 'sandmen' under the guidance of Martin Carver), which surround a probable gallows site, indicate that judicial execution by hanging and beheading was carried on in Suffolk in Offa's time and later. A demonstrative overlord might exact such penalties at Rædwald's tomb in symbolic degradation of the Wuffing state.

Æthelberht's romance sends him to Offa's court to seek his daughter's hand in marriage. (Where the kings of Wessex and Northumbria had won Offa's favour, an East Anglian might have hoped to follow.) He conceives the plan in consultation with his thegns, and explains his intentions to his mother queen Leofruna at Beodricesworth. In the *Passio Sancti Athelberhti* preserved in a twelfth-century manuscript (based on traditions collected around Hereford), two of his company entertained him on his journey with royal songs about his lineage. He rewards them with a bracelet and the promise of other gifts on their return home. Sam Newton warms to this reference to a lost body of Wuffing genealogical verse. Such literature must have fuelled East Anglian expectations.

The later *Lives* fix the crime upon Offa's queen, Cynethryth. Claiming that his wooing-journey is a pretext to survey Mercian defences, she urges her husband to secure East Anglia by destroying the prince. Offa angrily refuses and welcomes him with feasting, music and dancing. In one account Cynethryth has a pit dug beneath a seat in his bedchamber; when Æthelberht retires he falls in and is stifled by her villainous agents. Roger of Wendover, who selected this version for his chronicle, was eager to show obedience to his abbey (St Albans) and to honour its royal founder. He also includes the fictitious story of Offa's pilgrimage to Rome. The older truth is that Offa ordered Æthelberht to be beheaded. The legend concludes that Offa mustered a large force and subdued East Anglia. Early chronicles do not record this action, but local tradition rumours that Offa fought a battle at Blood Hill in Claydon near Gipeswic.

The response in East Anglia was invocatory: a martyr-cult was rapidly promoted through numerous dedications to Æthelberht. The sites of one at Falkenham overlooking the lower Deben (later a berewick of Walton, the Roman fort estate, and associated with Rochester) and another at the presumed royal dwelling at Albrighteston, Bramford, suggest patronage by the indigenous East Anglian powers. An important dedication stood at Hoxne, a possession of the bishops of Elmham, and there are others in Suffolk at Herringswell, Tannington and Hessett. One at Larling (Norfolk) shows a contemporary connection. A delicately-sculpted bone plaque found in the churchyard, perhaps from a book-cover or small casket, includes a detail of the Romulus and Remus scene very like Lul's die, the wolf's face lowered and frontal. Somehow this image is tied up with the confrontation between Offa and Æthelberht.

Very accomplished stone-sculptors were then employed, probably by Offa, to create decorative shrines and friezes for the abbey at Medeshamstede, for the tombs of the Mercian royal saints Cyneburh and Cyneswith (daughters of Penda) at Castor nearby, and elsewhere. The stone hilltop church at Breedon monastery (where Tatwine had lived), overlooking the Trent valley in north-west Leicestershire, already possessed superb friezework by a sculptor, probably not English, closely familiar with Byzantine and Syrian art. The Medeshamstede

Ivory plaque from a box or book-cover, found near the Church of St Æthelbert, Larling (Norfolk). *Norwich Castle Museum: Norfolk Museum Service*

sculptors knew this work, and developed it: the Gandersheim casket might be their work, and the Larling plaque resembles it. Such artistic endowments presented a magnificent aspect to Offa's kingdom. He is credited with having re-founded St Albans Abbey (Verulamium) at the first British martyr's tomb, in atonement for Æthelberht's death. The legend of his discovery of St Alban's bones is doubtful, but Offa understood the Christian primacy of this site, and brought that into his kingdom's service. In the south-west, he founded a nunnery at Winchcombe (Glos.).

The death of King Offa

In the year of Æthelberht's execution a new insurrection arose in Kent led by Eadberht, nicknamed Præn. His dynastic claim is unknown, but may have been distant from Wihtred's descendants. Kent and East Anglia no doubt remembered their former alliances. Alfhun, as Bishop of Dommoc until his death in 798, witnessed Offa's last subjection of East Anglia. The moneyer Lul continued to issue East Anglian coins for Offa. Moneyers often survived serving rebel kings and were not necessarily implicated in revolt, despite their important role. Offa died in 796, at the height of his authority, as Kent was gathering towards Eadberht.

ECGFRITH, KING OF MERCIA 796, OVERLORD OF EAST ANGLIA

Ecgfrith, Offa's anointed son, inherited his father's power but died only a few months later: and so the male bloodline from Eowa, so carefully developed by Æthelbald and Offa for 80 years, was suddenly eclipsed. If he ever issued an East Anglian coinage, which is extremely doubtful, no example survives to show it.

EADWALD, ?790s–810s
COENWULF, KING OF MERCIA 796-821, OVERLORD OF EAST ANGLIA

The Mercian dynastic crisis gave an opportunity to the East Angles, and to all of Offa's other dependencies. In Northumbria, King Æthelred was almost immediately murdered, and his rival Eardwulf, favoured by Charlemagne, was consecrated his successor. Eadberht Præn, who had earlier issued his own three-line coinage using Jænberht's Canterbury mint, was in revolt in Kent. Beorhtric in Wessex looked isolated. Mercia soon found a new blood-claimant in Coenwulf, a descendant of Penda's brother Coenwalh. Coenwulf's father Cuthbert was perhaps the ealdorman to whom Abbot Beonna of Medeshamstede leased 10 farms at Swineshead (Lincs.) in his suspicious charter of 777.

The East Angles now obtained King Eadwald as their ruler, who issued a series of coins in his own name. They were minted by Wihtred and Lul in the style of their three-line issues for Offa, and by Eadnoth, some of whose designs were like Lul's. Eadnoth also produced circumscription types for Eadwald. Wihtred's reverse showed his name in a fully runic inscription between the arms of a centrally-voided cross. Examples of Eadwald's pennies have been found at Ipswich, Coddenham, Wetheringsett and Brandon in Suffolk; at Norwich, Oxborough, Cringleford and Sedgeford in Norfolk; at Tilbury and Richborough; and as far away as Bidford-on-Avon, a productive site in Warwickshire. With three moneyers providing such circulation, King Eadwald seems more successfully established than Æthelberht. His coinage and his moneyers belong to the period following 796.

The old suggestion that Eadwald was related to Ecgberht of Wessex is not proven. If Ecgberht's father, Ealhmund, had been established in Kent before 784, a friendly connection between the dynasties is possible. Ecgberht was exiled to Charlemagne's court for three years from 789-92, but returned while Beorhtric was still ruling in Wessex. Eadwald's coinage is not extensive, and Lul and Wihtred are soon found minting for Coenwulf, together with Botred, who had also worked for Offa. Coenwulf showed his mettle by harrying the people of Kent and Romney Marsh, and suppressed their revolt in 798. He captured King Eadberht, led him bound and mutilated into Mercia, and gave the kingdom of Kent to his own brother Cuthred. A fine portrait-penny of Cuthred (d. 807) was excavated at Burrow Hill.

Loyalty of the East Anglian Church
Increasingly, it is in the life of their Church that one sees the East Anglian protest for independence. Bishop Alhheard of Elmham had attended the Legatine Council in 786 with Heardred, Alfhun's predecessor, and had therefore witnessed

Penny of Eadwald (c.796-?), moneyer Eadnoth. (diam. 1.9cm) *The Fitzwilliam Museum, Cambridge*

the kingdom's changing fortunes. In 798, within his more northerly diocese, it was decided to disinter the body of Wihtburh, the former royal abbess of East Dereham, who had died there in 743. The purpose was no doubt to enshrine her and to create a focus of veneration for the last of the daughters of King Anna. As sister of the foundresses of Ely and Sheppey, her body might be a potent symbol of the Wuffing and Æscing dynastic rights and a reminder of Mercia's former aggressions. Wihtburh was found miraculously free from corruption after 55 years in the tomb. In the same year Bishop Alfhun died, and was buried at Dommoc.

The *Anglo-Saxon Chronicle* records that Alfhun died at Sudbury. Archaeology has revealed the presence of a large Iron Age ditch, but not, as yet, the Anglo-Saxon defences implied by 'burgh', a fortified stronghold, at Sudbury. Its important relation to the Stour is manifest, a frontier citadel with its west side around the church of St Gregory facing across into Essex. The site controls access of river transport upstream towards the confluence of the river Glem at Long Melford, where there is also a significant road intersection. (Hadleigh, called a royal *vill* during the next century, similarly controls the upper reaches of the Brett.) The dedication to Gregory in such a place surely belongs to the earliest phases of Christian rulership, perhaps part of the work of Felix; a religious foundation added to an existing royal stronghold of strategic importance during the seventh century. Sudbury has a long market tradition, its marketplace set back at the central road convergence beside St Peter's church. Here is a prime candidate for one of those 'hinterland wics' of which we have heard, especially if St Gregory's possessed a clerical or monastic community placed (like St Peter or St Mildred at Gipeswic) so as to oversee trade. A large patron residence was no doubt associated, which King Eadwald's bishop might visit in the course of his affairs much as King Ealdwulf's bishops may have done a century earlier. The chronicler of 798 named Sudbury knowing that it was a place worth mentioning even in so concise a record.

Archbishop Æthelheard had to abandon Canterbury during Eadberht Præn's revolt, but returned in 798. The creation of the Archbishopric of Lichfield had broken Pope Gregory's original intention to establish two archbishops' seats in England, one at York and one in London (for which Canterbury, where Augustine died, had been substituted). To some, the heathen assaults on Lindisfarne and Jarrow, and the early death of Ecgfrith, seemed to show divine displeasure at the creation of a third. Coenwulf opened communication with Pope Leo III, seeking to revoke the Lichfield archbishopric but to transfer the Canterbury see to London (within Mercian control). After Charlemagne's coronation as Holy Roman Emperor had proceeded in 800, Æthelheard travelled to Rome in 801, and was given hospitality at Alcuin's cell of St Judoc near Quentovic on his way there. In the following year he received papal confirmation of his authority over all the historic dominions of Canterbury. At a council at Clofesho in 803 it was decreed that Augustine's see should not again be diminished, and the Lichfield archbishopric was to be held invalid. The transfer to London was not sanctioned, and Hygeberht of Lichfield had already resigned.

The diocese of Dommoc was represented in these decisions by its new bishop, Tidfrith, who succeeded Alfhun in 798 and held it until at least 816. Bishop Tidfrith was among the first who, upon election, was required to make a written declaration in Latin of his orthodox belief and obedience to his archbishop, and this text still survives in a collection headed by the profession of Bishop Eadwulf of Lindsey. Eadwulf boldly announced his allegiance to the see of St Augustine, despite the earlier example of some others. Tidfrith, having affirmed the single Divine Being of God in the three Persons of the Trinity, follows Eadwulf in stating to Æthelheard his lifelong obedience to the see of Canterbury in all its authority everywhere. Thus, the leading churchmen of Coenwulf's dependent provinces declared their loyalty to Canterbury even before the Lichfield see was reduced to its former status. Tidfrith and Bishop Alhheard were present together at Clofesho in 803 to ratify the important declaration, along with their parties of attendant clergy.

The East Anglian bishops derived support from Alcuin, whose influence in Charlemagne's court had become most pervasive. An abbot named Lull, who ruled one of the monasteries in the Dommoc diocese, had visited Alcuin abroad (probably as Tidfrith's emissary) to explain the condition of the East Anglian Church. Abbot Lull also told him of a distinguished (but otherwise unknown) East Anglian named Ardberht. Alcuin wrote a letter to Tidfrith and Alhheard, referring to his meeting, encouraging them in their duties and asking for their prayers. Two abbots from the Dommoc diocese, Lull and Wulfheard, accompanied Tidfrith to Clofesho in 803, together with the priests Ceolhelm, Cynulf, Eadberht and Tilberht. Alhheard was accompanied by two deacons, Beornhelm and Hunferth, and the priests Eadberht, Folcberht, Freothoberht and Wulflaf. Professor Whitelock inferred from this that the two most important monasteries in East Anglia were probably in the diocese of Dommoc, and thought deacon Hunferth probably the same who later became Bishop of Elmham. It was unusual for so full a list of churchmen to be recorded among those attending a Council.

Was Abbot Lull the same person as the moneyer Lul? The name was not uncommon, and one can only speculate. Lull's role as abbot, emissary to Alcuin and episcopal attendant makes him a central and trusted figure. Coenwulf was the last king for whom Lul the moneyer minted coins. Coenwulf's East Anglian pennies carry a portrait on the obverse, with the regal legend (COENWULF REX M) circumscribed in Latin characters. The design is basically like those of Canterbury, showing a centralised policy. On the reverse, Lul's name as usual appeared in a large quatrefoil with one letter in each leaf and a cross in the fourth: that was the style imitated by Eadnoth for King Eadwald. Botred and Wihtred, working for Coenwulf, generally placed their own names surrounding a central motif or crosslet contained in a circle, and this was adopted by a new moneyer named Hereberht. Another, Wodel, arranged the letters of his name more freely around the arms of a cross, and Wihtred used similar designs. A moneyer named Wighere briefly appears. Lul's coins were of higher quality than the others, some of which were quite crude. Botred, Wihtred, Hereberht and Wodel, and another named Werbald, all continued to mint in East Anglia into the following Mercian reign.

Penny of Coenwulf (796-821), moneyer Wodel. (diam. 1.8cm) *The British Museum*

Penny of Coenwulf (796-821), moneyer Wihtred. (diam. 1.8cm) *The Fitzwilliam Museum, Cambridge*

Mercian power confronting the Church

The general acclamation of King Ecgberht in Wessex in 802, following the death of Beorhtric, ended the Mercian ascendancy there. In the first years of the ninth century Coenwulf, having stabilised Kent and East Anglia, was preoccupied with Northumbria. Alcuin and Charlemagne had taken an interest in its extremely confused dynastic feuding. In around 800 Coenwulf gave hospitality to a rival of King Eardwulf's, Ealhmund, who was gathering an army in readiness to attack Northumbria. Eardwulf pre-empted him, invaded Mercia and slew Ealhmund, who was commemorated by the Mercians as St Alkmund at Derby, then called *Northworthig*, in a church dedicated to him. The richness of ninth-century carvings found there, some by sculptors who also produced works at Repton and Breedon, shows that Ealhmund's cult became important to Mercia: several decades later his church was thought a noble place to be buried. Ealhmund's father Ealhred was the king who had sent Alubert to the Old Saxons some 30 years before. Although Eardwulf was deposed in 808, he was protected in exile by Charlemagne at Nymwegen, and reinstated in the same year with the Emperor's help: after his death in *c.*810 his son Eanred maintained rule in Northumbria for 30 years.

Wulfred, Æthelheard's archdeacon, succeeded him at Canterbury in 805 and held it until his death in 832. After Cuthred's death in 807 the Kentish succession remained under Mercian control and devolved upon Baldred, possibly Cuthred's son, who ruled there into the mid-820s. Wulfred introduced to Canterbury a reform of communal life for the cathedral clergy – the priests or canons attending the bishop – using the code which Chrodegang, Boniface's successor, had compiled for his cathedral at Metz. Canon life was becoming loosely observed. Although communal, it differed from the contemplative life of monks, and clear distinctions between them had been decreed at the Legatine Council of 786. Through the influence of Alcuin (who died in 804), the English Church was seeking renewal by the continental example. Wulfred declared his reform in a charter of 813. The Emperor died in 814, and was succeeded by his son Louis the Pious (r.814-40). Three years later at the synod of Aachen, Louis further decreed that the Rule of St Benedict should be universal for the life of monks (but not the canon clergy) within his empire.

The East Anglian dioceses may have attempted their own canon reforms out of allegiance to Canterbury. Both Tidfrith and Alhheard were fully aware of their apostolic debt to St Felix and his royal patrons, an obligation newly acknowledged in the translation of St Wihtburh within Alhheard's episcopacy. We have seen that South Elmham, centred upon Flixton, was probably the original home of the *Helmham* bishopric of 673, even if it later migrated to North Elmham. A century on, Bishop Alhheard therefore possessed at South Elmham an ecclesiastical centre of twofold apostolic meaning for East Anglian Christianity. Its unusual structure of small parishes forming a deaconry might suggest a complex functioning in relation to its collegiate clergy. When Alhheard brought two deacons, but no abbots, to Clofesho in 803, the presbyters in their company were presumably of their canon community, as presbyters are described in the articles of the Legatine Council.

Deacon Hunferth apparently progressed to be Bishop of Elmham. Bishop Sibba is recorded in 814, and probably soon after this Hunferth succeeded him. His profession made to Archbishop Wulfred is the first to survive for the Elmham bishopric. The text is composed in rhythmical phrases: even in so short a document we have a clue to the Elmham style. First he explains the custom of Profession. He speaks of God's merciful appearance in the flesh, and of the procurement by His Sacred Blood of the Holy Catholic Church, to which He has sent prophets and elected teachers to maintain orthodoxy of faith. When divine providence destines (*praedestinat*) a man to be ordained bishop he must show, by a text of obedience, that he has learnt right belief and religious life, and recognises his duties impartially. The allusion to Sacred Blood echoes the trauma of Æthelberht's martyrdom some 20 years earlier. One can believe that the royal martyr was invoked in prayer with indignant fervour in the community to which Hunferth was so long attached.

East Anglian and Kentish interests were embedded in church and dynasty. Queen Seaxburh, who was buried at Ely, remained a powerful symbol of that alliance. The houses of Reculver, Minster-in-Thanet and Wakering (in Essex), as well as her own house at Sheppey from which Eormenhild and Werburgh had succeeded her at Ely, could all see her in the light of a patroness. The cult of Mildred was observed at Gipeswic. Following the last great Council of the Mercian supremacy, in 816 at Chelsea, a very dramatic dispute arose between Archbishop Wulfred and King Coenwulf. This related directly to two of these Kentish houses, Reculver and *Suthmynstre* (Minster-in-Thanet). The argument reached its height in the last years of Tidfrith's episcopate.

Coenwulf was then campaigning in Wales towards Snowdonia and in Dyfed. He had taken over certain possessions and rights at Reculver in Kent, founded by Ecgberht (Seaxburh's son) in 669, which possessed a magnificent early stone church. It was to the abbot of Reculver that Ealhmund, probably father of King Ecgberht of Wessex, had granted land without reference to Offa in 784. Now Coenwulf's daughter Cwendritha had become abbess of *Suthmynstre* in Thanet. She was also probably abbess of Winchcombe in Gloucestershire, Offa's nunnery foundation of 787, where in 798 Coenwulf had added a monastery of monks. Cwendritha acquired possessions of Winchcombe, to which the mausoleum of Coenwulf and his family was soon attached, and at which important Mercian records were held. Reculver and Southminster had become secularised monasteries, their revenues and domestic rule now directly in the hands of a Mercian royal proprietress. Wulfred, spurred by the Frankish reform of 817 decreeing universal Benedictine observance, claimed 'lordship' of these communities with their lay clergy. Coenwulf reacted furiously, even seeking to enlist papal support, and Wulfred was effectively disbarred from his duties until an agreement, not very favourable, was imposed upon him in 821, the year of Coenwulf's death. Coenwulf would not bow the head to Canterbury, because he knew that the spiritual might of Louis' Empire, and the dynastic pretensions of the king of Wessex, stood behind it.

ÆTHELSTAN, ?821-45
CEOLWULF, KING OF MERCIA 821-3, OVERLORD OF EAST ANGLIA

Coenwulf died near the Welsh borders in 821. He was in due course succeeded by his brother Ceolwulf, who was consecrated King by Wulfred at Canterbury. The one great action of his reign was to continue the assault on Wales, reducing the kingdom of Powys to subjection. Although the *Anglo-Saxon Chronicle* makes Ceolwulf his brother's immediate successor, legend (summarised, for instance, by Wendover) interposes the story of St Kenelm, son of Coenwulf, a child-king (*cynebearn*) who was murdered shortly after his accession. Cwendritha, who had been a central player in the drama relating to Minster and Reculver, is made the villain of the legend. Her lover is Æscberht, the tutor of Cynhelm (Kenelm), and she incites him to murder her young brother. He conceals the headless corpse in a cow-bothy in Clent, but the crime is revealed miraculously in Rome when a dove drops a parchment inscribed with a couplet of Anglo-Saxon verse on the altar of St Peter's. When the body is discovered and brought to Winchcombe, Cwendritha rejoices by reciting backwards from the Psalter. Thereupon her eyes burst out onto the page from which she reads and incants her devilish inversion of the holy text.

This disturbing narrative might be well-received in East Anglia. Perhaps a son of Ceonwulf's named Cynhelm did fall victim to dynastic feuding and was buried at Winchcombe. Nothing in contemporary sources supports the story. In the west, Cwendritha's land-grants caused wrangles between the double monastery of Winchcombe and the canon community of Worcester for several decades. A rood-screen painting of St Kenelm from Woodbridge shows that the cult was renewed in East Anglia during the later Middle Ages. Kenelm's legend no doubt also encouraged opposition to Mercian authority in the west, where the oldest monasteries like Much Wenlock remembered the patronage of independent rulers and their former East Anglian friendships.

East Anglian impatience was growing, but Mercia competed with its subject states. Stone minsters on the western Fen Edge at Edenham and South Kyme (Lincs.) were enriched with ornamental sculpture in Coenwulf's time, probably for Mercian royal patrons. Six magnificent brooches found at Pentney (Norfolk), with representations of the 'Anglian' biped creatures, show artistic links both to these and to sculpture continuing at Medeshamstede. Little survives to show similar developments at Ely. The East Angles had no freestone nor a school of sculptors, but doubtless they had other artistic wealth. The church dedication

at March (Cambs.) to the otherwise shadowy St Wendreda suggests that this
Cwendritha established a religious house there. March, a western Fen isle
smaller than Ely, must have been occupied before, but this expansion from
Medeshamstede would remind the East Angles of Mercian interests in Ely.
Hence the conflicting portraits of Cwendritha as saint and murderess may reflect
early ninth-century rivalry between the East Angles and Mercians.

The Brandon finds revealed the comparative prosperity of an East Anglian
patron-centre in the age of Mercian dominion. A more widespread prosperity
is suggested by the metal tags which formed part of the secular costume. These
decorative strap-terminals for the tunic or overshirt were worn throughout the
English regions. Usually of bronze (more rarely silver), they are commonly about
1cm wide and perhaps 4cm long, with an animal-head terminal and ornamented
on one flat surface. Many Suffolk examples show a distinctive regional style,
with tiny silver-wire spirals set into inlaid fields of black niello, doubtless very
smart when newly-made and polished. Their distribution, especially around the
estuaries and inner reaches of the Deben, Orwell and Gipping, may partly reflect
patterns of modern collecting.

Other types without niello and silver are reported from the same areas, and
their focuses of distribution reinforce the impression of middle or wealthier
status activity at such places as Badwell Ash, Ixworth, Icklingham, Freckenham

Four Suffolk strap-ends, from Chelmondiston and Felixstowe (eighth- to ninth-century). *Ipswich Borough Museums*

and Brandon. Their variety within general design principles suggests the emergence of a class habitually so attired, and perhaps engaged in clerical, professional, courtly or mercantile affairs. Their miscellaneous distribution suggests the mobility of their wearers, or of their vendors. Spurs are extremely rare in this period, but a group of examples found in Suffolk at Yaxley, Pakenham and Icklingham indicate specialised horsemanship. Like the strap-ends they have soft-featured animal-head terminals with large round ears, a much-repeated motif in East Anglian metalwork through the ninth century.

Ceolwulf clearly expected to maintain authority in East Anglia, where Coenwulf's moneyers continued to mint portrait coins for him, styled 'Rex M' – King of the Mercians. Wihtred, Hereberht and Wodel adopted a new reverse with the moneyers' name written in three lines between crook-ended bars: Werbald did likewise, but without the bars and somewhat randomly. Botred is presumed the same as 'Fotred', who maintained a circumscription reverse for Coenwulf and Ceolwulf. A new moneyer (with a career ahead of him) was Eadgar, perhaps identical with another who wrote his name 'Eacga'. Since Ceolwulf's reign lasted only two years, there appear to have been at least six mints running concurrently in East Anglia in his time: Wihtred and Botred

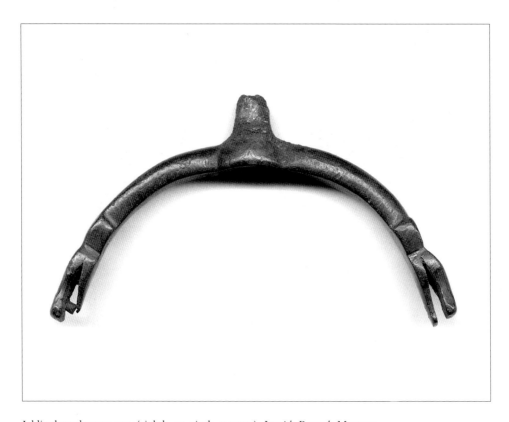

Icklingham: bronze spur (eighth- to ninth-century). *Ipswich Borough Museums*

Penny of Ceolwulf (821-823), moneyer Wodel. (diam. 1.9cm) *The Fitzwilliam Museum, Cambridge*

Ship-type penny of Æthelstan, ?*c*.821, moneyer Eadgar. *Norwich Castle Museum: Norfolk Museum Service*

had both struck for Offa. Without its coinage, and the scrupulous caution of numismatists, ninth-century East Anglian chronology would be extremely bare. On existing evidence, specialists hesitate to connect King Eadwald's moneyer Eadnoth with another of that name who worked in East Anglia after 823. We cannot safely infer that Eadwald was still ruling in Ceolwulf's time.

Indeed, there is a rival claimant for that distinction. Marion Archibald's study of a coin of King Æthelstan, who ruled after 827, suggests he was in place as early as 821. He might well have emerged in the uncertain times surrounding Kenelm's death. The penny, found at West Harling (Norfolk), was struck by Eadgar and shows the king's name and title, 'RE+', circumscribed around the image of a ship, a type unprecedented in Anglo–Saxon broad–flan coinage. It has a high silver standard, 94 per cent, but the dies are crudely cut, setting it apart from other Æthelstan/Eadgar issues. It imitates Carolingian 'ship' deniers minted in small numbers at Quentovic and Dorestad in the last years of Charlemagne and the early years of Louis, who succeeded in 814: it most resembles Louis' Dorestad type. East Anglia's long-established maritime trading partnership informed the monetary expression of Æthelstan's aspiration to kingship. It was a harbinger of much greater things to come. Ceolwulf was deposed as King of Mercia after two years' rule, in 823.

7

The triumph of faith

ÆTHELSTAN, ?821-845
BEORNWULF, KING OF MERCIA 823-5, OVERLORD OF EAST ANGLIA

The powers which overthrew Ceolwulf set Beornwulf in his place. Roger of Wendover tells that Beornwulf 'claimed the kingdom of East-Angles as his own from the time of Offa, and was ever seeking to invade it'. Does that mean he claimed it as Offa's successor, or did so even when Offa was ruling? His name suggests a connection with Beornred, expelled from Mercia by Offa in 757, and so also with King Beonna, from whom a prior Mercian claim in East Anglia might be derived. The later Mercian Kings Beorhtwulf and Burgred could be members of the same family, a Mercian 'B-dynasty'. Had Beornwulf long fomented his plot, as Wendover suggests? A Mercian ealdorman Beornwulf was a junior witness to a charter for Coenwulf in 812, and again for Ceolwulf in 823 on the eve of his fall. We know from the *Anglo-Saxon Chronicle* that there was a king and 'court' in East Anglia during Beornwulf's overlordship, and that they opposed him. That king may well have been Æthelstan.

Coinages of Offa, Coenwulf and Ceolwulf were struck in Kent, East Anglia and London, but Beornwulf has only East Anglian issues, apart from one or two doubtful London strikes. His power was therefore heavily dependent upon that control. Wihtred, Botred, Hereberht and Wodel did not strike for him and cease to appear, leaving Eadgar ('a notoriously careless moneyer') and Werbald using three-line reverses similar to those they produced for Ceolwulf. These portrait issues in the Mercian style were also struck by Eacga (?Eadgar) and two new moneyers, Monna and Eadnoth (?II), with circumscribed reverses around a cross-crosslet in the central circle. They foreshadow the typical ninth-century circumscription obverse and reverse. In Beornwulf's time Baldred ruled in Kent with Mercian support and issued coinage along similar lines.

Penny of Beornwulf (823-25), moneyer Werbald. (diam. 1.9cm) *The British Museum*

Suffolk's Church was in transformation. At Dommoc Bishop Wermund had succeeded Tidfrith sometime after 816 and attended Clofesho in 824 where he witnessed a charter. His tenure was brief, for in 825 his successor Wilred appears first as *electus* (chosen but not yet consecrated) and then as bishop. Wilred's installation at Dommoc may signal an independent turn in East Anglian affairs: he was Æthelstan's bishop for many years afterwards. Some sources have Hunberht already Bishop of Elmham in 824, who apparently survived until 869. Forty-five years is a long but not impossibly long tenure: otherwise his name may be mistaken for Hunferth's in 824, or perhaps was later borrowed from an imperfect list for inclusion in Eadmund's legend. At the Council of Summer 825 the remaining business of Wulfred's dispute was mostly resolved. At that moment Beornwulf's authority was still acknowledged in East Anglia, Kent, Essex and Middlesex.

Ecgberht, by right and consent King of the West Saxons, great-great-grandson of Ingeld brother of King Ine, of the bloodline of Cerdic, had held his throne for 21 years when Beornwulf seized the kingdom of Mercia. Thirty-four years had passed since King Offa sent him into exile, where he received direct impressions of Charlemagne's occult magnificence. The long period of his early reign in Wessex included a military campaign in 815 which placed Cornwall under his lordship, just over a century after Ine had done the same in Devon. If Arthurian legends were nurtured there, as by Nennius in his collections, they may have implanted Britannic ideals in Ecgberht's vision of rule. He maintained independence from Coenwulf: now Beornwulf's accession showed Mercian rulership divided by feud and increasingly remote from ancestral legitimacy.

Late in 825, Beornwulf having attacked Ecgberht, their armies met at *Ellandun* near Swindon and Beornwulf was defeated amidst great slaughter on both sides.

Ecgberht, his strategy already prepared, sent a large army into Kent led by his son Æthelwulf, Wulfheard ealdorman of Hampshire, and Ealhstan, a fighting man consecrated Bishop of Sherborne in 817. This military, royal and spiritual ensemble fell upon King Baldred and drove him north across the Thames. The people of Kent, and those of Surrey, Sussex and Essex, submitted to Ecgberht because (so the *Anglo-Saxon Chronicle* states) they had been forced away wrongly in the past from their allegiance to Ecgberht's kinsmen (meaning presumably Ealhmund his father, suppressed after 784). That is the language of the victor: the West Saxon conquest is portrayed as a liberation.

'In the same year the King of East Angles and his court turned to Ecgberht as protector and guardian against the fear of Mercian aggression ...' It is typical of the *Anglo-Saxon Chronicle* to give so grudgingly brief a notice of a great East Anglian event. After the foregoing silence we are gratified to learn that they even had a king, let alone a court to endorse and carry through so mighty a decision. If not already rebellious what did they have to fear other than the militarisation of their southern boundary? Beornwulf, so weakened at Ellendun, failed to deter their revolt. Expecting his hostility the king and court made a stand for independence trusting in Ecgberht's support. Ecgberht assented to their request and readily engaged to stand by his petitioners to the end (adds Florence of Worcester). Their expectations were soon realised: 'In the same year the East Angles slew Beornwulf, King of the Mercians,' the *Chronicle* notes. Beornwulf may well have died during an expedition into the kingdom to coerce them into allegiance, as Florence and others record.

ÆTHELSTAN, ?821-45
LUDICA, KING OF MERCIA 825-7

Despite their success, the East Angles did not immediately throw off their Mercian overlords. Beornwulf was succeeded by one of his ealdormen, Ludica, who had risen to importance only during the year preceding these events. It is impossible to tell whether the embattled Mercians chose him by right of blood or expectation of leadership: perhaps both. The tiny number of his surviving coins were all struck by the same East Anglian moneyers who had worked for Beornwulf – Eadgar, Eadnoth and Werbald – but at present there is no example by Monna. These were portrait issues with circumscription reverses, apart from Werbald's, who kept his three-line reverses as before. Werbald, who first struck for Coenwulf, does not (on present evidence) appear for the East Anglian kings Eadwald or Æthelstan. Was he a Mercian partisan? The evidence is too scanty to be sure.

The sizeable hoard from Delgany (Co. Wicklow, Ireland), deposited *c*.828, contained East Anglian coins of Ludica and his predecessors but none of his East Anglian successor Æthelstan. On this evidence the East Anglian coinage

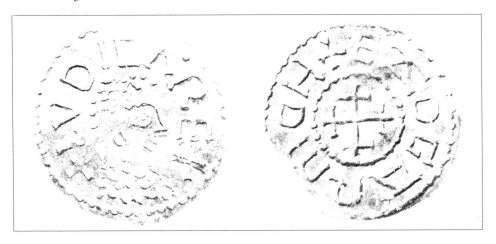

Penny of Ludica (825-827), moneyer Eadgar. (diam. 2cm) *The Fitzwilliam Museum, Cambridge*

remained under Mercian control, to the exclusion of the local ruler, for a short period further. King Ludica was slain with his five ealdormen in 827, an act which (according to Wendover) was encompassed by King Ecgberht. Ludica's Mercian successor Wiglaf (827-40) produced no East Anglian coins, but those of Æthelstan begin at about this time. The East Angles therefore gained independence of moneying rights from Mercia in 827 in consequence of Ludica's death and Ecgberht's protection.

Æthelstan's reign: Rex Anglorum

Æthelstan maintained control of East Anglia's coinage until the early 840s. The moneyer Werbald ends with Ludica, but Monna, Eadgar and Eadnoth strike for Æthelstan, beginning with circumscription types (often with portraits), Eadgar and Monna sometimes using a three-line reverse. In subsequent issues a barred letter 'A', probably for 'Anglorum', replaced the portrait, making Æthelstan's coinage state a direct claim to his kingship of the Angles, as the Mercian coinage had often used a barred 'M' for 'Merciorum'. This is reinforced by later issues in which the reverse bears the legend 'REX ANG' around a barred letter 'W'. Hence the two faces show A and W, the Christian formula, though one wonders if the W does not also represent literally the overthrown barred M to signify the reversal of Mercian power. These coins have rather primitive lettering and design, and resemble the work of Torhthelm, Rerhelm and Rægenhere who struck in Æthelstan's middle and later periods, sometimes still using runic letters. Raegenhere (an English form of the Danish name Ragnar) also struck in the following reign, and was probably related to Rerhelm (an abbreviated name), both rune-using officials for King Æthelstan.

This title *Rex Anglorum* was therefore used in Æthelstan's middle or later reign, after Ecgberht had completed his assault on Mercian power. Wiglaf,

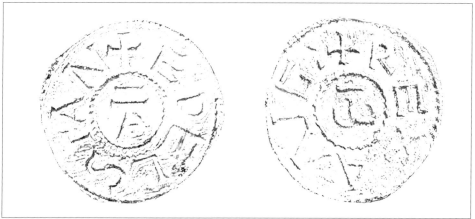

Above top Penny of Æthelstan (*c.*821–845), moneyer Eadnoth. (diam. 1.9cm) *The British Museum*

Above Penny of Æthelstan (*c.*821–845), 'Rex Anglorum' type. (diam. 1.9cm) *The British Museum*

Ludica's successor, reconstructed Mercia after its defeat and recovered part of its former importance. But his first efforts, probably directed against the East Angles, failed when Ecgberht led all his forces against Mercia in 829. The late Crowland historian ('pseudo-Ingulph') makes Wiglaf take refuge there for four months with Abbot Siward. He encounters Offa's daughter, the intended bride of Æthelberht of East Anglia and the cause of Mercia's downfall, now a recluse. Siward intercedes with Ecgberht to reinstate him as a tributary king. More dependable sources show that Ecgberht, leading an army which had already conquered four kingdoms, entered Northumbria in violence and obtained King Eanred's submission and tribute to him as overlord. Ecgberht struck coins at London bearing the style *Rex Merciorum*. In 830 Wiglaf regained Mercia and rebuilt his authority there, but he did not recover East Anglia from Æthelstan nor did the Mercians ever conquer it again.

James Campbell develops the theory that the great epic poem *Beowulf* took shape in Mercia at this time. A Mercian patron is suggested because the poem's references to Offa of Angeln concide with his appearance in the Mercian dynastic tally and reinforce his importance. Charlemagne took a great interest in heroic literature and Offa presumably cultivated it for similar reasons. But Sam Newton has demonstrated the rich East Anglian vein of interest in *Beowulf* and its possible Wuffing affinities. Where the imagery of treasure-ships and funeral hoards find so many echoes between *Beowulf* and Sutton Hoo, he reminds us that such genealogically-based heroic literature is necessarily and causally rooted in the cultures which practised mound-burial of that elaborate kind. If, therefore, we are right in tracing Beornwulf's East Anglian claim back through a 'B' dynasty to Beonna, and perhaps even to Beodric (whose *worth* King Sigeberht occupied at Bury), then East Anglian heroic traditions were in part their own. The poem's closing episode revolves upon Beowulf and his faithful accomplice Wiglaf. Did it finally take shape at King Wiglaf's court in homage to the heroic antecedents of Beornwulf, for whom no tally survives?

Canterbury was adjusting to new masters. Despite his conflict with Coenwulf, Archbishop Wulfred had gained a settlement under Beornwulf: but he ceased to mint coins altogether when Ecgberht began to issue them in Kent, and Ecgberht seized certain Canterbury possessions. In 832 Wulfred died, and after an interval he was succeeded by Archbishop Ceolnoth who ruled the see until 870. Within Mercia Wiglaf's power was quickly restored, for in 831 he had authority in Middlesex and had re-established himself in London. He summoned important Councils during the 830s, and the friendship of Ceolnoth was not taken for granted by Ecgberht and Æthelwulf.

Relations between Canterbury and Mercia (especially Lichfield and Worcester) are shown by surviving books which reveal patronage, piety and splendour. They include several prayerbooks for private devotion including the Book of Cerne, the painting of which we have loosely compared to the Brandon plaque of St John. The Book of Cerne was probably made for Bishop Æthelwald of Lichfield (818-30) who introduced reforms there after Archbishop Wulfred's. It has artistic links to the great 'Royal' Bible, a sumptuous volume drawing on Carolingian models, for which either Mercia or Canterbury is a possible origin. The art of both books has counterparts in stone-carvings (crosses and slabs) at Breedon, Derby and Repton, major Mercian sites in the sphere of Tamworth: other carvings at Breedon share the Carolingian mood. But the Brandon plaque does not look to a Mercian artistic precedent, any more than reforms of the Elmham community need have awaited a Mercian initiative. King Æthelstan's relations with Canterbury are unrecorded, but both his bishops, Hunberht of Elmham and Wilred of Dommoc, attended the Council of all bishops south of the Humber *æt Astran* in 839.

In the late sixth century the heirs of Woden had looked upon that divine legendary ancestor as the parent of their blood-right and kingship. The coming of Christianity had effected transformations in arts, law, urban life, literacy, organised commerce, statehood and ecclesiastical structure, all embedded in the East Anglian state. It was therefore in defence of their way of life, their domestic, mercantile, ecclesiastic and royal communities, that the English responded to the onslaught of attacks by murderous pagan warrior-troupes of looters. They were confronted by a terrifying new reality.

To Sheppey in Kent, site of the famous double monastery founded by Queen Seaxburh, a horde of ship-borne Danes came in search of booty, and devastated it, in 835. In the next year 25 ships disgorged hundreds of Danes at Carhampton (near Minehead, beside the Bristol Channel) who fought King Ecgberht there, made a great slaughter, and had possession of the battlefield. A great host came to Cornwall in 838, joined with the British and fought against Ecgberht, who defeated them in a major expedition. These freebooters had been marginalised by the dynastic overlordship which held the Danish peoples together, and formed leagues seeking adventure and plunder. They ransacked Dorestad several times, news of which must soon have reached Gipeswic. At the same time they were assaulting the Frankish and Irish coastlands. As Frisian control of the seaways had declined, the wealthy coastal towns, monasteries and estates of the southern powers lay undefended against the highly-developed Danish raiding longships. They came dedicating their adventures and victims to Odin, a god himself transformed from the Woden of earlier centuries.

King Ecgberht died in 839, and his son Æthelwulf, the conqueror of Kent, became King of Wessex. Æthelstan, Æthelwulf's son, succeeded to the rule of Kent, Surrey and Sussex. Some suggest he was the same man as Æthelstan of East Anglia, and that he now assumed dominion over both kingdoms. This claim, open to endless speculation, cannot be proved: if true, he must have been a very young king in East Anglia. Some wish him to be the brother rather than the son of Æthelwulf (as the northern *Chronicle* variant asserts), but Sir Frank Stenton considered the evidence for such a brother inadequate. There is slight support in Huntingdon's statement, 'the Estangle kingdom was for a period subjected to other rules in various ways: sometimes the kings of Wessex or Kent held it in dominion, and sometimes they gave it to another or to others. Thus at one time there was one king there; at another there were many lesser kings.' A connection with Ecgberht's family is quite possible. Later West Saxon rulers claimed kinship with Eadmund, who ruled East Anglia from 855.

King Æthelstan's late East Anglian coinage was struck for him by Rægenhere, Æthelhelm and Tuduwine. Monn, Eadgar and Eadnoth (the last that had worked for Mercian rulers) retire from the scene, and Torhthelm may appear only in Æthelstan's middle period. In a hoard of over 240 coins deposited in *c*.840-2 and discovered in 1893 at Hare Court, Middle Temple, London, 66 were Kentish, London or East Anglian coins of the time of Beornwulf or earlier. Ecgberht and Æthelwulf's coins mostly account for the rest, with a few for Wiglaf and the archbishops, but a rather high proportion, 39, were East Anglian coins of Æthelstan. Seven of the 'REX ANG' type show he maintained this title during the 830s. Two others bore the king's name on both sides. H.E. Pagan, noting the continuity of moneyers, types and styles into the succeeding reigns, recognised that all were controlled by one minting organisation. Using only one die-cutting workshop at any one time, four or five moneyers worked concurrently, perhaps mainly at Gipeswic. After some interruption, *c.*845, Æthelstan's last moneyers minted for his successor Æthelweard. No coinage is known for the Kentish King Æthelstan.

East Anglia attacked from the sea

The interruption and the burial of this hoard might be connected. In 840 the Viking raiders struck twice on the Wessex coast, attacks involving hundreds of men. At Hamwih, the West Saxon *wic*, the ealdormen and his levies drove them off with great slaughter; but at Portland the men of Dorset were defeated, their ealdorman was slain, and the raiders had possession of the battlefield. In the next year they raged through Lindsey, East Anglia and Kent, while others gained a foothold at Dublin, and also sacked Rouen. In 842 they butchered and plundered in London and Rochester, and Hamwih was struck again. They also crossed the Channel and did the same at Quentovic, the north Frankish port for English traffic. London and Rochester, seats of ancient bishoprics, were home to two of the principal mints. The first Viking sack of London therefore shortly preceded the burial of the Temple hoard, drawn to the sum of one pound from mixed currency. In 843 the Vikings were back at Carhampton near Minehead, and there defeated an English force personally led by King Æthelwulf.

The *Anglo-Saxon Chronicle* tells that many men were slain by the host in the assault on East Anglia of 841. Roger of Wendover describes the Viking force as a marching army. All the other large trading emporia had been ransacked or looted: it seems very likely that Gipeswic, and perhaps the growing settlement of Norwich, the *North wic*, were their targets. In the Blyth estuary the tombs of King Anna and his son probably held precious furnishings free for the taking. The *civitas* of Dommoc, the tombs of the bishops, the church, palace, library and community stood vulnerably beside its haven. All the estuarine settlements from the Stour to the Wash, the long-established centres of wealth and communication around the coast, were similarly exposed. Ely and Medeshamstede must have trembled, if they were not actually attacked through the Fen.

Bishop Wilred of Dommoc and Hunberht of Elmham attended a meeting held by Archbishop Ceolnoth in London in 845. The occupation of the royal estates around Rendlesham was perhaps reshaped in the wake of the 841 raid. Burrow Hill in Butley, its ditches now inconveniently rubbish-filled, seems to be abandoned permanently around this time: and it has the legend of a battle. Did Rendlesham no longer require that seaward vantage-point beside the Butley estuary? At Iken, by the Alde estuary, a related story unfolds. This famous monastery had flourished into the ninth century, though little more than a bronze stylus from neighbouring Sudbourne survives to show it. But by the 940s all of the Wicklaw, from the Orwell to beyond the Alde, and inland to Debenham and Framlingham, was administered from Sudbourne. Had the English rulers of the ninth century – Æthelstan, perhaps – already transferred the focus of their local power to Sudbourne, close by Iken monastery and sheltering in the hinterland of the Ness, the shingle bar between Aldeburgh and Orford? Yet the defence of the Deben was still paramount.

In 1972 Stanley West found part of a stone cross reused as building stone in the medieval fabric of Iken church. This extraordinary object, originally some 3m tall, came from a Midland quarry, and its sculptor was familiar with the crosses made for east Mercian monasteries of the earlier ninth century. It is the only example of that date in Suffolk. Its monolithic rectangular shaft, with carved ornament on all four sides, is shaped into a tenon at the base for fixing into a socket-stone. The top of the shaft and the cross head are broken off and lost. Carvings of whorled dragons on one face and a circular cross-motif on the other establish the date and style of the work. The animals compare in specific details to others at Elstow (Beds.), Glatton (Hunts.) and Moulton (Northants.),

Above left Iken: shaft of a ninth-century stone cross. *Suffolk County Council*

Above right Iken: detail of cross showing animal ornament. *Drawing: Author*

all related to a further example at Brixworth (Northants.). These boldly linear, almost heraldic, Mercian animal-carvings derive their anatomical details from the formal style in late eighth-century English metalwork. They are works in the vernacular manner, not the high-relief sculptural values of the Breedon and Medeshamstede carvings. Brixworth and Elstow had important minsters, and their carvings belong to the early ninth century.

The Iken stone might have been brought to Suffolk for a Roman building and afterwards reused, but it originated in the region where such Anglo-Saxon carving was produced, and may have been specially imported in the ninth century. In either case its transport (?by coast lighter from the Fen) and rearing at Iken demanded immense coordination, not least in loading and unloading. After the 841 raid, new priorities and emergencies affected relations between Mercia and East Anglia. King Beorhtwulf succeeded Wiglaf in Mercia in 840 and in 851 assisted Æthelwulf against the Vikings in Kent. An old statute of Archbishop Theodore's decreed that whenever a church and altar were removed a cross should be erected in that place.

Crosses were raised for many purposes, but this was an exceptional long-distance commission. Two centuries later, Folcard (*Life of Botolph*) heard that Iken was abandoned in 870. The cross itself suggests that the monastery and its inmates fell victim to the Viking assault of 841. Dr West excavated the footings of an earlier wooden building beneath Iken church. The Norman wall was built above a pit containing severed human limbs which were articulated at the time of burial. An iron sword found long ago on Yarn Hill was perhaps a relic of the incident. The series of Beonna's coins from Burrow Hill imply that he'd had interests in this region, perhaps at Rendlesham, Sudbourne or Benhall. Beorhtwulf may have had a family connection with those interests. The Iken cross is a puzzle, but also witness to the continuing fame of Botolph's cult, the rising importance of Sudbourne, and to an act of patronage in which Mercian and East Anglian interests were combined at a high, perhaps royal, level. Botolph's bones remained at Iken until the late tenth century when they were translated to Grundisburgh: during the eleventh they were transferred to Bury St Edmunds.

ÆTHELWEARD, *c*.845-855

Whether King Æthelstan died sometime after 842, or did in fact become the King of Kent in 839 and lived on with authority over both kingdoms, we cannot tell. In either case, East Anglia needed its own leader. Æthelstan of Kent had seen his kingdom raided in his second year, and both Rochester and London sacked in his third. King Æthelwulf could not easily oversee the defence both of Kent and the Devonian peninsula (where the Cornish Welsh joined the pagans against him), though he had Bishop Ealhstan of Sherborne to lead the rout of the Danes at the river Parrett. Neither Wessex nor Kent were adequate bases from which to mount a sudden defence of East Anglia when needed. East Anglian interests were closely allied to Kent's. In Northumbria in 845 a certain Redwulf drove out King Æthelred, Eanred's son, only to be slaughtered at once with most of his followers by a pagan army. Æthelred resumed his rule, but met a similar fate three years later. Under such conditions, unity was essential to the security of East Anglia.

During the 840s a king named Æthelweard obtained control of the minting organisation which had served Æthelstan. Although Æthelweard is not mentioned in early records, he must be considered the primary ruler in East Anglia until the close of his coinage in *c*.855. The issues of the two do not seem to overlap, so either Æthelstan was dead or had relinquished monetary control. Rægenhere, Tuduwine and Æthelhelm resumed their offices, and Æthelhelm was still striking later in the reign when three others named Dudda, Twicga and Eadmund appeared. The coinage of Æthelweard, and of his successor King Eadmund, was well produced and was struck on blanks of a better metallurgical quality than those issued by Æthelwulf and others in Kent during the 850s. Although the central letter 'A' appears on some obverses, Æthelweard is styled 'Rex' but not 'Rex Anglorum'.

No further Viking assault on East Anglia is recorded in his time. The enemy, however, intensified and focused its efforts. The men of Devon repulsed a fresh attack in 850, but in Kent a major threat was looming. That winter for the first time the Danes made their quarters in England, on the Isle of Thanet. We may guess that the monastery of St Mildred and its inmates did not escape their attention, if it had been spared so long. When the winter storms had subsided a fleet of 350 ships, representing an army of perhaps 6,000 men, put in to the mouth of the Thames and stormed both Canterbury and London. King Beorhtwulf, coming with the Mercian army, was defeated and driven off. The Danes then marched into Surrey where the West Saxon armies led by King Æthelwulf and his son Æthelbald met them and had the victory: an immense number of invaders were slaughtered. King Æthelstan of Kent and ealdorman Ealhhere intercepted a large party of Vikings off

Penny of Æthelweard (*c*.845-855), moneyer Twicga. (diam. 2cm) *Ipswich Borough Museums*

Sandwich and fought them in ships. Nine enemy craft were captured and the rest driven off. That is the last real sight of Æthelstan, and Ealhhere died two years later fighting the heathen in Thanet.

There are however three legends relating to Æthelstan: he was killed fighting a Pict called Hungus and his head was impaled on a stake on a sea-girt rock at Queensferry, an object of curiosity for years afterwards; or, he made a pilgrimage to Jerusalem and did not return; or indeed, he retired to a monastery and as (St) Neot became the tutor of Ælfred the Great in his childhood. St Neot's has a suitably East Anglian setting: but in a confusion of Æthelstans, the reader may choose which tale to pin to each of them.

Renewed confidence in southern Suffolk
The Mercian overthrow of 825-7 had changed the political character of the southern East Anglian boundary along the river Stour. Its settlement is concentrated on the north bank, suggesting East Anglian confidence there. Since the late seventh century the East Saxon kingdom had been a satellite of Mercian power. Under King Offa's rule during the 760s, the distinction between the two subject-kingdoms was not dissolved. As we have seen, Sudbury, strongly-defined by 798, stood at a river-crossing and probably owed its foundation to seventh-century royal patronage. After 823-7 the boundary fell under Ecgberht's protection. Under Æthelstan and his successors the river and its Suffolk hinterland became the focus of renewed activity as a province withdrawn from the dangerous coast and sheltering against a friendly border.

Hadleigh, midway between Gipeswic and Sudbury, was as old as either of them (it has early cremations), but its importance is not apparent until the ninth century. It is first mentioned (in the *Annals of St Neots*, as *Headleage*) in *c*.891, when Guthrum, the Danish King of East Anglia, was entombed (*mausoleatus*) at a *villa regia*, a royal dwelling there. The old historian Cox thought that the Anglo-Saxon kings were also buried there. There are persistent reports of masonry foundations, perhaps of a stone church or mausoleum, in the churchyard south of the present church. D.E. Davy recorded in 1827 that a chapel had been excavated there: massive foundations were remembered in 1926, and grave-diggers have since reported similar obstacles. No plan, or evidence of date, exists. There is very little evidence for stone architecture in Suffolk before the tenth century, though North Elmham (Norfolk) may have had an eighth-century structure. Since stone-sculpture of the tenth or early eleventh centuries exists at Aldham (i.e. old *ham*) nearby, Hadleigh's lost church could have been at least that old. If so, it was a very significant building, and at this *villa regia* may have commemorated a much earlier importance.

Metalwork finds suggest wealthy and militarised activity nearby in the decades before Viking occupation. A brooch from Elmsett (near Aldham) shaped as a circular cross with splayed arms was discovered during the 1990s. The form, with a similar smaller cross inset diagonally, is cut out in openwork, and the surface is decorated with animals and interlaced knots in silver inlaid with niello. This is typical work of the early-middle decades of the ninth century, and the main cross outline is closely like that carved on the Iken cross-shaft. A central faceted stud compares to the silver pin-heads of the period, and the clasp-pin is attached with an animal head, like the niello-inlay brooches from Pentney in Norfolk. Another openwork circular-cross brooch with silver-niello foliate ornament, formally very like Elmsett, was found at Chediston on the middle reaches of the river Blyth. These two important recent finds together suggest a silversmith of quality operating in south-east Suffolk in the time of Æthelstan or Æthelweard.

Silverwork of similar kind and date is inlaid on the finger-guard of an English sword found at Kersey, just north-west of Hadleigh. It may well have been lost in a fight: Vikings were then the expected enemy. Swords were always valuable objects, but this ornament reflects the West Saxon fashion of the famous Wallingford (Oxon.) sword, and related silverwork (including horn-mounts) from that region later hoarded as scrap at Trewhiddle in Cornwall, perhaps after a plundering raid. Our sword could show a noble West Saxon visitor presence near Hadleigh, though the style became widespread, and (like the brooch-makers) new finds may enlarge our view of East Anglian production. An English sword

Elmsett: silver-niello openwork disc-brooch. *Ipswich Borough Museums*

recovered from the river Orwell was undecorated. Barham's triangular nielloed fasteners in Trewhiddle style show it busy through the middle of the ninth century. Wealthy folk were also upstream from Sudbury at Poslingford, where one lost a superb gold ring with panels of animal and plant decoration around the hoop. They were perhaps among the early patrons of Clare, which possessed an important religious house before the Norman Conquest.

Gipeswic was the likely point of entry for small circular brooches depicting the bust of a saint, continental imports based on a type known from Paderborn (Germany), which found their way to Barham and to Wetheringsett-cum-Brockford north along the Pye Road. The raids on London, Kent and East Anglia had doubtless been savage and destructive, but Canterbury and London (at least) recovered their minting functions rapidly and restored their former activities. Whatever had befallen it, Gipeswic was facing the need for redevelopment, though some decades and great upheavals passed before it was achieved. The new town laid out in Ælfwald's time had now acquired a dense, crowded appearance: along St Stephen's Lane near its centre, adjacent buildings had walls fronting directly onto the streets as workshops or residences (probably both). In these close quarters, where cattle and livestock were driven along the metalled road past buildings in commercial use, a genuinely urban environment had arisen.

Comb manufacture in Gipeswic reflected changing fashions. Dr Taylor's example from the foot of Providence Street, found with two elegant bone needles, is probably ninth-century, of long bowed form with animal-head finials above at each end. A dog's skeleton from Martin's Bank points to ninth-century domestication. Further from the centre less cluttered habitations were spreading east of Foundation Street. By the end of the century the town centre buildings were being replaced with a new type of cellared house, positioned well back from the streets in more spacious enclosures. At that time town-like environments were also being developed at Beodricesworth, Thetford and Norwich. But in the mid-ninth century Gipeswic was still East Anglia's primary commercial and industrial capital and its gateway to international communications.

Silver-niello ornament from a sword found at Kersey. *Ipswich Borough Museums*

The Potteries, still the town's foremost industry and the most significant production centre in central and eastern England, had spread north-eastwards from Carr Street. Their updraught kilns and increasing control of the wheel had achieved consistent output and very wide distribution. Within 50 years a fast wheel would transform production, introducing shapes with a higher centre of balance and better collaring, the thinner fabric drawn up with even throwing-ridges and a narrower foot achieved without secondary paring, wired off the wheel flat under the base. These improved products, also made at Thetford, were less widely distributed as industries developed elsewhere in the early tenth century. But those developments still lay ahead: meanwhile Rhenish wares from Badorf, Pingsdorf and elsewhere continued to arrive in Gipeswic. The quayside, advancing into the channel through successive siltings and re-embankments, remained the hub of water-borne commerce, where merchants or overseers busied their stevedores and reckoned their wares and tariffs. Gipeswic probably shared the London custom of payment for use of authorised weights and measures.

Clerics from St Mildred's and St Peter's and harbour officials or port-reeves were among the population. Kings and ealdormen must sometimes have inspected their operations. A penny of Æthelweard's was excavated in Gipeswic. If his moneyers struck here, we do not know whereabouts. If (as suggested) Corn Hill was already a market area and administrative focus around St Mildred's Church, it may have been used for public meetings and proclamations. But St Margaret's Green acquired the name Thingstead, showing that in the tenth century if not before it was used for a 'Thing', a formal moot or assembly. On the top side of town, between the principal

Ipswich, Providence/Westgate Street: comb and two needles. *Ipswich Borough Museums*

north roads, this field rose to an apex where Soane Street reaches St Margaret's, perhaps marking an early religious focus to the Thing. In 1200 when Ipswich received its Charter, proclamation took place inside the Viking Age defences at St Mary-le-Tower churchyard. John Fairclough suggests that the Thingstead (close to the Woodbridge road) related to Wicklaw administration, not merely to Gipeswic. But we do not know how this area was used in the ninth century.

In 852 King Beorhtwulf of Mercia died. His son Beorhtferth reputedly murdered Wiglaf's son, Wigstan, who was buried near Wiglaf in the royal mausoleum at Repton and became the subject of a successful martyr-cult. Beorhtwulf was therefore succeeded by Burghred (852-874) who married Æthelswith, King Æthelwulf's daughter, at Chippenham. Mercian and West Saxon friendship was renewed, and in 853 the two kings joined forces to mount a swingeing attack on the Welsh of Powys. But in 854 the Danish host was back in Kent and made winter quarters there a second time, in Sheppey.

Wessex and Mercia in alliance

King Æthelwulf had five sons, namely Æthelstan (of Kent, probably dead by 854), Æthelbald, Æthelberht, Æthelred, and Ælfred. He deposed that they should succeed him in priority of age. Early in 855 he left Æthelbald in charge of Wessex and made a pilgrimage to Rome where he remained a year. During that summer the pagan armies made an appearance in west Mercia around Wroxeter (Salop.). Returning in 856 Æthelwulf stayed with Charles the Bald (King of the West Franks since 840) and married his 13-year-old daughter Judith. Æthelbald and other West Saxon leaders, including Bishop Ealhstan, determined that he should not return as their king. It is claimed that Æthelwulf had taken, or afterwards sent, his youngest son Ælfred to Rome to be anointed his successor, and also that he allowed Judith to sit by him at table as his Queen, a thing intolerable to the West Saxon nation. An agreement was reached that he should rule in Kent and the south-eastern kingdoms and that Æthelbald should rule Wessex. Meanwhile, in 855, the reign of King Æthelweard of the East Angles ended: if this was connected with the crisis in Wessex, there is nothing but the coincidence in date to suggest it.

EADMUND, 855-869

The gold-lustre of legend clings to Eadmund's name, and we struggle to see the man himself for the brightness of it. His most famous contemporary, Ælfred the Great (r.871-899), is remembered as the man who saved and began to rebuild England. Eadmund is his spiritual counterpart, the youthful king as defender of his people's faith, the culminating example of the first great era of English Christianity, and in his martyrdom the consecrated symbol of its passing.

King Eadmund's birth and origins

King Eadmund appears to have succeeded to East Anglian rulership immediately after the end of Æthelweard's reign. With regard to his origins, our earliest authority is Abbo, an eminent churchman who wrote his *Passio Sancti Eadmundi* for the monks of Ramsey, with whom he was staying in 985-7. We are told this is the first written account. On the key question of Eadmund's descent he tells that Eadmund was 'sprung from the noble stock of Old Saxons' (*ex Antiquorum Saxonum nobili prosapia oriundus*). This only means 'East Anglian', for nearby he explains that East Anglia was settled by the Saxons, not the Angles. Abbo adds that Eadmund was descended from a line of kings, but that he was not so much elected from family succession, as seized upon by the unanimous choice of all his fellow countrymen, to rule over them with the sceptre. This formula was meant to emphasise his popularity, not to question his dynastic right. The term *comprovinciales* is decisive that Eadmund was East Anglian, but the expression 'Old Saxons' led some early writers to think he was of continental Saxon, not East Anglian origin. Perhaps, by the late tenth century, they wished to associate him with the Old Saxon connections developed in 928 by the marriage of Otto I and Edith, the children of Henry the Fowler and Eadward the Elder.

Geoffrey of Wells, an early twelfth-century Thetford writer, addressed to Abbot Ording of Bury a collection of stories current in his time. By his account Eadmund was the younger son of a King of the continental Saxons. An East Anglian king named Offa, his kinsman, had no heir and decided to make a pilgrimage to Jerusalem. On his way he visited his kin, formed a liking for Eadmund, and gave him a ring. While returning he became mortally ill, and sent a token (a second ring) to Eadmund to signify that he should inherit East Anglian rule. (Most accept that this story probably arose from a misunderstanding of Abbo's statements. If there was such a person as King Offa, there are no coins and no other records of him: if he was a junior king under Æthelweard, how could he designate East Anglian succession?) Eadmund was brought to *Maydenebure* (Maiden's Bower) in Norfolk, where miracles occurred, and founded a royal dwelling at Hunstanton nearby. He then dwelt at Attleborough (Norfolk) for a year and committed the complete Psalms of David to memory, before being conveyed into Suffolk for his consecration as King of the East Angles. These details presumably derive from regional twelfth-century tradition. Geoffrey's story gained currency, and Offa's image appeared in a window of Blythburgh Church during the later Middle Ages. The names 'Alcmund and Siwara' for Eadmund's parents, in later accounts, are imports from Folcard's *Life of Botolph* and have no credibility.

An older source, the *Annals of St Neots* compiled early in the eleventh century probably at Bury, records that Eadmund acquired the throne in 855, and this is also stated by Florence of Worcester. The *Annals* appear to be based on a narrative and tell us that Eadmund succeeded on Christmas Day, 25 December 855, at the age of 13, and exactly one year later was anointed and consecrated by Bishop Hunberht of the East Angles at the royal villa of *Burum* in Suffolk amid great rejoicing and the greatest honour. It is from these same *Annals* that we have reference to King Guthrum's burial at Hadleigh in *c*.891, so we rest on the one authority for both stories of royal villas in central southern Suffolk. We know that Sudbury was already long-established, and have seen other reasons to think this area had importance in Eadmund's time. Geoffrey of Wells adopted the *Bures* identification, adding his topographical evocation as 'the known bound between Essex and Suffolk, and situate upon the Stour, a river most rapid in summer and winter.' Hamlet Watling, the Victorian antiquary, established the general belief that the site was that of Chapel Barn (a medieval chapel now restored) on a hill crest just north of the village at the top of Cuckoo Hill. This overlooks the Stour valley across Bures towards Wormingford, and has a natural command when seen from the valley below, especially from the East Saxon side. But Cyril Hart finds the place name *Burum* an error for *Burna* and, surveying a range of possibilities, suggests Bourne near Gipeswic. (There is in fact a Maiden's Bower, *Maidenhall*, beside the Orwell at Stoke. Eadmund is sometimes called *Mayde*, because martyrdom earned spiritual virginity.) Sudbourne might also be considered. Bures understandably clings to its 1,000-year legend.

The early St Neots narrative, therefore, asserts that Eadmund was a child-king. Abbo (who does not tell us this) refers to the loveable perfection of his Christian humility and grace even in childhood, of his liberal and unassuming behaviour towards his subjects of whatever station, and of his wisdom in avoiding the sophistries of wickedly-disposed people. The great homilist Ælfric, who reworked Abbo's *Life*, implies that Eadmund was born as late as *c*.848. A catalogue of his personal virtues, the mildness and comeliness engendered by his youth and spiritual nature, accrued to his legend. There is nothing inherently unlikely in the tradition that he became king when a child. Legend also assigns to him a brother named Eadwold, a sister Botild, a nephew (her son) Fremund, and another nephew Reginhere. However, their stories (of which Eadwold's may be the least dubious) relate to the period after Eadmund's death.

Eadmund's kingdom

Eadmund took control of the East Anglian minting organisation. His coinage is fairly extensive, and a greater number of moneyers struck for him than for any of his East Anglian predecessors. One of them, Æthelhelm, had operated continuously since Æthelstan's time: Eadmund also inherited Æthelweard's moneyers Dudda, Eadmund and Twicga, but not Rægenhere or Tuduwine. He therefore began with at least four working at once, and later at least seven others also struck for him. All his coins have circumscribed legends both obverse and reverse, and some continue the central obverse letter 'A'. Eadmund resumes the style 'REX AN-' for *Rex Anglorum*, King of Angles, and the good metallurgical quality introduced by Æthelweard is maintained. Eadmund's accession date is inferred from a hoard found at Dorking (Surrey), deposited *c*.860-62, which among many West Saxon coins included a small East Anglian group. Two were struck for Eadmund by his early moneyers Eadmund and Dudda.

Penny of Eadmund (*c.855–869*), moneyer Beornferth. (diam. 2cm) *The Fitzwilliam Museum, Cambridge*

King Æthelwulf, who had liberated Kent in 825 and had ruled Wessex from 839 to 855, now held only Kent, Essex, Surrey and Sussex until his death in 858. His second son Æthelberht succeeded him there while the eldest, Æthelbald, who ruled in Wessex, took to wife Judith, his Frankish stepmother now 15 years old. Union in this degree was expressly banned, but here tolerated in both kingdoms. Presumably they hoped to unite the blood of the two houses. There were mystical interests in Charles' court, which found their way to Wessex: the bond was renewed in 926 when the Holy Lance was given to Æthelstan, Ælfred's grandson. However, Æthelbald died in 860, Æthelberht reunited the southern realms under his rule, and Judith eloped with Baldwin of Flanders. Æthelberht is said to have kept a good peace in great tranquillity, although a large heathen host who stormed Winchester had to be met in battle and defeated during his reign. There are no accounts of raids in East Anglia during the first 10 years of King Eadmund's reign, and it seems likely that the borders of his kingdom with Burghred in Mercia and with Æthelwulf's sons in Essex were at last maintained in peaceful co-existence. It was the calm before the storm.

Bishop Hunberht of Elmham, who appears to anoint Eadmund at his consecration in 856, had presumably done so as the senior churchman of the kingdom. (His name is preserved in *Homersfield*, one of the South Elmham parishes.) He had been with Bishop Wilred of Dommoc at the London meeting of 845, in the wake of the assault on East Anglia in 841. Wilred's is the last name to appear in the episcopal lists for Dommoc (as is Hunberht's for Elmham), compiled by medieval chroniclers from whatever records had then survived the intervening conflagrations. Nonetheless we know that Wilred had a successor, Æthelwald, for his profession to Archbishop Ceolnoth survives. It is brief, affirming his creed in God the Father, the consubstantial Word of the

Father, which is the Son, and the coessential Spirit proceeding from the Father and the Son; and that in this Triune Nature is constituted the single perfection of Godhead. He notes his eternal obedience to Ceolnoth and his successors at Canterbury.

Furthermore, the actual matrix of his episcopal seal survives, having been found many years ago at Eye. Cast in bronze, it is conical in shape, almost 3 inches tall, with three tiers of openwork arcading enclosing small animal heads, a most sophisticated production. The circular seal-die on the base has a circumscribed legend within a beaded margin, reading + SIG EÐILVVALDI EP- , with a floriated cross set with four leaves between. The die is expertly cut, and the foliate cross resembles the central reverse motif on the second coinage of King Æthelberht of Wessex, c.863-5.

The inset animal heads of this seal-handle, with their glass eyes, are very similar to those of a mount from a hanging vessel found at Barningham (beside Coney Weston, supposed a royal house). Chip-carved interlace runs continuously and ingeniously around the various modelled and gilt surfaces of the casting. A fine beast's head forms the suspension hook, and smaller glass-eyed faces project as lugs. The seal-handle's ornamental themes also recur on a bronze censer bowl with openwork arcaded rim and animal-headed suspension fittings, found beside North Elmham church in 1786. The High Mass at North Elmham with its incense-laden air, gleaming wrought vessels hanging aloft, and Æthelwald's Dommoc authority stamped in wax upon its official parchments are the vivid impressions of Eadmund's kingdom afforded by these finds. At the same time, we know that his coinage was under the supervision of new men, presumably of honoured and powerful families: Eadberht, Eadwald and Ethelulf; Sigered; and Bæghelm, Beornferth and Beornhæh.

A Viking host, having made its winter-quarters in Thanet, was promised money by the people of Kent, who thought this would protect them from attack. But the host went inland secretly by night, and ravaged all the eastern part of that kingdom. In the same year, 865, King Æthelberht died and his next brother, Æthelred, became King of Wessex and the southern realms.

Then the thunder struck. That autumn a great army, prepared for a lengthy campaign in a foreign country, arrived in East Anglia in a mighty fleet. They were led by a man named Ivar, nicknamed 'the Boneless' by his own people, perhaps because he had no love-lust. Also in the campaigns which followed over the next decade were his brothers Halfdan and Ubbi, and probably his brothers Bjorn Ironside and Sigurd Snake-eye: but the East Anglian sources, of which the earliest is Abbo's *Passio*, identify the leaders of this first arrival as 'Hinguar and Hubba', that is, Ivar and Ubbi. So far as can be discerned from legend, they were the sons of Ragnar Lothbrok, the most famed Viking of the ninth century, who was later celebrated in the Norse sagas. The dynastic power which had held the peoples of Denmark together a generation before, and had opened them to the early missionary work of St Anskar, had suddenly collapsed in 854 with the murder

Above left Eye: seal-matrix of Bishop
Æthelwald of Dommoc, *c*.865 (handle). *The
British Museum. Photograph: R. Carr*

Above right Eye: seal-matrix of Bishop
Æthelwald of Dommoc, *c*.865 (die). *The
British Museum. Photograph: R. Carr*

Left Barningham: chip-carved suspension
mount for a vessel. *St Edmundsbury Borough
Council / Moyses Hall Museum*

of their senior ruler, Horik, and all his household; and in the decade which followed, the nobles and fighting men attached to the various rival families had burst forth from their lands in pursuit of wealth and adventure. Their exploits can be traced in the Frankish annals, including those of Reginheri (?Ragnar) on the Seine in 845, and those of Bern (?Bjorn) there in 855 and in the Rhone and in north-west Italy by 860. Ivar may be the same as the famous Viking of that name who was active in Munster and Meath in Ireland between 857 and 863.

But this arrival in East Anglia was no mere raiding exploit: it was the first step in a war of invasion which was to bring England to the brink of destruction, though that may not have been its original purpose. Various legends assert that Ragnar Lothbrok had been killed in England, and that the first motive was revenge. A famous story preserved in Saga, generally disbelieved, tells that he was thrown into a pit of snakes in York. (There is some slight evidence of human pelts, reputedly of Vikings, being nailed to church doors in south-eastern England.) But the tradition connected with East Anglia is that Ragnar came to Eadmund's court and was received with courtesy. While on a hunting expedition he was slain by Berne (?*Beorn*), one of Eadmund's royal huntsmen, who was jealous of his skill. The crime was concealed, but Ragnar's faithful hound appeared and led them to the body. Berne was set adrift in Ragnar's boat, which came ashore in Denmark, and there he told the sons that Eadmund had slain their father. Yet another story tells that Ragnar, hearing of Eadmund's fame, goaded his sons to their exploit.

The *Anglo-Saxon Chronicle*, and the tenth-century West Saxon chronicler Ethelwerd using a very early source, bring the Danish fleet first to East Anglia in autumn 865, where they made a peace with the people of that kingdom and set up winter-quarters. The East Angles also provided them with horses, which shows the intention to make a mounted assault across land. (The name of Wickham *Skeith* contains a Scandinavian word signifying a racecourse.) Abbo does not record this episode, but states that they first attacked and burnt a city (*civitas*), inflicting indiscriminate slaughter on its inhabitants and harrying the countryside. Eadmund, he says, was unable to raise an army against them, because Ivar had sought out and slain his best fighting men to forestall a resistance. Geffrei Gaimar naughtily identifies this city as Orford, which was suitably coastal, but did not come into being as a town until the twelfth century when its castle was built. That strategic haven was, however, part of Sudbourne, which may certainly have been a royal centre then. The one East Anglian place consistently termed *civitas* is Dommoc; but Abbo's version seemingly telescopes the historical events, and Geffrei probably embroidered what he read in Abbo and in the early chronicle he possessed.

The next spring, the army took their horses over the mouth of the Humber to York and occupied it. Osberht, Northumbrian ruler since Æthelred's death in the late 840s, was out of favour and some had accepted Ælla, not of royal birth, to rule them. It was not until March 867 that the Northumbrians settled their differences, gathered their levies and stormed the city. Some got inside the walls, but the English were slaughtered in immense numbers both within and outside, and those who were left alive came to terms with Ivar. Both the English kings died: according to the Icelandic poet Sighvat, writing in *c.*1030, Ivar had an eagle carved on Ælla's back, which killed him. Ivar, leaving an Englishman named Egbert as his tax-king in York, led his army to Nottingham in Mercia late in 867 and made winter-quarters there. According to Geffrei Gaimar, Ube (Hubba, Ubbi) was with him there. King Burgred entreated help from his brother-in-law, Æthelred of Wessex, who came with Ælfred and the West Saxon levies. (Ealhstan, the fighting Bishop of Sherborne, had died in 867.) A siege was laid, but the Danes stayed within their fortifications and would not meet them, and eventually Burghred agreed terms for peace. Late in 868 the army returned to York and wintered there.

Then in autumn 869 Ivar and his army rode back to East Anglia through Mercia, presumably travelling west of the Fen and joining the Icknield Way. They chose Thetford for their winter-quarters, favouring its navigable river access. Thetford controlled the Little Ouse and provided central access to the kingdom. In the years since their first arrival, Eadmund had managed to muster sufficient forces to attempt to oppose them. The *Anglo-Saxon Chronicle* records that he fought against the Danes, to which Ethelwerd adds that he fought for a little time against them during that winter. These engagements may have been at some distance from the winter-quarters. By its statement that 'the Danes had the victory', the *Chronicle* implies that there was a set-piece battle, which Roger of Wendover expands into a bloody conflict lasting from dawn till dusk in which countless men perished. He numbers the Danish army in tens of thousands. Hamlet Watling used to locate this at Stone Bridge below Columbine Hall, Stowupland, where it might be defending Thorney and the Gipping valley from Thetford. A battle-grave yielding horseshoes, iron weapons and human skeletons lying on a paved surface under a mound, now lost, was broken up during Victorian earth-clearances there. The *Chronicle* adds that the Danes killed the king, and conquered all the land. But there must be an interval between the battle and Eadmund's death because the story of the martyrdom is not set on the battlefield, and it has a seemingly unimpeachable authority.

Abbo's Preface to his *Passio Sancti Eadmundi*, which he dedicates to Dunstan, Archbishop of Canterbury, explains that Dunstan himself has told him the story of the martyrdom. Dunstan heard it in his youth, in person, from a decrepit old man as he related it to King Æthelstan, probably soon after 925. This man declared on oath before the king that he had been armour-bearer to King Eadmund on the actual day on which he died, and he told his account simply and in good faith. Dunstan had been moved to tears by the tale, and had often repeated it. Since Abbo addressed the work to Dunstan, this most unusual warranty leaves no doubt that the meeting really took place. However, Abbo does not describe a set-piece battle.

He relates that Ivar, establishing winter-quarters at Thetford, proceeded to ravage the district. Eadmund was then at a villa called *Hægilisdun* some distance from the town, beside which was a woodland of that name. Ivar sent a messenger to announce his presence, requiring an account of Eadmund's hereditary possessions and ancient wealth, which he should share with him, to rule thereafter under his authority. Eadmund summoned his bishop, his confidential adviser, who counselled him to submit to Ivar for his own safety: but the king, tormented by the suffering of his people, expressed the wish to die on their behalf. He declared that nothing would separate him from the love of Christ, having been consecrated to the faith of the Holy Trinity by the triple unction of baptism, confirmation and anointing to the sovereign power of the East Anglian kingdom. Having dedicated himself before his whole court to live and rule under Christ alone, he could not now serve two masters, but must make himself the example, rather than the ruler, for his people. He sent the messenger off with a stern refusal to submit, unless Ivar should consent to become a Christian.

Geffrei Gaimar and Roger of Wendover, seeking to reconcile Abbo with the Chronicle, place this interview before the battle which they next introduce. At its close, Eadmund withdraws with the survivors to the stronghold at *Hægilisdun*. Ivar is joined by Hubba, who has been campaigning in Mercia, and together they march on Hægilisdun, where Eadmund has taken refuge in the church at the bishop's suggestion. They surround the place with their soldiers, and Eadmund, having resolved never again to take up arms against the pagans, casts aside his weapons and prays for constancy of faith in his coming ordeal. Gaimar tells that a heathen came in search of the king and, not recognising him, asked him where Eadmund was. Eadmund replied, 'When I was in flight Eadmund was there; when I turned, he turned; I know not if he will escape you.'

The armour-bearer resumes his narrative. At a distance, Ivar had followed the messenger with a force to Hægilisdun. No sooner had the messenger left the king, than he met Ivar and conveyed Eadmund's answer. The palace was surrounded by the Danes, and orders were given that only the king was to be captured, who had defied the conditions set down. Eadmund was taken, pinioned and bound with chains, and was made to stand before his imperious captor. There he was mocked and savagely beaten. Then they bore him off to a tree nearby, near the edge of the wood, where a witness of the events which followed lay in hiding. Eadmund was tied to the tree and scourged for a long time, during which he called repeatedly on the name of Christ in a broken voice. Enraged by this, the pagans began to shoot arrows at him as if practising at a target, firing off one after another until he was bristling with them, and scarcely able to draw breath. Realising that Eadmund would never yield, Ivar commanded his executioner (whom Gaimar calls Coran Colbe) to cut off his head. The king was wrenched from the tree, hardly standing but still alive, his ribs bare beneath the innumerable gashes. They bade him stretch forth his head, that royal head which had been thrice anointed and had worn the diadem. Meek, yearning to be released into eternal life, Eadmund was refreshed by the Grail vision of inner light: the words of prayer were on his lips as Coran Colbe struck the single blow.

Adveniat Regnum Tuum

Epilogue

Thus Eadmund achieved his martyrdom. Ivar's men threw his head into the brambly undergrowth of Hægilesdun woods so that the English could not find it. They were observed, and when the English returned and found the body, they searched in the woods for the head. They went in a party, calling out to each other 'Where are you?' to keep their bearings, and the replies came 'Here, here, here.' So they came together at a certain place, and there they found Eadmund's head, which had itself spoken the summons in a rasping voice. It lay securely between the paws of a huge wolf of the forest which crouched like a guardian behind it. The wolf, the last appearance on Earth of the totem-spirit of the Wuffings, surrendered its trust and followed the expedition home anxious after its sacred morsel. Eadmund's head and body were reunited and buried with honour in a small church at Sutton nearby.

Where were Hægilisdun woods? For many centuries the martyrdom was believed to have taken place at Hoxne, where Eadmund is supposed to have hidden after the battle under a bridge crossing the Goldbrook. There is no doubt as to the early importance of Hoxne, on its knoll near Oakley overlooking the confluence of the Waveney and Dove out among the level and willowy pastures. But Hoxne's claim was probably invented in the eleventh century, displacing the distinguished cult of St Æthelberht which certainly existed there 70 years after Eadmund's death. Hellesdon near Norwich was long favoured as the only East Anglian place name likely to derive from Hægilisdun. But the existence of a Hellesdon Wood at Bradfield, out on the claylands south-east of Bury, was noticed by Stanley West and offers a much more convincing identification. Close by is a place called Kingshall, and also a Sutton which would take account of the place of Eadmund's first burial. If the central plateau of Suffolk was its defensive stronghold, with important positions above the Black Bourne vale at Tostock, above the Gipping at Haughley, and above the Lark and Brett at Bradfield, one may readily believe that Eadmund took his last stand there.

The version of the *Anglo-Saxon Chronicle* associated with Peterborough tells that the Viking host in East Anglia destroyed all the monasteries they found. At the same time they burned and demolished Medeshamstede, slew the abbot and the monks, and reduced to nothing what had formerly been a very wealthy foundation. Did the chronicler exaggerate? The 'Hedda Stone' (a late eighth-century carved shrine-cover) and other early sculptures at Peterborough Cathedral show signs of having been burnt at some time, perhaps in this onslaught. A similar fate is supposed to have befallen Ely and Beodricesworth, and, as Malmesbury describes, at Soham. Iken, Brandon and Burrow Hill were deserted, and Dommoc vanished so completely that its true location is still uncertain. Symeon of Durham, in his account of the martyrdom, has the Danes also slay the bishop, whom he identifies as Hunberht (of Elmham). Lands and endowments were stripped away and allocated to secular patrons. Gipeswic, however, survived, for its commerce was as valuable to the new rulers as to the old. The town centre was soon being reconstructed with new buildings. Legend asserts that Eadwold, Eadmund's brother, was offered the kingdom but declined it. Fremund retired to Cerne Abbas in Dorset.

A century later there were other wars. But the great body of East Anglian literature, charters and deeds, libraries, religious and vernacular writings, and the art, ornament and treasures of its holy places, had already been dispersed or destroyed. The dislocation was profound, and the varied legends of Eadmund and the gleanings of the later chroniclers only underline the discontinuity in written historical tradition. The impact of the ninth-century Viking conquest of East Anglia was not superficial: it was in many ways cataclysmic. As a new study of East Anglian monasticism shows, the continuity of Christian thought remained with the people through these experiences, when its whole physical apparatus had been devastated.

The Danish army, having advanced to Repton in Mercia in 873, divided into two sectors. The south-eastern party returned to Cambridge led by three kings named Guthrum, Anund and Oscytel. Over the following decades this army conducted the principal campaigns against the West Saxons. In 878 Guthrum came to an accommodation with King Ælfred (the Great) at Athelney in Wessex, and was baptised. He returned to the systematic occupation of East Anglia, which became a Danish stronghold for assaults into Kent and elsewhere: in 883 Ælfred sent a fleet to the mouth of the Stour and captured 16 ships, slaying their crews at Shotley. In 886 the English peoples as a whole accepted Ælfred's overlordship, and soon afterwards he concluded a treaty with Guthrum in which England was partitioned broadly on a line between London and Chester. It was also disposed that in the two social classes of Guthrum's kingdom, English and Dane should have parity of worth – Danish freedman and English ceorl renting land from a lord in the lower; Danish and English nobles, Danish peasant settlers and English ceorls farming their own land in the upper. Guthrum, the Danish King of the East Angles, died *c*.891 and was buried at Hadleigh in Suffolk, as we have already told.

After prolonged wars, King Ælfred authorised the Kentish issue of a memorial coinage in the name of St Eadmund. Similar coins were also struck and circulated in East Anglia, even before English control was wrested back by Eadward the Elder, Ælfred's son, early in the tenth century. St Eadmund's body was transferred to Beodricesworth, afterwards called Bury St Edmunds, where it was tended and became the focus of a national, royal cult. After Swegn Forkbeard approached the relics blasphemously, Eadmund appeared to him in a dream and transfixed him with a spear. Swegn actually died soon afterwards, and King Canute, his son, showed his respect by completely refounding the abbey at Bury in 1020.

When Abbot Samson opened the shrine in 1198, St Eadmund's body lay in a wooden coffin with iron rings at either end, like a Danish chest. On its lid near the breast was a golden image of the Archangel Michael, a foot long, the figure having a sword in one hand and a standard in the other. Above was written 'Lo, the image of St Michael keeps the martyr's corpse'. Below was a hole through which the relic might be touched. The celestial dragon-slayer stood on guard.

Archaeology and myth are closely interwoven. In 1687 a silver crown was dug up at Rendlesham. Those who saw it before it was melted down stated that it was of Anglo-Saxon type. It may have been a diadem, a relic of the ancient power. But what need a silver crown? Eadmund's martyrdom for his Kingdom became the culminating example of England's first Christian age. Through Danish rule and settlement, and the English reconquest, the old kingdom gave way to new realities: during the tenth century it re-emerged in a new guise. The division of the country east of the Fen into South and North Folk gave to Suffolk many of the places with most notable royal and ecclesiastical associations. When Ely received its grants in 970, its relation to East Anglia was recast. While the regional life, including that of Gipeswic, continued under changing authorities, the royal and saintly histories of Rendlesham, Beodricesworth, Iken, Hoxne or Dommoc had already resolved into foundation-myths of the Suffolk countryside.

Original impression of a thirteenth-century *Secretum* seal of Bury Abbey, showing the martyrdom of St Eadmund. *Ipswich Borough Museums*

Sources and further reading

Alcock, Leslie, 1971 *Arthur's Britain, History and Archaeology AD 367-634* (London)

Alexander, M.R., 1966 *The Earliest English Poems* (London)

Anderton, M. (ed.), 1999 *Anglo-Saxon Trading Centres – Beyond the Emporia* (Glasgow)

Anon, 2004. Prittlewell: Treasures of a King of Essex, *Current Archaeology* 190 (Feb. 2004), 430-436

Archaeology in Suffolk – Yearly Reports in *Proc. Suffolk Institute of Archaeology & History*

Archibald, M.M., 1985 The coinage of Beonna in the light of the Middle Harling hoard, *British Numismatic Journal* 55, 10-54

Archibald, M.M., 1982 A Ship-type of Athelstan I of East Anglia, *British Numismatic Journal* 52, 34-40

Archibald, M.M., Fenwick, V.H. and Cowell, M.R., 1996 A sceat of Ethelbert I of East Anglia and recent finds of coins of Beonna, *British Numismatic Journal* 65, 1-19

Arnold, T. (ed.), 1890 *Memorials of St Edmund's Abbey* (London)

Bailey, R.N., 1996 *England's Earliest Sculptors* (Toronto)

Bailey, R.N., 2000 The Gandersheim Casket and Anglo-Saxon Stone-Sculpture, in R. Marth (ed.), *Das Gandersheimer Runenkastchen. Kolloquiumsband 1 des Herzog Anton Ulrich-Museums* (Series editor J. Luckhardt), 43-51

Bakka, E., 1963 Some English decorated metal objects found in Norwegian Viking graves, *Arbok for Universitet I Bergen (Humanistisk Serie)* 1963 no. 1, 4-66

Bassett, S. (ed.), 1989 *The Origins of Anglo-Saxon kingdoms* (Leicester)

Birch, W. de Gray (ed.), 1883 Cartularium Saxonicum, 3 vols (London)

Blackburn, M.A.S. and Dumville, D.N. (eds.), 1998 Kings, Currency and Alliances: History and Coinage of Southern England in the Ninth Century, *Studies in Anglo-Saxon History* 9 (Woodbridge)

Blake, E.O. (ed.), 1962 *Liber Eliensis*, Camden 3rd Series, XCII (London)

Blatchly, J.M. (ed.), 1982 A Journal of Excursions through the County of Suffolk 1823-1844 by David Elisha Davy, *Suffolk Records Society* 24

Blunt, C.E., 1961 The coinage of Offa, in R.H.M. Dolley (ed.), *Anglo-Saxon Coins – Studies Presented to F.M. Stenton* (London)

Blunt, C.E., Lyon, C.S.S. and Stewart, B.H.I.H., 1963 The coinage of southern England, 796-840, *British Numismatic Journal* 32, 1-74

Blunt, C.E., 1969 The St. Edmund Memorial coinage, *Proc. Suffolk Institute of Archaeology & History* 31 Part 3, 234-255.

Boulter, S., 2003 Flixton Park Quarry: A Royal Estate of the first Anglo-Saxon Kings? *Current Archaeology* 187 (August 2003), 280-285

Brand, J., 1813 Popular Antiquities, 2 vols (London)

Brenan, J., 1991 *Hanging Bowls and their Contexts*, BAR British Series 220 (Oxford)

Briscoe, T., 1979 Some Anglo-Saxon finds from Lakenheath and their place in the Lark Valley context, *Proc. Suffolk Institute of Archaeology & History* 34 Part 3, 161-169

Brown, B.J.W., Knocker, G.M., Smedley, N. and West, S.E., 1954 Excavations at Grimstone End, Pakenham, *Proc. Suffolk Institute of Archaeology & History* 26 Part 3, 188-207.

Bruce-Mitford, 1975, 1978, 1983 *The Sutton Hoo Ship-Burial* (3 Vols in 4) (London)

Bruce-Mitford, R.L.S., 1974 *Aspects of Anglo-Saxon Archaeology. Sutton Hoo and Other Discoveries* (London)

Campbell, J., (ed.), 1982 *The Anglo-Saxons* (Oxford)

Carr, R.D., Tester, A. and Murphy, P., 1988 The Middle Saxon Settlement at Staunch Meadow, Brandon, *Antiquity* LXII, 371-77

Caruth, J. and Anderson, S., 1999 RAF Lakenheath Anglo-Saxon Cemetery, *Current Archaeology* 163 (June 1999), 244-250

Carver, M.O.H. (ed.), 1992 *The Age of Sutton Hoo: the Seventh Century in North-Western Europe* (Woodbridge)

Carver, M.O.H. (ed.), 1993 *Sutton Hoo Research Committee Bulletins 1983-1993* (Woodbridge)

Carver, M.O.H., 1998 *Sutton Hoo − Burial Ground of Kings?* (London)

Coatsworth, E., and Pinder, M., 2002 *The Art of the Anglo-Saxon Goldsmith* (Woodbridge)

Colgrave, B. (ed.), 1927 *The Life of Bishop Wilfrid by Eddius Stephanus* (Cambridge)

Colgrave, B. (ed.), 1956 *Felix's Life of Guthlac* (Cambridge)

Colgrave, B. and Mynors, R.A.B., (eds.), 1969 *Bede's Ecclesiastical History of the English People* (Oxford)

Cramp, R.J., 1977 Schools of Mercian Sculpture, in A. Dornier (ed.), *Mercian Studies*, 191-233 (Leicester)

Cummings, D.R.F., 1991 Finds of Anglo-Saxon and other Metalwork from Coddenham, Suffolk, 1987-1990, *Ipswich Numismatic Society Notes* 12, Special Publication 2b (Ipswich)

Dahl, L.H., 1913 *The Roman Camp and the Irish Saint at Burgh Castle* (London)

Darby, H.C., 1934 The Fenland Frontier in Anglo-Saxon England, *Antiquity* 8, 185-201

Davy, D.E., MS. Collections for Suffolk, Carlford and Colneis Hundreds (BL Add. MS 19,086-87).

Dickinson, T. and Harke, H., 1992 Early Anglo-Saxon Shields, *Archaeologia* Vol. 110 (London)

Dümmler, E. (ed.), 1895 Alcuini Epistolae. *Monumenta Germaniae Historica: Epistolae Karolini Aevi* II (Berlin)

Dumville, D.N., 1976 The Anglian Collection of Royal Genealogies and Regnal Lists, *Anglo-Saxon England* 5, 23-50

Evans, A.C., 1986 *The Sutton Hoo Ship Burial* (London)

Fairclough, J. and Hardy, M., 2004 *Thornham and the Waveney Valley: an historic landscape explored* (King's Lynn)

Fairclough, J. and Plunkett, S.J., 2000 Drawings of Walton Castle and other monuments in Walton and Felixstowe, *Proc. Suffolk Institute of Archaeology & History* 39 Part 4, 419-459

Fenwick, V.H., 1984 Insula de Burgh: Excavations at Burrow Hill, Butley, Suffolk 1978-1981, *Anglo-Saxon Studies in Archaeology and History* 3, 35-54

Filmer-Sankey, W. and Pestell, T., 2001 Snape Anglo-Saxon Cemetery: Excavations and Surveys 1824-1992, *East Anglian Archaeology* 95

Fletcher, R., 1997 *The Conversion of Europe from Paganism to Christianity 371-1386 AD* (London)

Folcard (Abbot), *Life of Botolph*, in J. Mabillon (ed.), *Acta Sanctorum Ordinis S. Benedicti* (Paris, 1668-1701) III, 1-7

Fox, C., 1923 *The Archaeology of the Cambridge Region* (Cambridge)

Garmonsway, G.N., 1953 *The Anglo-Saxon Chronicle* (London)

Gibbon, E., 1910 *The Decline and Fall of the Roman Empire* (1st edn. 1776-88 Everyman Edition, 6 Vols with O. Smeaton's notes, 1910) (London)

Giles, J.A., 1849 *Roger of Wendover's Flowers of History* (Translation - 2 Vols) (London)

Godman, P. (ed.), 1982 *Alcuin: The Bishops, Kings and Saints of York.* (Oxford)

Gordon, R.K., 1954 *Anglo-Saxon Poetry* (London)

Green, C., 1963 *Sutton Hoo: The Excavation of a Royal Ship-Burial* (London)

Green, B., Milligan, W.F. and West, S.E., 1981 The Illington/Lackford workshop, in V.I. Evison (ed.), *Angles, Saxons and Jutes: Essays presented to J.N.L. Myres.* (Oxford)

Grierson, P. and Blackburn, M., 1986 *Medieval European Coinage I: The Early Middle Ages* (Cambridge)

Haddan, A.W. and Stubbs, W., 1871 *Councils and Ecclesiastical Documents Relating to Great Britain and Ireland*, 3 Vols (Oxford)

Hamerow, H. and MacGregor, A. (eds), 2001 *Image and Power in the Archaeology of Early Medieval Britain — Essays in Honour of Rosemary Cramp* (Oxford)

Heaney, S., 2002 *Beowulf: A New Translation* (London)

Hele, N.F., 1870 *Notes or Jottings about Aldeburgh, Suffolk* (Ipswich)

Henderson, G.D.S., 1987 *From Durrow to Kells: The Insular Gospel-Books 650-800* (Oxford)

Henderson, G.D.S., 1999 *Vision and Image in Early Christian England* (Cambridge)

Hervey, Lord Francis, 1907 *Corolla Sancti Eadmundi: The Garland of St Edmund, King and Martyr* (London)

Higham, N., 1992 *Rome, Britain and the Anglo-Saxons* (London)

Hines, J., 1993 *Clasps, Hektespenner, Agraffen: Anglo-Saxon Clasps of Classes A-C of the Third to Sixth Centuries AD. Typology, Diffusion and Function* (Stockholm)

Hines, J., 1997 *A New Corpus of Anglo-Saxon Great Square-Headed Brooches* (Woodbridge)

Hodges, R., 1982 *Dark Age Economics: The Origins of Towns and Trade AD 600-1000* (London).

Hodges, R., 1988 *The Anglo-Saxon Achievement* (London)

Hope-Taylor, B., 1977 *Yeavering, an Anglo-British Centre of Early Northumbria* (London)

Hurst, J.G. and West, S.E., 1957 Saxo-Norman pottery in East Anglia. Part II: Thetford Ware, with an account of Middle Saxon Ipswich Ware, *Proc. Cambridge Antiquarian Society* 50, 29-60

James, M.R. (ed.), 1917 Two Lives of St Ethelbert, King and Martyr. *English Historical Review* 32 (1917), 214-44

Johnson, S., 1984 Burgh Castle. *East Anglian Archaeology* 20

Kendrick, T.D., 1938 *Anglo-Saxon Art* (London)

Kirby, D.P., 1991 *The Earliest English Kings* (London)

Klaeber, Fr. (ed.), 1950 *Beowulf and the Fight at Finnsburg, 3rd Edition* (Lexington)

Layard, N.F., 1907 An Anglo-Saxon Cemetery in Ipswich, *Archaeologia* LX, 325-352

Leahy, K., 2004 *Anglo-Saxon Crafts* (Tempus)

Lethbridge, T.C., 1956 The Anglo-Saxon Settlement in Eastern England — a Reassessment, in D.B. Harden (ed.), *Dark-Age Britain: Studies Presented to E.T. Leeds*, 112-122 (London)

Levison, W., 1946 *England and the Continent in the Eighth Century* (Oxford)

Lucy, S., 2000 *The Anglo-Saxon Way of Death. Burial Rites in Early England* (Stroud)

Malster, R., 2000 *A History of Ipswich* (Chichester)

Markham, R.A.D., 2002 *Sutton Hoo through the Rear-View Mirror 1937-1942* (Sutton Hoo Society)

Matthaeus Westmonasteriensis, *Flores Historiarum... de Rebus Britannicis usque ad MCCCVII: Et Chronicon ex Chronicis ad MCXVIII deductum*, auctore Florentio Wigorniensi (Frankfurt 1601)

Mayr-Harting, H., 1972 *The Coming of Christianity to Anglo-Saxon England* (London)

McGrail, S, 1990 Maritime Celts, Frisians & Saxons *CBA Research Report* 71

Meehan, B., 1996 *The Book of Durrow. A Medieval Masterpiece at Trinity College Dublin* (Dublin)

Metcalf, D.M., 2000 Determining the mint-attribution of East Anglian sceattas through regression analysis, *British Numismatic Journal* 70, 1-11

Metcalf, D.M., 1993 *Thrymsas and Sceattas in the Ashmolean Museum, Oxford* (3 Vols) (London)

Moir, J.R. 1921 Excavation of two tumuli on Brightwell Heath, *Journal of the Ipswich & District Field Club* 6, 1-14

Moore, I.E., Plouviez, J. and West, S.E., 1988 *The Archaeology of Roman Suffolk* (Ipswich)

Morris, J., 1973 *The Age of Arthur. A History of the British Isles from 350 to 650* (London)

Morris, J., 1980 *Nennius: British History and the Welsh Annals*, edited and translated (London and Chichester)

Mundell Mango, M., Mango, C., Evans, A.C. and Hughes, M., 1989 A sixth century Mediterranean bucket from Bromeswell parish, Suffolk, *Antiquity* 63 (1989), 295-311

Myres, J.N.L., 1986 *The English Settlements* (Oxford)

Newman, J., 1993 The Anglo-Saxon Cemetery at Boss Hall, Ipswich, in M.O.H. Carver (ed.), *Sutton Hoo Research Committee Bulletins 1983-1993*, 32-36 (Woodbridge)

Newman, J.A., 1995 The true provenance of the Woodbridge sceatta 'hoard', *British Numismatic Journal* 65, 217-218

Newton, S., 1993 *The Origins of Beowulf and the Pre-Viking kingdom of East Anglia* (Cambridge)

Newton, S., 2003 *The Reckoning of King Rædwald* (Brightlingsea)

North, J.J., 1980 *English Hammered Coinage* (2 Vols. New Edition) (London)

Pagan, H.E., 1982 The coinage of the East Anglian kingdom from 825 to 870, *British Numismatic Journal* 52, 41-83

Page, R.I., 1965-66 Anglo-Saxon Episcopal Lists, *Nottingham Medieval Studies* 9, 71-95, and 10, 2-17

Page, R.I., 1973 *An Introduction to English Runes* (London)

Pestell, T., 2004 *Landscapes of Monastic Foundation. The Establishment of Religious Houses in East Anglia, c.650-1200* (Woodbridge)

Plummer, C., 1896 *Venerabilis Bedae Historia Ecclesisticam… una cum Historia Abbatum Auctore Anonymo* (2 Volumes) (Oxford)

Plunkett, S.J., 1994 Nina Layard, Hadleigh Road and Ipswich Museum, *Proc. Suffolk Institute of Archaeology & History* 38 Part 2, 164-192

Plunkett, S.J., 1994 *Guardians of the Gipping. Anglo-Saxon Treasures from Hadleigh Road, Ipswich* (Ipswich)

Plunkett, S.J., 1998 The Mercian Perspective, in S.M. Foster (ed.), *The St Andrews Sarcophagus – A Pictish Masterpiece and its International Connections* (Dublin), 202-226

Plunkett, S.J., 1999 The Anglo-Saxon loom from Pakenham, Suffolk, *Proc. Suffolk Institute of Archaeology & History* 39 Part 3, 277-298

Plunkett, S.J., 2001 Some recent metalwork discoveries from the area of the Gipping valley, and their local context, in P. Binski & W. Noel (eds.), *New Offerings, Ancient Treasures – Studies in Medieval Art for George Henderson*, 61-87 (Stroud)

Rapin, Thoyras, 1723 *Histoire d'Angleterre*, Tom. I, Liv I-V

Rigold, S., 1961 The Supposed See of Dunwich, *Journal of the British Archaeological Association* 24, 5-59

Rigold, S., 1974 Further evidence about the site of Dommoc, *Journal of the British Archaeological Association* 37, 97-102

Rollason, D.W., 1982 *The Mildrith Legend – A Study in Early Medieval Hagiography in England* (Leicester)

Sadler, J., 1990 The Suffolk 1998 Find of one Merovingian Cut Quarter, Eight Anglo-Saxon Shillings and Other Artefacts of Gold, *Ipswich Numismatic Society Notes* 11, Special Publication 2a (Ipswich)

Savile, H., (ed.), 1596 *Rerum Anglicarum scriptores post Bedam praecipui, ex vetustissimi codicibus* (London) (Latin editions of Malmesbury, Huntingdon, Hoveden, Ingulf, Ethelwerd)

Scarfe, N., 1976 The Place name Icklingham: a Preliminary Re-examination. With an Appendix on the Icklingas by E.A. Martin, *East Anglian Archaeology* 3 *Suffolk* (Ipswich), 127-134

Scarfe, N., 1982 *Suffolk – A Shell Guide* (3rd Edition) (London)

Scarfe, N., 2002 *The Suffolk Landscape* (New Edition) (Chichester)

Scarfe, N., 2004 *Suffolk in the Middle Ages* (New Impression) (Woodbridge)

Scull, C., 1985 Further evidence from East Anglia for enamelling on early Anglo-Saxon metalwork, *Anglo-Saxon Studies in Archaeology and History* 4, 117-124

Scull, C., 1993 Archaeology, Early Anglo-Saxon Society and the Origins of Anglo-Saxon kingdoms, *Anglo-Saxon Studies in Archaeology and History* 6, 65-82

Scull, C. and Bayliss, A., 1999 Dating burials of the seventh and eighth centuries: a case study from Ipswich, Suffolk, in J. Hines, K. Hoyland Nielsen and F. Siegmund (eds.), *The Pace of Change: Studies in Early Medieval Chronology* 80-88 (Oxford)

Smith, R.A., 1911 Anglo-Saxon Remains, *Victoria County History for Suffolk* I, 325-355. (HMSO)

Smith, R.A., 1923 *British Museum Guide to Anglo-Saxon Antiquities* (London)

Spelman, H. (ed.), 1639 *Concilia, decreta, leges, constitutiones, in re ecclesiarum orbis Britannici*, Vol I (to 1066) (London)

Stenton, F.M., 1971 *Anglo-Saxon England* (Third Edition) (Oxford)

Stenton, F.M., 1959 The East Anglian kings in the seventh century, in Clemoes, P. (ed.), *The Anglo-Saxons: Studies presented to Bruce Dickens* (London)

Stevenson, F.S., 1922 St Botolph (Botwulf) and Iken, *Proc. Suffolk Institute of Archaeology & History* 18 Part 1, 30-52

Stolpe, H. & Arne, T.J., 1927 *La Necropole de Vendel* (Stockholm)

Tangl, M. (ed.), 1916 S. Bonifatii et Lullii Epistolae, *Monumenta Germaniae Historica, Epistolae Selectae*, I

Taylor, H.M. and J, 1965 *Anglo-Saxon Architecture*, 2 Vols (Cambridge)

Wade, K., 2001 Gipeswic – East Anglia's first economic capital, 600-1066, in N. Salmon and R. Malster (eds.), *Ipswich from the First to the Third Millennium* (Ipswich), 1-6

Wade, K., 1993 The Urbanisation of East Anglia: the Ipswich Perspective, in J. Gardiner (ed.), *Flatlands and Wetlands: Current Themes in East Anglian Archaeology. East Anglian Archaeology* 50, 144-151

Warner, P., 1996 *The Origins of Suffolk* (Manchester)

Webster, L., and Backhouse, J., 1991 *The Making of England. Anglo-Saxon Art and Culture AD 600-900* (London)

West, S.E., 1963 Excavations at Cox Lane (1958) and at the Town Defences, Shire Hall Yard, Ipswich (1959), *Proceedings of the Suffolk Institute of Archaeology* XXIX Pt 3, 233-303

West, S.E., 1983 A new site for the martyrdom of St Edmund? *Proc. Suffolk Institute of Archaeology & History* 35 Part 3, 223-225

West, S.E., 1985 West Stow: The Anglo-Saxon Village. *East Anglian Archaeology* 24 (Suffolk County Council)

West, S.E., 1988, Westgarth Gardens Anglo-Saxon Cemetery, Suffolk: Catalogue, *East Anglian Archaeology* 38 (Suffolk County Council)

West, S.E., 1998 A Corpus of Anglo-Saxon Material from Suffolk, *East Anglian Archaeology* 84

West, S.E., Scarfe, N. and Cramp, R.J., 1984 Iken, St Botolph, and the coming of East Anglian Christianity, *Proc. Suffolk Institute of Archaeology & History* 35 Part 4, 279-301

Whitelock, D., 1969 Fact and fiction in the legend of St. Edmund, *Proc. Suffolk Institute of Archaeology & History* 31 Part 3, 217-233

Whitelock, D., 1972 The Pre-Viking Age Church in East Anglia, *Anglo-Saxon England* 1, 1-22 (Cambridge)

Whitelock, D., Douglas, D.C. and Tucker, S.I., 1961 *The Anglo-Saxon Chronicle - a revised translation* (London)

Whitwell, J R, 1917 Bronze patera found at Wickham Market, Suffolk, *Proc. Suffolk Institute of Archaeology* XVI Pt 2, 179-80

Wilson, D M, 1965 Some neglected late Anglo-Saxon swords, *Medieval Archaeology* IX, 32-39

Wilson, D.M., 1981 *The Anglo-Saxons* (2nd edn.)

Wilson, D.M., 1984 *Anglo-Saxon Art from the Seventh Century to the Norman Conquest* (London)

Winterbottom, M., 1972 *Three Lives of English Saints* (Toronto)

Winterbottom, M., 1978 *Gildas: The Ruin of Britain and other works*, edited and translated (London and Chichester)

Yorke, B., 1990 *Kings and kingdoms of early Anglo-Saxon England* (London)

Online Resources

Dr Sam Newton's Wuffings Website. (www.Wuffings.co.uk)

Portable Antiquities Scheme Finds Database. (www.finds.org.uk)

Fitzwilliam Museum, Cambridge: Corpus of Early Medieval coin finds, and Sylloge of Coins of the British Isles (www.fitzmuseum.cam.ac.uk/coins/emc)

Index